Advance Praise for Playing Sick? by Marc D. Feldman, M.D.

"*Playing Sick?* is a brilliant portrayal of people on a quest to be noticed, no matter the costs. Factitious disorder, Munchausen syndrome, Munchausen by proxy, and malingering are all splendidly described with numerous case descriptions and dialogue. The book is a fascinating read, authoritative from start to finish. The case material provides a riveting thrill ride into the depths of deception, masochism, and manipulation so characteristic of these individuals.

"In this masterful and unprecedented book, Dr. Marc Feldman has captured the essence of feigned illness and the underlying motivations for assuming the sick role. The origins and impact of 'playing sick' are clearly depicted with practical advice for those affected and a sensible approach to healing."

David G. Folks
Chair, Department of Psychiatry, University of Nebraska at Omaha

"Dr. Marc Feldman has done it yet again. He has turned his sophisticated insight to illuminate these frustrating and often infuriating problems. At the same time, he tells stories of medical mystery and intrigue that rival the most riveting novels—yet his accounts are true. In *Playing Sick?*, he offers practical suggestions for intervention and treatment where few existed before. Offering face-saving techniques where instinct might suggest confrontation will go a long way toward humanizing the interaction of physicians and patients."

Allen R. Dyer, M.D., Ph.D.

Co-Author, *Concise Guide to Ethics in Mental Health Care*

"This is a thoughtful, well-written and very useful contribution to the study of factitious disorder, Munchausen syndrome, Munchausen by proxy, and malingering. These have been 'orphan' phenomena too often misunderstood by the medical community. *Playing Sick?* is essential reading for health care professionals and the vast numbers whose lives have been touched by these difficult, often harrowing conditions."

Michelle Riba, M.D., M.S.

President, American Psychiatric Association; Co-author, *Primary Care Psychiatry*

"In his masterly book, Dr. Feldman offers a unique and fascinating look at factitious disorder and related phenomena. I enthusiastically recommend it both to professionals in the medical field and to lay persons who provide healing or are interested in these difficult-to-understand conditions."

Pedro Ruiz, M.D.

Vice President, American Psychiatric Association

"Factitious disorder and its relatives in the domain of medical deception are frustrating, resource-consuming, sometimes life-threatening conditions. Aside from admonitions about not tricking patients into revealing that they do not have the signs and symptoms they claim, there has been precious little to inform medical caregivers, mental health professionals, or the public about these medical mysteries. Dr. Marc Feldman's book addresses that gap, offering explanations, practical treatment suggestions, and hope for those who suffer or have been victimized, their families, and their doctors."

Nada L. Stotland, M.D., M.P.H.

Secretary, American Psychiatric Association

"The world's foremost expert on these befuddling conditions, Dr. Feldman here gives engaging, indeed spell-binding accounts of real cases that are just as fantastic as the tales of Baron von Munchausen himself—but here the accounts are all true stories. And, although the fictional benign exploits of the Baron occurred centuries ago, Dr. Feldman documents how these modern medical hoaxers are today even employing the World Wide Web, thereby increasing costs to their unsuspecting victims and to society at large. Whether you are a physician, mental health worker, or simply interested, this book will prove a worthy read."

Lewis R. Baxter, Jr., M.D.

Professor of Psychiatry, University of Florida; Adjunct Professor of Psychiatry, UCLA

"Dr. Feldman offers a rare glimpse into the bizarre but compelling world of people who feign or produce illness: people with disorders of health care simulation. A fascinating story teller, Dr. Feldman enlarges our understanding by recounting the dark, personal stories of patients who play sick, often to a life-threatening extent, to gain attention and nurturance, to exert control, or to express rage. Meticulous research overlays the stories to create a powerful work that is both intelligent and intriguing."

Marlene M. Maheu, Ph.D.

Editor-in-Chief, *Self-Help and Psychology Magazine*

Co-Author, *Infidelity on the Internet: Virtual Relationships and Real Betrayal*

"Rich in case studies and loaded with balanced, informed commentary, *Playing Sick?* sheds light on some of the most confounding disorders in the field of psychiatry. An essential contribution to the literature, and a compassionate one as well."

Thomas N. Wise, M.D.

Medical Director, Behavioral Services, Inova Health Systems

Co-Editor, *Restoring Intimacy* and *Psychiatry for Primary Care Physicians*

"In clear, concise language, Dr. Feldman provides astounding insights into some of psychiatry's most poorly understood and medically perplexing disorders. Rich clinical material keeps one riveted, while his mastery of the subject and lucid writing provide never-before-published information for even the most experienced clinician—not to mention the general public."

Stephen M. Goldfinger, M.D.

Professor and Chair of Psychiatry, State University of New York, Downstate Medical Center

"Dr. Feldman's book, *Playing Sick?*, reveals the minds of patients with some of the oddest conditions the medical field has ever faced. This book brings understanding to the novice as well as the professional. A must read for students, professionals and the curious alike. A total revelation!"

Vicki Villegas Westfall
Author, *Almost Love, Almost Death*

"It is time for the medical community and the media to stop either marginalizing or sensationalizing these disorders. It is time to start *treating* them, and treating them with respect. *Playing Sick?* is a smart, provocative book that will open a lot of people's eyes and save lives."

Stephen Fried
Author, *Bitter Pills: Inside the Hazardous World of Legal Drugs;* Adjunct Professor of Journalism, Columbia University

Playing Sick?

Playing Sick?

*Untangling the Web of Munchausen Syndrome,
Munchausen by Proxy, Malingering &
Factitious Disorder*

Marc D. Feldman, M.D.

Routledge
Taylor & Francis Group
New York London

Published in 2004 by
Routledge
711 Third Avenue, New York,
NY 10017, USA

Published in Great Britain by
Routledge
27 Church Road
Hove, East Sussex
BN3 2FA

Routledge is an imprint of the Taylor & Francis Group, an informa business

Library of Congress Cataloging-in-Publication Data
Feldman, Marc D., 1958-
    Playing sick? : untangling the web of Munchausen syndrome,
Munchausen by proxy, malingering, and factitious disorder / Marc D.
Feldman ; foreword by James C. Hamilton.
      p. ; cm.
Includes bibliographical references and index.
    ISBN 13: 978-0-415-94934-7 (hbk)
    1. Factitious disorders. 2. Malingering. 3. Munchausen syndrome. 4.
Munchausen syndrome by proxy.
    [DNLM: 1. Munchausen Syndrome. 2. Factitious Disorders. 3.
Malingering. 4. Munchausen Syndrome by Proxy. WM 178 F312pg 2004]
I. Title. RC569.5.F27 F453 2004 616.85'86--dc22
                                                      2003025175

Dedications

To my family—Jackie, Lee, and Sara—for supporting my relentless, admittedly curious passion to chart the worlds presented in this book.

To my indefatigable agents, Katherine Boyle of the LitWest Group in San Francisco and Whitney Lee of the Fielding Agency in Beverly Hills, for embracing this project with their remarkable intelligence, skill, and warmth.

Contents

Author's Note

The essential psychological issues in each case in this book reflect real-life events. Except when accurate names and identifying characteristics of persons and institutions were already provided elsewhere in the scientific or general media, they have been changed to protect individual privacy and anonymity.

Recognizing that language reveals key elements of personality and culture, the author has preserved individuals' own voices as they recount their stories. Dialectical and grammatical idiosyncrasies are therefore incorporated into the narrative where appropriate. Infrequently, dialogue has been created de novo to enhance the interest and immediacy of case reports.

The author has exerted every effort to ensure that treatment options and recommendations set forth in this text are in accord with current recommendations and practice at the time of publication. However, in view of ongoing research, changes in government regulations, and the constant flow of information, and because human and mechanical errors sometimes occur, the author recommends that readers follow the advice of a physician directly involved in their care or that of a member of their family.

Foreword

James C. Hamilton, Ph.D.
Associate Professor of Psychology
University of Alabama
Tuscaloosa, Alabama

New scientific theories arise from puzzles or problems that existing theories are unable to explain. Whole new scientific disciplines arise when the solutions to those puzzles cause humankind to become aware of previously unimaginable dimensions of the natural world. The fields of particle physics and cell biology are good examples. At the end of the 19th century, physicists realized that the behavior of magnetic fields and light was inconsistent with the prevailing view of physical matter. Their observations led them to postulate the existence of atoms and subatomic particles, the eventual discovery of which led to the creation of the discipline of particle physics. Around the same time, biologists scratched their heads over two seemingly unrelated problems: explaining contagious diseases and explaining how things decay. Louis Pasteur and Joseph Lister solved the second problem, which then led to the solution to the first. They discovered that rotting—things growing moldy—reflected the proliferation of microscopic single-celled organisms, and then they deduced that similar microscopic organisms might spread invisibly from person to person and proliferate into observable diseases. Their work led to the development of germ theory and subsequently to the disciplines of cellular and molecular biology. Thanks to them, developed countries have massively reduced mortality related to infectious diseases such as tuberculosis.

Around the same time, a neurologist in Vienna was puzzling over a group of medical patients who presented with a range of typical neurological problems—deafness, blindness, paralysis, and so forth—for which the young doctor could find no physical cause. After observing that the problems of these patients abated when the patients were given the opportunity to talk about their most secret wishes and darkest fears, Dr. Freud began to suspect that the apparent physical problems of these patients were somehow a product of mental disturbances. The work of Freud and his contemporaries evolved into psychoanalytic theory and spawned a whole new medical specialty, psychiatry, dedicated to studying the causes and treatments of mental disorders.

However, the story of psychiatry differs from the stories of particle physics and cell biology. In both physics and biology, the original problem has been solved and work on the theories that developed from the early efforts has progressed in a steady and orderly way. In contrast, the story of psychiatry is a collection of winding and ironic twists and turns. For example, one irony is that psychiatry was born out of attempts to understand apparently physical problems, not classic psychological disorders like depression or schizophrenia. A second irony is that these "classical" mental disorders turn out after all to have a significant biological component. But the most compelling irony is that, unlike particle physics and cell biology, psychiatry has not yet solved its original problem. Although more than a century has passed, neither psychoanalytic theory nor any other psychological theory has produced an adequate, empirically supported explanation for why some people behave as if they are medically ill when, in fact, they are not.

This book represents a return to the oldest puzzle in psychiatry, the explanation of illness behavior that occurs in the absence of true medical disease or injury. In the chapters that follow, Dr. Marc Feldman shares the remarkable stories of people with factitious disorder, Munchausen syndrome, Munchausen by proxy, and malingering. These are people whose lives have been consumed by their desire to occupy the sick role or the role of caregiver to a sick child. These individuals have intentionally subjected themselves or their loved ones to all kinds of pain and discomfort for the primary purpose of playing these roles. Aside from simple malingering, the primary motive behind these examples of medical deception appears to be psychological. But what are the psychological benefits of playing these roles and why are some people are so strongly drawn to them? That is the ultimate puzzle.

Although the medical literature contains hundreds of case reports of patients with factious illness behavior, those reports typically are written by physicians for the purpose of alerting fellow physicians to the signs and symptoms with which the patients presented, and to the strategies that were effective in uncovering the deceptions. Seldom do these publications provide detailed information about the social or emotional context of the patients' fraudulent illness behavior. They are medical detective stories, not stories of people's lives. The fact is that these patients rarely admit to their deceptions and almost never cooperate with psychiatric evaluations. The unfortunate result is that we know very little about the psychology of these patients, and we rarely get the opportunity to appreciate the tragic dimensions of their suffering or the suffering that they inflict upon the people in their lives.

The case descriptions in this book are the stories of people whose lives have become entangled in the lies and manipulations of factitious illness behavior. Based on Dr. Feldman's reputation as an internationally renowned expert, many of these people have willingly shared their stories with him. These never-before-told stories are rich in detail, often deeply personal, and frequently expressed in the patient's own voice. In addition to the accounts of the patients themselves, the book presents many cases from the perspective of friends and family members who describe the anguish of believing that a loved one is terminally ill, only to learn that they have been cruelly deceived. Few medical or psychiatric professionals will ever have the opportunity to become so intimately knowledgeable about even a single case of factitious disorder from their own practices. The combination of the patients' stories and Dr. Feldman's expert commentary provides the reader with an unprecedented glimpse into the lives of dozens of persons with factitious illness behavior. Dr. Feldman resists the temptation to indulge in the regurgitation of old or untested theories for why people feign illness. Instead, he takes a mostly descriptive approach. In effect, he gives us the raw data to examine and analyze for ourselves and gently helps us along.

Although these stories make for captivating reading, is there any more important reason to learn about these individuals? I believe that there is. To fully appreciate the value of this book, it is important to understand the dimensions of unnecessary, excessive, and inauthentic illness behavior of the sort that captured Freud's curiosity. It is also important to understand why so little progress has been made toward the scientific understanding of this particular psychological problem.

Each year, U.S. residents make approximately 820 million doctor visits. Research based on the medical records generated from these visits consistently indicates that in 20 to 30 percent of these encounters doctors are unable to find a physical cause for the patient's complaint. In addition to doctor visits, Americans annually log roughly 108 million emergency room visits and 35 million hospital stays. For roughly 16 percent of the emergency department visits, the primary diagnosis is listed as "Signs, Symptoms, and Ill-Defined Conditions." In other words, no clear medical problem was found. The same is true for about 6 percent of the hospitalizations. These facts mean that in a given year, Americans make 150 million unnecessary doctor visits and 17 million unnecessary emergency room visits, and they experience 2 million unnecessary hospital admissions. The annual health care costs for these unnecessary medical encounters probably range between 10 and 20 billion dollars.

There is no reason to suspect that all of these unnecessary medical encounters constitute the sort of willful abuse of health care resources carried out by psychologically troubled patients like those described in this book. Indeed, many medical encounters are revealed to be unnecessary only after the fact. For example, many emergency department visits that do not result in a definitive diagnosis are made by patients who experience chest pain and mistakenly fear that they are having a heart attack. Far from being psychologically troubled, most of these patients are regular folks who are merely following the advice of public health officials who have urged people to seek immediate treatment if they experience the symptoms of heart attack. So, unnecessary does not mean excessive or illegitimate.

Another portion of the unnecessary medical encounters reflects psychological problems, but not like the ones that characterize the patients described in this book. These are medical encounters initiated by patients who have excessive and irrational fears of illness. It is these patients to whom the term "hypochondriac" can be accurately applied. Although the medical encounters that these patients initiate could be fairly described as both unnecessary and excessive, it is not fair to call them illegitimate. These patients genuinely believe that they are seriously ill and their illness behavior reflects a genuine desire to receive an accurate diagnosis and proper treatment. In other words, they are motivated by a desire to maintain or restore their health.

The remaining unnecessary health encounters can be described as illegitimate. That is, they represent the use of health care resources for reasons other than restoring or maintaining physical health. It is impossible to determine the exact proportion of unnecessary medical encounters that fall in this category. However, even if these illegitimate encounters account for only ten percent of all unnecessary health care encounters, the price tag for the problems addressed in this book would be one to two *billion* dollars per year.

On the other hand, there is no reason to assume that all of the fraudulent health encounters instigated by psychologically troubled patients are captured in the statistics on unnecessary heath care use. The individuals whose cases are presented in this book alone have probably been responsible for thousands of unnecessary medical encounters that would not be detected in large studies of medical records. These people were able to accurately simulate a genuine disease and would have received a definitive diagnosis (or misdiagnosis). Also, it is generally true within the medical community that there is a bias toward making a definitive diagnosis even when the physician has doubts about the authenticity of the patient's complaints. This bias reflects fears of legal actions by patients and concerns that insurance companies will not authorize payment for services rendered to those who do not have a true medical problem. No one has any guess at the proportion of illegitimate medical encounters that go undetected for these reasons. However, we know that the scope of the problem is much greater than would be indicated by the number of people who are formally diagnosed with factitious disorder or related conditions. Finally, doctors and nurses are trained to trust and respect their patients. Factitious illness behavior is so far outside of their expectations of the doctor-patient relationship that health care professionals are blind to the possibility that their patients could be willfully deceiving them.

Beyond the financial costs to society, factitious illness behavior causes tremendous human suffering. The lives of those who perpetrate factitious illness behavior are often totally consumed by their sick role enactments. They sacrifice careers, family relationships, and other valued activities that typically bring joy and meaning to life. In their zeal to simulate medical illnesses, they often cause actual disease and disability, if not death. These outcomes are particularly tragic when the victim is the child of a "caregiver" with Munchausen by proxy. In these cases, approximately ten percent of the child victims die as a result of the caregivers' attempts to make them ill. The personal suffering caused by factitious illness behavior also extends to all those in the orbit of the patient. Friends and family members put their lives on hold and make sacrifices of money, time, and emotional investment to provide aid and support to the patient. Doctors and nurses experience guilt and self-doubt over their inability to provide cure or comfort in these cases.

It is reasonable to assume that factitious illness behavior results in personal and financial costs that are comparable to medical problems that are regarded as serious public health problems. *The estimates of cost, for example, would place factitious illness behavior problems in the same league as medical problems like Parkinson's disease, multiple sclerosis, liver disease, ovarian and cervical cancers, and epilepsy.* Certainly, no one would argue that these other diseases are trivial medical problems. In 1999, the National Institutes of Health spent 132 million dollars on research and other programs related to Parkinson's disease, 81 million dollars on epilepsy, and 96 million dollars on multiple sclerosis. Yet, a search of federal funding databases reveals that between 1973 and 2003 not a single research grant was awarded to study factitious disorder. That is to say, for at least 30 years the United States government has not spent a penny to understand a behavior pattern that, in the U.S. alone, may have resulted in 30 to 60 billion dollars of wasted health care services over that same time period.

Why has there been so little research and so little research funding for a problem of such importance? There are at least two factors that have stifled scientific investigation into the causes of factitious illness behavior. The first has to do with the politics of research funding. In the U.S., Congress establishes research funding priorities. These decisions are made by politicians who are influenced by various constituencies that lobby for their favorite causes. For example, the growing ranks of elderly Americans represent a powerful voting block that has successfully lobbied for better funding of research on Alzheimer's dementia and other issues that are particularly important to older adults. The National Alliance for the Mentally Ill has succeeded in shifting the research agenda of the National Institute of Mental

Health toward studies of the biological bases of bipolar disorder and schizophrenia. As you will come to understand by reading this book, there is no organized constituency that is invested in promoting the understanding of factitious disorder. The patients who perpetrate medical deceptions are certainly not going to take up the cause. And unlike issues such as pedophilia, factitious disorder—along with Munchausen syndrome and malingering—do not have direct victims who are invested in promoting a better understanding of the problem. No advocacy groups have ever existed for the living adult victims of Munchausen by proxy and victims' voices remain mostly silent. Doctors, family members, friends, and employers are all emotionally or financially violated by the lies and deceptions carried out. Again, however, none of these groups has come together to demand that the government do more to understand and prevent factitious illness behavior. The victimization is spread too thinly to cause any one single victim to invest his or her precious time and energy to mount a campaign to stop factitious illness behavior.

The second reason why so little research has been done is that the individuals discussed in this book are seldom willing to cooperate with psychiatric examinations or psychological research. Patients whose deceptions are so audacious that they can be "caught in the act" have typically committed fraud against their employers, their health insurance providers, doctors, and hospitals. Theoretically, they are subject to civil suits and in some states they could be prosecuted for criminal fraud. Under these conditions it is no surprise that they typically flee when their ruses are uncovered. On the other hand, patients whose medical deceptions have not risen to the level of criminal fraud may be more amenable to participate in psychological research. Examples of such patient populations might include some chronic pain patients, some patients with chronic fatigue syndrome, and some patients with "functional" abdominal pain. The key word is "some." How do we know which patients are engaging in authentic illness behavior that is motivated solely by a genuine desire to restore their physical health, and which ones are motivated to some degree by other psychological incentives for enacting the sick role? The answer is that we don't know. The frustrating fact is that the more certain we are that a patient is engaged in medical deception, the less likely the patient is to cooperate in research, and vice versa.

The scientific progress of clinical psychology and psychiatry is often compared unfavorably with sciences like physics and biology.

Neither atomic particles nor single-cell organisms willfully evade the researchers who seek to understand them. Biologists and physicists can apply the full measure of their creativity and cleverness to coax their subjects to reveal their secrets. However, psychologists and psychiatrists must work within the parameters of legal and ethical principles that protect all people from the uninvited intrusions of scientists. Despite the fact that persons engaged in factitious illness behavior consistently break important social contracts in their relationships with their doctors, employers, and families, society must nevertheless provide them the same rights and protections to which all citizens are entitled. They cannot be forced to participate in research against their will.

On the other hand, the difficult task of achieving a scientific understanding of factitious illness behavior is not so different from the challenges faced by the pioneers of particle physics and cell biology. Just as those pioneers formulated new questions about the physical world, they used their ingenuity to develop new methods for answering those questions, such as particle accelerators and the electron microscope. They were able to make these advances because they were able to persuade policymakers of the importance of their research problems, and they succeeded in securing the support needed to achieve their goals.

With the same support, psychologists and psychiatrists could certainly advance the understanding, assessment, and clinical management of factitious illness behavior. I believe that this book has enormous potential to stimulate this important research initiative. The case material in this book gives these patients faces and names, and makes tangible the problems that they cause themselves and those around them. They can be seen for the complex and troubled souls that they are, not merely petty cheats. The book also shows that these patients are not lost causes. There is hope for recovery for those patients who can be persuaded to seek professional help.

Hopefully this book will stir patients and their families to take steps toward recovery, open the minds and hearts of doctors and nurses who encounter these individuals, and move policymakers to take this problem for what it is—a serious and grossly under-researched public health problem.

Preface

Factitious disorder, Munchausen syndrome, Munchausen by proxy, and malingering are the four disorders of simulation. Each involves willful medical or emotional deception. Factitious disorder and Munchausen syndrome are mental disorders. Munchausen by proxy and malingering are not—but, as I will explain, they may become a focus of serious clinical attention regardless. Although it has been recognized among medical and psychological specialists for over a century, factitious disorder—when a person feigns or produces his or her own injuries or illnesses to meet emotional needs such as attention—is often misinterpreted as simple lying. Alternatively, it is viewed as a way to misuse physical or psychological complaints to take advantage of others. But factitious disorder and its more severe cousin, Munchausen syndrome, are much more complex than that and they reach further in their effects upon the general public. They partly overlap the other two phenomena I discuss: Munchausen by proxy maltreatment and malingering. Even workers in the field can become confused about these forms of health care trickery.

The central goal of this book is to bring these little-known phenomena to light, especially in the hope of helping affected patients and families as well as professional caregivers. Most of the information about these diagnoses is presented in professional journals or in psychiatric textbooks, thus making it generally unavailable to the public at large.

I will turn first to patients with factitious disorder and Munchausen syndrome. These individuals who, in my experience, are more commonly women than men, have voluntary and conscious control of the symptoms they flagrantly display, but they may lack insight into why they are doing what they are doing. Factitious disorder is formally recognized by the American Psychiatric Association in the *Diagnostic and Statistical Manual of Mental Disorders, Fourth Edition,* Text Revision (DSM-IV-TR) on the same tier as schizophrenia, major depression, bipolar disorder, obsessive-compulsive disorder, and other major mental disorders. The DSM-IV-TR also mentions and defined the term "Munchausen syndrome." However, both remain among the few disorders whose symptoms are not recognized by the general public or a startling number of clinicians.

As Dr. James C. Hamilton describes in his foreword to this book, research into the motives, prevalence, characteristics, and treatment of medical deception—especially factitious disorder and Munchausen syndrome—remains in its infancy. Researchers, advocacy organizations, public and private funding sources, and insurance companies have largely ignored it. It remains as stigmatized both inside and outside the health care profession as kleptomania. But even kleptomania is better known among health care providers and the general public.

Patient and family advocacy groups have never championed factitious disorder and Munchausen syndrome, nor have they explained why. To date, the American Psychiatric Association and the American Psychological Association lack any patient or family education materials on the subject; this may change as new leaders set their priorities. An absence of knowledge and understanding appears to be at the root of this problem, and it is the patients, families, friends, and uninformed medical personnel who suffer from the lack of readily available information.

Health care training tends not even to touch on the subject of factitious disorder and other unexplained medical complaints (UMCs), so caregivers generally shun these patients due to their own discomfort and sense of having nothing to offer. They also fear professional embarrassment if they take on the care of such patients, only to find out that weeks or months of work were "wasted" chasing stories and symptoms that the patients have invented as part of their mental illnesses.

Psychological tests that can reliably quantify improvement (or deterioration) among these patients are essentially nonexistent, further complicating research and clinical care. Patients themselves may fear legal repercussions for lies told, and many decline for this reason and others to enroll in any studies that are proposed. A work-around to preserve confidentially was formally presented to the U.S. federal government: to create an Internet website where patients or their doctors could fill out anonymous questionnaires to create a standardized database about these patients' lives. The government declined to provide any support.

Moving on to Munchausen by proxy and malingering, they remain hidden worlds much like factitious disorder and Munchausen syndrome. This "Gang of Four" may be the most taboo list of diagnoses in all of medicine, as if patients were branded with a scarlet F or M (for "factitious," "Munchausen," or "malingering") and to be cast away. They remain "orphans" even as very uncommon, even esoteric diagnoses (such as multiple personality disorder) have become the focus of scholarly debate and national conferences, and commonly receive financial support from the government, private foundations, and wealthy philanthropists as well as profligate media attention. Advocacy organizations have never replied in any way when patients, their associates, or I have asked them to help us create patient/family resources or support other projects in this field.

The typically female perpetrators who engage in Munchausen by proxy also play sick, but cruelly use the bodies of others—usually young children—to meet their needs to be perceived as virtuous, indefatigable caregivers who merit our respect and compassion.

The term "malingering" may be familiar to those who have heard of military recruits or those charged with or convicted of a crime who have sought to evade their responsibilities through disease forgery. Malingering appears to be plied by men more than women. It is understandable, albeit illegal, that those not wishing to serve in the military or in prison might manipulate their way out by pretending to be physically or emotionally sick or by inflicting self-injury. Others do so to accrue disability payments or opioid medications. However, patients with factitious disorder and Munchausen syndrome simulate disease when the payoff for appearing sick is not obvious. Despite their theatrical charades, for instance, it is often impossible not to have some sympathy for these patients when their childhood backgrounds have been harsh—if not overtly abusive, then emotionally neglectful. They have often learned that whatever nurturance they could receive would have to come from doctors, nurses, or other care-givers only when they appear—or are—ill. These patients' genuine emotional pain must be acknowledged and dealt with before their frantic attempts to alleviate it can be halted. However, difficult child-hoods have many different outcomes, including complete normality. The matrix of factors leading to macabre outcomes remains concealed in all-too-many cases.

There are unpublished findings that medications such as serotonin reuptake inhibitors and low-dose antipsychotic medications have helped a few afflicted individuals. However, there are no medications that have proved consistently effective in treating medical deception and its sometimes deadly consequences. For this reason, supple-mented by patients' hesitance to come forward and comply with drug-study protocols, pharmaceutical companies—whose check-books are wide open when it comes to researching other mental disor-ders or paying for junkets to tout their products in lush resort settings—disregard these patients, their families, and those doctors eager to help. In a vicious cycle, the lack of funding for research ensures that medication and other therapeutic options remain undis-covered, except perhaps by chance. This orphan has had little chance of ever finding a home due to lack of awareness or to derision and short-sightedness despite the billions of dollars the U.S. economy alone loses each year due to UMCs.

Insurance companies have been co-conspirators in this wall of silence. Many of them routinely use sophisticated computer systems to identify enrollees who jump from hospital to hospital or who have had repeated surgery for reasons that remain unclear. Rather than confront the matter or accumulate databases that could be studied for patterns, however, they quietly pay the bills accumulated. They fear the notoriety of rejecting the claim forms of patients who can be vociferous, even litigious if questioned about their misuse of health care resources. They also worry about public opinion if they were to adopt aggressive efforts to root out fakers. The government, in the form of Medicare payments and Medicaid disbursements, does the same. Payers may view even full-blown Munchausen syndrome as a problem of little consequence in terms of their vast budgets, but in doing so they overlook the slow leakage of expenditures for patients who engage in medical deception only sporadically (e.g., at times of severe stress) or who seek repeated care from the same local doctors and hospitals. This book is a call to action to advocacy groups, professional societies, payers, drug companies, health care providers, educators, and policymakers finally to take notice.

Revelation that an illness is invented has a tumultuous effect on all who rendered emotional, medical, and, in many cases, financial support to the person who has been consciously deceiving them. *Playing Sick?* explores the thoughts and feelings of these caregivers, offering the reassurance that they are neither alone nor wrong to be loving human beings who trusted another. As mentioned, the book also provides abundant actual, true case studies, including first-person accounts, of those with factitious disorder and Munchausen syndrome, and those who engage in Munchausen by proxy maltreatment and malingering to help alert readers to their symptoms and manifestations. In that respect it is unique, though at least six novelists have applied their talents to create fictional works about those who play sick (see Suggested Readings at the end of this book). I emphasize that every case in this book is true, because the behavior of these individuals is so foreign to the average person that it is hard to overcome the reader's incredulity. It is almost a miracle that I have been able to accumulate so much experience with these phenomena. I have earned the reputation of caring deeply about those involved, and those affected seem to find me. As a result, this book contains more cases, especially first-hand accounts, than any other ever produced.

For patients seeking recovery from the psychiatric ailments factitious disorder and Munchausen syndrome, the first step is to realize they cannot heal themselves alone because they are often unaware—or only vaguely aware—of their motivations for the deceptive behavior in the first place. Though seeking therapeutic help is a hurdle they inevitably find intimidating, they must reach out to someone. Because Munchausen by proxy involves the abuse and/or neglect of another person, it is typically handled through the intervention of child protective services and family courts. When it is detected, malingering tends to follow circuitous paths through the civil court system.

Factitious disorder, Munchausen syndrome, Munchausen by proxy, and malingering are exaggerated and sometimes twisted, dangerous outgrowths of a relatively harmless, normal behavior of playing sick, and that is what makes it at once frightening and familiar. The primary distinction, however, between most folks and medical tricksters is that the latter take playing sick to pathological extremes, profoundly affecting their lives as well as the lives of others.

This book is an effort to enlarge the awareness of the powerful effects that illness deception can have on the lives of others. Although it is not an academic treatise, it points out that more sophisticated exploration is required to help professionals understand these individuals and learn how to meet their needs more effectively. Additionally, this information will help family members and others learn to handle their own frustrations and pain as they attempt to break the cycle of participation in these deceptions.

Factitious disorder and the other disorders of simulation are among the trickiest of psychiatric ailments to address. Whether offered by a therapist, a relative, or a friend, help must be informed and humane. Some readers may be as curious as I have been about medical deception in all its forms. Others may be particularly concerned about behaviors in friends, family, co-workers, patients, or themselves that fall under the rubrics of factitious disorder, Munchausen syndrome, Munchausen by proxy, or malingering. Still others may feel comfortable that they understand the central issues in diagnosis, but are hungry for education about intervention and treatment. Whether one chooses to read the book from cover to cover or seek out specific sections, I hope that this book will help patients and families heal themselves and their loved ones, as well as aid professionals in identifying the symptoms earlier.

The book concludes with suggestions for further reading, including worthwhile websites dealing with the phenomena discussed in this book. I think you will find yourself intrigued and informed. If it serves no other purpose, I hope that this book will counter the isolation of those convinced that they are the only ones who have been "conned" in this way.

M.D.F.
Birmingham, Alabama

Acknowledgments

I extend my heartfelt thanks to the numerous colleagues who have shared their thoughts and experiences over the years. The phenomena explained in this book can be understood only by our continually talking together, appreciating the similarities and differences in our perspectives, abandoning turf battles, and working as a team to develop research strategies to advance the field. Special appreciation goes to Louisa Lasher, M.A. and Mary Sheridan, Ph.D., whom I met through my activities in Munchausen by proxy and who give me big, wonderful (but all-too-often "virtual") hugs whenever I need them. My friend Roxenne Smith could not have been more helpful. Roxie, I love the purity and directness of your literary voice as well as your soothing, caring, and kind spirit. I genuinely appreciate the journalists from all media who have allowed me to reach large audiences in my effort to open the closet door. I am indebted to George Zimmar and Shannon Vargo of Brunner-Routledge for lugging my unruly first draft into the bright light of day. Shannon, I will miss those e-mails chock-full of great suggestions! Thank you to the marketing team at Taylor and Francis: a book is only happy when it is being read. Love to my relatives, who provide the netting that will always keep me from falling too far. Unbridled appreciation goes to Susan Reynaud, my eleventh-grade English teacher who, three decades later, remains my friend and avid supporter. I have saved my deepest appreciation for last: thank you, thank you, thank you to the patients, family members, and others who have so graciously opened their lives to me during the past 15 years. It is because of your bravery, eloquence, passion, insight—and yes, often your sense of utter aloneness—that this book was written. You have taught me so much.

1

Dying for Attention

This chapter starts with a true case and asks you to take a starring role. You have a co-worker who takes you into her confidence, gradually revealing that she's still recovering from a horrible car accident and is now suddenly coping with her mother's cancer diagnosis. You become her confidante and feel protective. Suddenly she develops cancer, is raped, and finally suffers a miscarriage. At this point you have the slowly dawning realization that there are holes in your friend's stories and that she may not be the person you believed her to be. You feel devastated. Through these intimate, real-life scenarios, this chapter reveals the awful impact of factitious disorder and Munchausen syndrome. The chapter discusses the artistry of patients in their disease portrayals and why it is easy to fool even doctors. Through detailed case narratives the reader observes patients going about their everyday lives as elaborate disease forgers. Underlying factors that contribute to factitious disorder and its relationship to borderline personality disorder are also discussed.

Imagine. You have a co-worker who sometimes joins you for coffee in the break room and, over time, you become well–acquainted. You even think of her as a friend. This person takes you into her confidence, telling you small secrets about her life that are emotionally charged: For instance, she is about to lose her beloved grandmother and doesn't know how she will bear it. Little by little, her stories gain momentum and the dilemmas become even more severe. She was abused as a child and has a hard time trusting people, but you are different, she says. Two years ago she was raped and lives daily with the fear that she might run into the rapist because he was never caught. Finally, when she has your total trust, she reveals the most devastating problem of all: She has just been diagnosed with cancer and the prognosis is not good.

What would you do? Would you stick by her? Would you offer emotional support and maybe even a helping hand? Even for one moment, would you doubt her latest account or any that came before?

Thankfully, human nature is mostly generous and a compelling story of suffering often brings out the best in us. But people with factitious disorder—briefly described in the Preface along with *Munchausen syndrome, malingering,* and *Munchausen by proxy*—practice a kind of thievery. They "play sick," telling lies about personal illness or crisis and secretly misusing others to gain the attention and nurturance missing from their lives. In most cases, their suffering is indeed genuine, but it is not the physical suffering of cancer or the grief of a lost loved one. It is the emotional suffering that comes from a profound perception of being unloved and unlovable.

Rhonda's story illustrates a mental illness that devastates the lives of those who come within its circle. Even though the account is inherently dramatic, it is true but for changes to protect anonymity. It is also stunningly representative of how factitious disorder presents itself, plays out over time, and, in some cases, unravels. Despite the intensity of the deceptions, it is a case of factitious disorder, not Munchausen syndrome. Munchausen syndrome is the most severe subset of factitious disorder, in which patients evolve a lifestyle involving little but manufacturing illness. Generally, Munchausen patients travel continually to find new theaters in which to display their craft.

Rhonda's Case

Everyone who knew Rhonda agreed that she was a woman of amazing spirit. What they didn't know was that she was a master story-teller—a woman who was remarkably and skillfully deceptive. Rhonda had earned the admiration of her fellow nursing students and instructors with stories of her valiant struggles. They heard that only three years prior, at the age of 28, Rhonda had overcome the devastating effects of a car accident that nearly claimed her life. With an iron will, she had defied her doctor's prediction that she was unlikely to walk again. Now the only visible remnants of her suffering were a leg brace and permanent limp—outward symbols of her inner strength and courage.

She claimed that she had barely recovered from the accident when another catastrophe struck: Her mother was diagnosed with an aggressive cancer. Rhonda watched her mother's swift, agonizing decline as she cared for her "only true friend" through the final stages of illness. On her nursing school application, she stated that these life events had changed her deeply and caused her to consider how she might use her experiences to benefit others. Although it is still unknown whether Rhonda lost a mother to cancer, it is almost certain that her depiction of her mother as her "only true friend" was Rhonda's idyllic fantasy.

Whatever the truth about her mother's death, she claimed that following this grievous loss, she could not bear to live in the same small town. She left West Virginia and enrolled in a college nursing program in a southern city far from home.

Rhonda was bright and eager to learn, but she had been out of school for so long that she worried she might not be able to meet the demands of a rigorous academic program. She heard about a special mentoring program for new student nurses and immediately signed up. Rhonda quickly made friends with one of the tutors, who responded to Rhonda's sharp mind and readiness to learn. Within a few visits, she had found a confidante in Louise and she began sharing secret and startling stories about her past. She was quick to tell Louise that their relationship was special. There were few people in her life with whom she could share such personal and painful accounts.

Louise had come to consider Rhonda as a friend and she cared deeply about her success as a student nurse. However, she was ill-equipped to handle Rhonda's ever-expanding need for attention. Rhonda began dropping in on Louise unannounced and expressed her displeasure at having to schedule appointments "like everyone else."

Two months after their first meeting, Rhonda came to Louise's office seemingly distraught and unable to speak her awful fear. The act of unveiling seemed an immense struggle for her, but with Louise's gentle encouragement, she finally revealed that she had discovered a lump under her arm and was terrified at what this might mean. Louise insisted that she have it evaluated promptly.

Rhonda had found an effective way to keep herself in the upper stratum of Louise's thoughts and concerns. How indeed could Louise expect her to schedule visits like everyone else when she was in such crisis? It was imperative to Rhonda that she be the most special of Louise's students, not merely a name in an appointment book. She hooked Louise even further by failing to schedule a doctor's appointment. None of Louise's urging could convince her to do so. She said she was too terrified. She cried inconsolably. She wanted her mother.

Seeing the anxiety and stress that she caused Louise gave Rhonda a heady confidence and she soon ratcheted up the crisis by revealing yet another terrible story. Something else had happened, so awful that she didn't know how to tell Louise.

Louise was a caring person who had been well-trained. She believed that she could help her students by always listening closely and offering carefully considered guidance, and so she fell easily for Rhonda's deceptions (though story after story eventually proved false). Nonetheless, the ruses still intact, Rhonda's latest tale emerged slowly and painfully with Louise's tender encouragement. Just as she had never actually spoken the word cancer, Rhonda apparently could not or would not say the word rape, but her meaning left no doubt. Her assailant was a stranger who threatened her at gun point. She cried audibly and convincingly, but Louise briefly registered that she saw no tears. A small doubt surfaced, but was quickly eradicated as Rhonda's saga unfolded.

With Rhonda's stress circuits so overloaded, Louise was determined that she seek professional help to deal with her dual crises. She insisted again that Rhonda immediately schedule an appointment to have the lump examined and that she work with a rape crisis counselor to deal with the trauma of her assault. Rhonda agreed to a physician's visit, but adamantly refused to reveal the rape story to anyone else. It was too shameful. Seeing a counselor was out of the question. She would not hear of it and told Louise that, if she really wanted to help, she must stop pressuring her and swear to keep the assault a secret.

On the day before her scheduled evaluation of the lump, Rhonda came to Louise's office stating that she felt weak. She had missed her period and was experiencing uterine pain. In this way, she diverted attention from the suspicious lump and had Louise reeling over the implications of the missed period. Louise guided her down the stairs and took her to an emergency clinic where an examination revealed a vaginal infection and an enlarged uterus. Louise had only Rhonda's word that a pregnancy test had been administered and that she could call later for the results.

Louise was amazed at how, despite her physical and emotional struggles, Rhonda was able to continue to succeed in school. How was she managing to attend all her classes, keep pace with the rigors of her program, and continue to perform adequately, if not excellently? Louise was mystified, but, rather than being warmly admiring, she found herself disturbed. Something didn't seem right. The jigsaw puzzle was missing too many pieces. Just as this doubt entered Louise's mind, Rhonda said that she had been to a doctor and was to begin aggressive treatment for breast cancer.

Louise never spoke with a doctor nor witnessed the actual treatments, just as she knew nothing about the obstetrician-gynecologist Rhonda had ostensibly seen, but she kept vigil with her friend following the treatments. She did witness firsthand the major effect of chemotherapy—one that could also have resulted from the syrup of ipecac available in every drugstore. Rhonda's vomiting was wretched and relentless, continuing into the night. She said that her headaches were even worse, like shards of hot steel. She writhed in agony and begged for release. In the face of such suffering, Louise felt desperate to help. She placed cool cloths on Rhonda's forehead and played soft music to ease her pain.

Rhonda continued to attend classes, looking weaker day by day, but determined to finish nursing school even if she did not live long enough to practice her profession. As her principal caregiver, Louise had seen all the signs of illness—the black ink marking on Rhonda's breast that guided the placement of the radiation scope, small clumps of hair in the bathroom sink, urinary incontinence following her treatments, and vomiting. There was no doubt in Louise's mind that this woman was sick, but it puzzled her that Rhonda remained so plump. These small, nagging thoughts were immediately censored by her compassion. Louise could certainly see for herself how sick this woman was.

Yet small inconsistencies continued to rise up into consciousness. Why did Rhonda continually put off applying for the cancer scholarship that Louise had recommended? Rhonda was a strong candidate and financially needy. Also, why was it that new crises arose just in time to sabotage any plans of resolving the old ones? Why didn't Rhonda allow Louise to speak with any doctor? Louise had become an integral part of her life and felt entitled to information, yet Rhonda was infuriated at the suggestion, stating that she was perfectly capable of conveying any medical data that Louise needed. Louise was growing resentful of the limits and of the burden she carried alone.

Rhonda was just finishing the last of her chemotherapy treatments when she received a call from a family member in West Virginia. Louise was visiting her when the call came in and she heard the whispers from the other room, the soft weeping, the click of the phone being placed back in its cradle. It seemed that Rhonda's sister had just died, totally unexpectedly. Louise comforted her friend in that moment, but she was worn out. One tragedy after another—it seemed there was no end to it.

Louise called a hospice bereavement counselor and asked for help. Several weeks later, the counselor called Louise and told her that she was not sure whether a sister had died and she flatly did not believe the cancer story. As an experienced hospice clinician with a background in the care of cancer patients, she told Louise that many—probably most—pieces of Rhonda's innumerable stories did not add up. The progression of her illness did not look like a true case of cancer. The story of rape and miscarriage—even her sister's death—contained inconsistencies and medical inaccuracies. Rhonda's evasion only added to her suspicions. Since Louise had made the referral, the counselor felt obligated to share her assessment, concluding that a psychiatric referral would be appropriate to see why Rhonda was almost compulsively inventing these overwhelming tales of woe.

When Louise confronted Rhonda with these suspicions, Rhonda responded with rage. She jabbed her finger at Louise and flung accusations without ever dealing with the substance of the doubts. She said Louise had betrayed her and she wanted nothing more to do with her. With Louise no longer willing to serve as a bin into which new ruses could be tossed, Rhonda broke all ties.

Rhonda apparently recovered from her "cancer," graduating with honors from nursing school and taking a position in a community hospital. Some months later, Louise heard through a colleague that Rhonda had found new friends; they had become the audience for her stories of endurance as a nurse even as she had just discovered a lump under her arm that proved cancerous, been raped, become pregnant, miscarried, and suffered the unexpected loss of two close relatives, including her sister. She had captured new admirers and spun her sad stories once again into a warm, nurturing blanket.

Rhonda wasn't the first patient to seek nurturance and even love by feigning cancer (as well as a host of other ailments and crises, as we saw), nor will she be the last. Cancer has been the disease of choice of a number of factitious disorder patients who consciously and intentionally lie about illness. Sometimes they actually injure themselves or induce physical symptoms and signs to gain sympathy, admiration, and concern. The heroic image that cancer survivors increasingly have is attractive to factitious disorder patients, as is the strong emotional response a cancer diagnosis is sure to draw from loved ones and associates.

A case reported in the psychiatric journal *Psychosomatics* by Dr. W. F. Baile and colleagues parallels Rhonda's in a number of ways. However, as I will discuss below, this woman exhibited stronger characteristics of full-blown Munchausen syndrome: Her life had centered on disease portrayals and essentially nothing else, while Rhonda was able to succeed in her studies despite her deceptions. In addition, the woman described in *Psychosomatics*, but not Rhonda, sought financial assistance for the maintenance of her ruses, raising the possibility that she was malingering for a financial windfall.

Libby's Ruse

A 38-year-old woman, whom I shall call Libby, traveled from town to town faking cancer and other equally dramatic illnesses and events. Although Libby's simulations became more intense and inventive as she grew older, her practice of playing sick had actually begun when she was in elementary school. The eldest of three children, this woman adored her father, a military officer who showered affection on her younger twin brothers but totally shut her out. She became jealous and temperamental and was physically abusive to her brothers.

After being enrolled in parochial school, Libby began playing sick to stay home as a way of getting extra attention from her authoritarian mother. She also used illness to try to evoke some positive emotion from her father, who remained cold and distant.

Libby continued playing sick as she got older. She saw a psychiatrist who was unable to curtail her charades, which increased after her father's death. Her mother knew that Libby was faking her ailments, but didn't know how to help or stop her.

Libby then created a new setting for her performances—another version of a family environment—by gravitating toward clergymen (father figures) and religious communities and parishes (second families). She entered a nunnery and became a novice. Though now surrounded by a nurturing, supportive "family," she soon resumed her sick role by feigning leukemia. She asked the other nuns to pray for her because she was fighting a terrible illness, but she never shunned her responsibilities, putting up a good front even though she was weak from "anemia." Libby's acting was convincing enough to draw pity and concern from the other nuns, and her ruse was discovered only after she told her Mother Superior that her cancer was in remission. When the older nun telephoned Libby's physician to applaud his success, she learned that Libby didn't have cancer or any other life-threatening illness.

Libby denied that she had pretended to be sick, but she soon left the nunnery with the explanation that such a life wasn't for her after all. She then moved from one Catholic parish to another under the guise of a terminally ill patient, often seeking counseling and guidance from priests while putting herself at odds with them if they dared to challenge or withdraw from her. In one parish, she successfully engaged the attention and pity of a priest when she revealed to him that she had AIDS. The priest attempted to help Libby in numerous ways and arranged for her to have psychological counseling to deal with her illness. Libby said she would take advantage of therapy, but she never showed up for any of her appointments, always making excuses about having bad days due to her illness.

Desperate to keep their audiences engaged, persons with factitious disorder often escalate their stories to include personal traumas beyond illness. The longer Libby remained in a place, the more outlandish her lies became. When she began circulating the rumor that she and a parish priest had had a torrid love affair, she raised the suspicions of the kind clergyman who had previously befriended her. He confronted her openly and Libby accused him of being indifferent to her problems. She insisted they were real, but the priest could no longer be swayed. Like a compulsive gambler gone bankrupt, Libby moved on to new sources of wealth in other venues. Back in action, she dealt new cards to unwitting players, now claiming that she had been raped and just suffered the loss of her mother and was seeking counseling and solace at a Catholic rectory.

Libby was given room and board by many parishioners who were moved by her story and wanted to help. When she sought financial assistance at a cancer center, Libby exposed herself to scrutiny. She told social workers there that she had been treated several years earlier for uterine cancer, but it had now spread to her liver and she had only six months left to live. They wanted to know where she had been treated so they could request her medical records, but she was vague and said that most of her medical care had been rendered in public clinics. She further explained that a doctor at the cancer center was treating her free of charge and, to avoid red tape, he had not registered her as a patient. She had convoluted answers for every question.

Lies to counselors snowballed into tales of tragic loss. She claimed that her fiancé had been killed in Viet Nam when she was 20, that a priest friend had been killed in Guatemala, and that her brother had died in an auto accident, which led to her mother's suicide. She exaggerated her education, saying that she had received bachelor's and master's degrees in nursing and had worked at several cancer centers before being called on to nurse her father following a heart attack. In her fantasies, the father who had shunted her aside needed her, but in reality, Libby neither nursed her father nor carried out any of the other heroic deeds for which she claimed credit.

Libby's appearance and her portrayal of illness were so convincing that even highly trained therapists were completely taken in. When they visited her for outpatient counseling, she was often bedridden and surrounded by gifts from parishioners. Libby appeared to be enduring chronic pain, yet she maintained such a positive attitude that her counselors asked if they could videotape her talking about her illness and funeral arrangements and bring her before a graduate social work class on death and dying. She readily agreed. The students were profoundly moved by Libby's presentation and, when she told them that one of her dying wishes was to ride in a hot air balloon, they collected $125 so that her wish could be fulfilled. There wasn't a dry eye in the house when Libby was finished.

Libby's needs were met beyond her expectations, but as the amount of attention she was receiving escalated, her story became increasingly inconsistent. A therapist started checking the facts and learned that Libby had never seen the doctor who was supposedly treating her. When Libby was confronted, she hinted that the doctor was lying for reasons which she could not divulge. But after the confrontation with the therapist, Libby never returned to the cancer center.

Libby lived with her parish friends for four months before her hoax was irrefutably uncovered and she moved on. During that time, she tried to elicit attention from priests whom she frequently called after hours, and used threats of suicide as leverage over them. She was devious and clever, but it was her mysterious trips out of town under the pretense of visiting other friends, whom she never satisfactorily identified, that aroused the greatest suspicion among her caregivers. Looking for answers, a group of parishioners hired a private investigator, who discovered her string of illness deceptions and located her mother, who was very much alive. The detective learned that Libby's employment history was a patchwork of short-term jobs, usually at doctor's offices or hospitals, which doubtless provided her with the information she needed to make her portrayals believable. After being discovered, Libby returned to live with her mother, who was not surprised to hear that her daughter was still faking illness.

Munchausen, Malingering, and Manipulation

In Munchausen syndrome, material needs, as well as burning psychological problems, can motivate a patient's behavior. Libby sought and realized some practical gain in the form of room, board, and gifts. But Libby was primarily a Munchausen patient, not a malingerer: She was motivated principally by her emotional needs rather than tangible reward. She played out her ambivalent feelings for her father through her relationships with clergymen and their parishioners. Overall, her material gains were merely means to an end—the credible portrayal of illness and crisis—rather than ends in themselves.

Even though Rhonda's deceptions were multi-faceted and lasting, I would diagnose her with factitious disorder but not with its most severe subtype, Munchausen syndrome. Feigned illness was not all there was to her life; in addition, she stayed in the same town and avoided any hospitalizations, her claims of illness notwithstanding. Unfortunately, like most factitious disorder and Munchausen patients, she refused to admit to the deceptions; therefore, she could not be treated for her true ailment, factitious disorder.

Libby and Rhonda suffered from additional mental disorders. The most important one—one that is seen in the majority of cases of factitious disorder and Munchausen syndrome—is *borderline personality disorder*. Borderline personality disorder usually appears before age 18 and interferes with an individual's ability to function well socially or in the workplace or it causes personal distress. It is characterized by most or all of the following criteria from the most recent edition of the definitive guide to psychiatric diagnosis, the *Diagnostic and Statistical Manual of Mental Disorders, 4th edition*:

- Frantic efforts to avoid real or imaged abandonment
- Unstable and intense interpersonal relationships in which idealization and devaluation of others alternate in the patient's mind
- Persistently and severely unstable sense of self
- Impulsivity
- Recurrent suicidal or self-mutilating behavior (self-mutilation, unlike factitious behavior, is readily acknowledged as self-inflicted; the patient does not attempt to conceal its cause)
- Instability of mood
- Chronic feelings of emptiness
- Inability to control anger
- Episodes of paranoid thinking

As both of these patients carried out their disease portrayals, they flitted around medical professionals like moths around a flame, taking risks and manipulating others as borderline patients typically do. Libby surrounded herself with counselors and therapists; Rhonda found a mentor who would become mother, sister, best friend, and guardian angel. Even though their dramas were carefully played out, the question still remains: How were they able to fool so many people, sometimes including highly trained professionals?

It isn't as hard to fool medical professionals as one might expect. Time and time again we see in the factitious disorder literature that patients expose themselves to multiple tests, exploratory operations, and diagnostic procedures. These tests may be done repeatedly, even by the same doctors.

As in any business, doctors want to please their customers. If a patient says, "You're missing something. I'm still in pain," doctors are likely to make every effort to please the patient, and so they conduct more tests. In other situations, a physician may say, "Everything looks normal, but since you're so sure of the ailment let's just go ahead and treat it." Having no cause to doubt their patients, physicians are motivated by a sincere desire to relieve the patient's suffering. Add to this

benign intent the fear of malpractice litigation in an increasingly scrutinized profession and the result is a treatment approach that leaves
no stone unturned. As a result, patients end up exposed to unnecessary medications, medical procedures, and even surgeries.

Sandra's Tale

Sandra presented herself as a member of a family so ravaged by
cancer that she underwent surgery to remove both her healthy
breasts and underlying tissue because of the apparent genetic risk of
future cancer. As awareness of hereditary cancers grows, individuals
who may be at risk on the basis of a family history are seeking a specialist's opinion to determine if medical or surgical intervention is
advised. For this reason, Sandra's case was viewed as fairly routine by
those treating her.

Sandra's husband contacted me to share the following heartbreaking
story, for which I had little advice to give. Sandra, a 40-year-old medical
transcriptionist, sought counseling at a genetics clinic. She expounded
upon the successful battle she had waged against ovarian cancer, first
diagnosed a decade earlier. She went on to claim that her mother had
died of breast and ovarian cancer several years earlier and that three of
her sisters had breast cancer, one of whom had undergone a bilateral
mastectomy. Sandra stated that her maternal grandmother, two maternal aunts, a niece, and a cousin had also had bilateral mastectomies
necessitated by cancer, and that a paternal aunt was suffering from ovarian cancer. She also claimed to have had five miscarriages. Eventually,
every bit of this information was proved false.

Based upon the history Sandra reported, the examiner concluded
that there was an overwhelming hereditary predisposition to breast
and ovarian cancer, and that Sandra's chance of carrying a corre-
sponding genetic mutation approached 90 percent. Prophylactic
mastectomy, about which Sandra had inquired all along, was
endorsed as an option. She was cautioned that outside records would
need to be obtained to ensure that there were no misunderstandings
about the various cancer diagnoses, but apparently this task was never
completed. Sandra was advised to undergo DNA testing but declined,
saying she could not afford the part not covered by insurance.

Sandra was next seen by a cancer specialist who, armed with the
genetic clinic report, agreed with her decision to proceed with the
removal of both breasts. He noted that several previous breast biopsies

had revealed only fibrocystic disease and that a specialized mammogram was negative. Regardless, Sandra reiterated that she preferred mastectomy over anti-estrogen medication and close follow-up. She had a bilateral radical mastectomy during the following month.

A later review of Sandra's records disclosed a long history of misinforming others that she suffered from illnesses such as diabetes. Over time, these assertions had been met with increasing complacency. She had also manufactured stories of personal crisis intended to mobilize friends' support. However, she was not known to have undergone any unwarranted surgery. Her family was unaware until after the operation that it had taken place.

During a four-hour "intervention" by her family and friends and her priest, Sandra could not offer any consistent or convincing explanation for her behavior; for instance, she claimed at one point that she hoped the surgery would lead her husband to divorce her, but could not elaborate. At the end of the meeting, she agreed to psychiatric care but changed her mind the next day and fled. Her whereabouts are uncertain.

As a result of Sandra's compelling reports, and the unlikelihood that a woman would seek the unnecessary removal of her breasts, her physicians took her reports at face value and did not carry out the process of objective corroboration and confirmation. The false premise under which surgery occurred was not discovered until afterwards.

Sandra's case reinforces the point that health care professionals are loath to question information supplied by patients. Their thoughts are not about whether someone is faking an illness or, in this case, a family history. Indeed, their blind trust and failure to follow through with plans to access records have placed them at legal risk in Sandra's case. Her husband, for one, has considered launching a malpractice suit against the surgeons.

The variations are ever-changing. For instance, this case, recounted directly to me by a co-worker, involved a British woman who feigned cancer (and bereavement) despite enviable social skills. Clearly, though, she needed the limelight always to shine on her.

Jackie's Guise

I met Jackie a few years ago when we worked in the same office. When I joined the department, I was told that poor Jackie had recently lost her live-in boyfriend as the result of a blood clot following a motorcycle accident. They had been together for the last 8 years. Jackie was keen to talk about his death. She went into great detail about the circumstances of finding him unconscious at home, calling an ambulance, etc. Of course, we all felt very sorry for her. She said that she had recently moved to our town and that her parents lived in Scotland where her father was a physician, so she knew very few people here and was lonely. Jackie also told us that she held a Ph.D. in Anthropology and lectured on this subject part-time at a particular university. Naturally, we all rallied around Jackie and included her in social events. We invited her into our homes for meals and to stay the night. Around Christmas time, Jackie held a party at her home and invited all her co-workers. We had a great time. Jackie was a charming, witty, and entertaining hostess and we all enjoyed her company.

I worried about what Jackie would do during the Christmas holidays, as I didn't like to leave her alone when she had so recently been bereaved. She assured me that she would be with her parents over the holidays but would be back shortly thereafter. On New Year's Eve, I telephoned her to ask how Christmas had been and what she was doing for the New Year's celebration. She sounded subdued and asked me not to tell anyone, but she had discharged herself from hospital that morning after undergoing emergency surgery for appendicitis the previous day. I was horrified that she was alone in her flat when she had just had a general anesthetic, so my boyfriend went round in a cab and fetched her back to my house to convalesce. She certainly looked as though she had just had surgery. She could not walk very well, was stooped, and had a large dressing on her abdomen. Of course, I told my boss at work, who insisted she remain home until she felt better. Jackie returned to work about a week later and seemed much recovered. The following Sunday, Jackie and I went to another friend's house for lunch. Jackie told us that 3 years previously she had suffered from leukemia and described the ordeal of undergoing chemotherapy and losing her hair. She told us that it was the second occurrence of the disease—she had also had childhood leukemia.

A couple of weeks later, Jackie was not at work and had phoned in sick. I phoned her to see if she was okay. She sounded really upset and was crying on the phone so I went round to see her. She was sobbing uncontrollably and told me that the hospital had contacted her and told her that during her treatment for appendicitis, they had taken blood tests which revealed that the leukemia had returned. This was devastating news and I offered to accompany her to the hospital, as she said she had to go for a lumbar puncture procedure the next day. She refused my offer, telling me that her friends from home were coming to be with her. Jackie came back to work in between chemotherapy sessions and had a bandage around one hand with a small IV spout attached. She said that she would have to keep it in place until the treatment was finished and that a nurse would visit her at home every day to change the dressing. She would phone us while the nurse was there and carry on conversations with this person, although we only ever heard her side of the conversation.

Jackie's hair became very clumpy and patchy. She had her hair cut at my house one day and my hairdresser commented that it seemed to be growing back very quickly as there were patches of stubble. Jackie explained that not everybody lost ALL their hair: It depended very much on the level of treatment. Around this time, she confided in another friend that she only had 8 months to live. Of course, our friend told us and once again we rallied around, taking her out, buying her gifts, and cooking her meals to tempt her to eat as she was by now very thin.

On one of our evenings out, Jackie had spent a long time talking to a friend of ours called Adrian. Adrian was charmed with Jackie and devastated that such a lively personality had such a short time to live. He used to e-mail her to check on her and often came to sit with us when we were in the pub. On Valentine's Day, Jackie came in to work with a card and red rose that she said had come from Adrian and that they were going out on a date that night. The following day, she came into work and described in hilarious detail how the date had gone, what they had eaten, what they had talked about, and how her father had come to collect her and insisted in sitting at the same table, proceeding to give Adrian the third degree. We all thought it sounded like a riot of an evening.

The following Friday, my boyfriend was down at the pub and bumped into Adrian. He asked him how his date had gone. "What date?" said Adrian. "Oh," said my boyfriend, "I must be mistaken." When he came home and told me this I was very confused. I thought maybe Adrian was just shy about the date and didn't want to discuss it.

The last time I saw Jackie was the day before I moved. She came around to see me and was very upset as our boss had told her that she was not to return to work until her treatment was finished and she was on the mend. Later that day, I received a call from my boss asking if I had heard from Jackie. I told her about Jackie's visit and she said, "I hope you're sitting down." She then proceeded to tell me that she had had doubts about Jackie for some time and so to put her mind at rest had done some investigating. She had started with the electoral register and found that Jackie had lived alone at that address for the last 2 years and that there was no mention of her late boyfriend. However, a man with the same name had lived in the same building for some time, and continued to do so. Death records were checked for the date Jackie's boyfriend had died and there was no record of any death. None of the hospitals in the area had any record of Jackie. The university she claimed to lecture for had her listed as a part-time student but had no lecturer by that name.

I was very hurt and confused. I couldn't believe that anyone could make up an entire life that was just a web of lies. I couldn't believe the time, emotion, and money I had put into trying to make her life easier. Looking back, I suppose some things didn't add up, but at the time I just didn't question it.

I didn't contact Jackie again and never heard from her. I guess she got the message that she had been found out. I thought that was the last any of us would hear of her and expected, given the tissue of lies she had told, she would move away and start over somewhere else.

This week, we had a new contractor start in our office. She picked up a stapler and saw Jackie's name written on the bottom. "I know her," she said. "She works at the place I just left. Did you know her boyfriend just died this year?"

Of course, we had to tell her what we knew. Apparently she is doing it all over again. All her new work mates offered to go to the funeral and support her but somehow never managed to find out when it was taking place. She recently had a party at her house to cheer herself up and said that, having just moved here, she doesn't know anybody. A new guy had also asked her out. She'll give them all the details of the date when she gets back. Oh, and by the way, this time her boyfriend had died of leukemia. Well there's a surprise.

The sad thing is that Jackie could have made and kept friends without having to tell all these ridiculous attention-getting tales. But I guess the glow of ordinary friendship didn't burn bright enough for her.

Jackie's story, as told by a friend and admirer turned saddened realist, gives us a valuable first-person perspective on the roller coaster of thoughts and emotions experienced by those who encounter factitious disorder patients. The notion that a person would lie about a serious physical affliction becomes even more befuddling when combined with lies about sudden bereavement and exciting romantic possibilities. It also shows that factitious disorder is very much an international phenomenon—in fact, reports have come from every developed country and even from developing countries such as Saudi Arabia, Nigeria, Kuwait, and Oman. Regardless of where cases arise, surprise, confusion, anger, sympathy, cynicism, hard-won wisdom—all are the effects factitious disorder patients leave in their wake. Jackie was skilled in making herself known, but, whether she intended it or not, she became unforgettable to everyone caught in her web.

Contributing Factors

This chapter presents patients with very different problems and circumstances, but the fundamental treatment question remains the same. Is there an underlying problem in which clinicians can intervene? It is important to acknowledge the various internal or environmental contributions to underscore that factitious disorder is almost never the sole problem.

We don't know why certain people react so differently from others in the same situation. Many people have grown up amidst strife, including childhood maltreatment, but never resorted to ruses of illness. Why did Rhonda, Libby, and Sandra choose their particular paths? What factors contribute to the development of medical deception? Is it a biological disorder? Is it situational? Is it related to early life experience? Or is it a combination? Studies suggest that all of these have been contributing factors in specific cases of factitious disorder, and I will provide illustrations throughout this book.

More than 3,000 reports on factitious disorder appear in the medical literature, but these reports are almost always incomplete because of the very nature of factitious disorder patients and the flight reaction that takes over when their hoaxes are discovered. Most of the articles describe single cases in idiosyncratic ways that prevent sound comparisons among patients. Those who have learned of my work have often chosen generously to share their own experiences with me, and I am grateful for their reports.

2

Disease or Deception? An Overview of the Issues

This chapter opens with the undeniably sad story of Gayle, who died as a direct result of her factitious disorder. But the chapter goes further to detail the other possibilities when a patient exhibits an unexplained medical complaint, including malingering and the somatoform disorders of somatization disorder, pain disorder, hypochondriasis, and conversion disorder. It provides a historical context for playing sick and describes how the research and medical communities classify such patients, whose numbers are far greater than most professionals might ever suspect.

The Encounter with Gayle

No one in the emergency department suspected anything unusual when the 31-year-old hospital security guard was admitted with flu-like symptoms. Complaining of chills, fever, and headache, Gayle described her symptoms persuasively and demanded that she be hospitalized. She was agitated and argumentative, stating that she had spent 8 days with the same symptoms in another Kentucky hospital; the hospital had treated her shabbily, she said, and the doctors there had failed to diagnose her illness. When staff pressed for specific details about her personal medical history, Gayle became suddenly quiet and seemed reluctant to say anything further.

While waiting for routine tests to be performed, Gayle excused herself to the ladies' room. When she did not return, a nurse decided to check on her and was horrified to find her dead. Scattered around her body were various drugs including antibiotics and laxatives, alcohol and iodine pads, a package of brewer's yeast, a syringe containing a whitish substance, and a paper bag containing a pale-colored powder.

Given Gayle's sudden, unexplained death, the articles on the bathroom floor were sent to a state crime laboratory where chemical analysis revealed that the syringe and bag contained ordinary corn starch. An autopsy disclosed that Gayle had been injecting yeast and corn starch into her veins, some of which had formed clots that traveled to her lungs and killed her. Apart from arteries that were clogged with yeast and starch, she showed no other signs of a physical problem.

Information that emerged after her death revealed that she had been hospitalized 11 times in 3 years in Texas and Kentucky for complaints ranging from back pain to bloody urine. She had undergone numerous exploratory operations and at one point had been referred to a psychiatrist, but she had not kept the appointment. The hospitalization about which Gayle had complained so vehemently shortly before her death had been even more dramatic than she admitted, for doctors there had discovered a needle, syringe, and yeast in her nightstand and confronted her with this evidence. Her ruse discovered, she fled the hospital against her doctors' wishes and went straight to the hospital where she died.

Gayle's personal background was as grim as her medical record, overshadowed by a dreary childhood spent in an orphanage and an adulthood marked by divorce and single parenthood. A post-mortem diagnosis of Munchausen syndrome was made by the coroner. The authors of the report about Gayle, which appeared over a decade ago in the *American Journal of Emergency Medicine*, accurately subtitled their article, "Sudden Death Due to Munchausen Syndrome."

In her desperation to be hospitalized and receive care in a dedicated, stable environment that starkly contrasted her own life, Gayle had found a way to use fairly innocuous substances to create serious-looking symptoms. She lied and misrepresented herself many times, not only to medical professionals, but also to her children and co-workers. It is doubtful that she intended to kill herself. In fact, her last effort to gain admission to the hospital may have come from an intuitive sense that she was in serious trouble. Unfortunately, we will never know. Her physical illness had been a forgery, manufactured for emotional gain; it turned into something all too real and ended as something all too tragic.

Creating Symptoms

Researchers classify patients with *unexplained medical complaints* (UMCs) into two general categories. One category includes patients who consciously create symptoms in themselves, either for secondary (material) gain as in malingering, or for more subtle benefits such as emotional support as in factitious disorder. The second category includes patients whose symptoms are purely unconscious expressions of stress, as illustrated by somatoform disorders. *Somatoform disorders* include *somatization disorder*, which is distinguished by a history of an inordinate number of unexplained physical problems; *pain disorder*, in which emotional distress is communicated through complaints of persistent pain; *hypochondriasis*, which is a faulty conviction, despite supporting aches and pains, that one is diseased; and *conversion disorder*, which involves a loss of or alteration in physical functioning, such as sudden paralysis, blindness, or mutism. Unlike the somatoform disorders, malingering and factitious disorder involve deliberate, willful disease forgeries.

Thus, UMCs range from malingering—in which the person knowingly lies and acts sick for obvious, tangible gains such as narcotics, malpractice payments, Social Security Disability dollars, or insurance compensation—to the aforementioned conversion disorder (further discussed below). Unlike conversion disorder, malingering may be viewed more as a crime than a psychological disorder, though it could suggest the presence of some underlying personality problem. Factitious disorder, which falls between malingering and conversion in the range of UMCs, is a conscious act as malingering is; however, the goal is intangible and psychologically complex, involving some form of emotional satisfaction. That duality places it in the middle.

Deliberate Disease Forgery

Intervention into a false illness requires a full understanding of the ailment's symptoms and how they came to be. The signs and symptoms of illness can be created in several ways: 1) *exaggerations*, such as the patient who claims to have devastating, incapacitating migraines but really has only occasional mild tension headaches; 2) *false reports*, as in the patient who groans about severe back pains but isn't really having any pain at all; 3) *falsifications of signs*, as in the patient who alters a laboratory report, manipulates a thermometer or spoils a urine specimen so abnormalities appear; 4) *simulations of signs and/ or symptoms*, such as mimicking the symptoms of a brain tumor or spitting up blood that was actually red fluid concealed in a rubber pouch inside the mouth; 5) *dissimulations*, which involve patients who conceal illnesses to allow them to progress before they seek medical attention (perhaps the most difficult to detect); 6) *aggravations*, such as rubbing dirt into a laceration from a spontaneous fall; and 7) *self-induced signs or diseases*, as in the patient who complains of fever and pain after actually inducing an infection by injecting herself with bacteria. As noted, sometimes the purposeful production of physical symptoms even becomes life-threatening, giving ironic truth to the original lie.

Individuals apply any or all of the preceding techniques. The extremes to which simulating patients go to create the appearance of illness seem to contradict everything we know about human nature. As I will show in subsequent chapters, their self-harming methods are often so bizarre, and yet so effective, that they defy the imagination, let alone medical knowledge. Many patients simulate disease by surreptitiously giving themselves medications. For example, one man displayed symptoms of what appeared to be hypoglycemia (low blood sugar), and doctors ultimately found out that he was injecting himself with insulin despite his not having diabetes. Some patients bleed themselves to simulate anemia; others inject anticoagulants into their systems to cause a bleeding disorder or use laxatives to produce chronic diarrhea. Doctors of such patients must be more than good diagnosticians; they must also be detectives.

A clinician who suspects that a symptom may be falsified or induced should be alert for various types of inconsistencies in the individual's evaluation. The individual's *reported symptoms* may contain obvious inconsistencies with his or her *behavior*. For example, a person may report that he or she is barely able to talk while speaking eloquently throughout the interview. The person who describes continuous disturbing hallucinations during the interview but shows no evidence of distraction illustrates this type of inconsistency. The behavior of a malingerer or factitious disorder patient may differ dramatically depending on whom he or she believes is watching. This disparity in presentation is illustrated by a person who acts in a confused, disoriented manner in the clinician's office but, shortly after leaving, is observed by ward staff winning a brilliant game of chess. The better a clinician understands characteristics of a true illness, the more likely he or she will be able to detect its forgery.

A cardinal difference between malingering and factitious disorder is that once exposed, malingering usually elicits feelings from doctors of irritation and of being wantonly scammed. Although factitious disorder can certainly elicit irritation as well, people also experience perplexity when they encounter it because the motives are not apparent. Gayle's sad case, which opens this chapter, is a prototypical example of factitious disorder; she never sought any goals other than a starched hospital bed sheet and the attention and care that came with it.

The following case illustrates the unique nature of malingering, the external goal that underlies it, and the unlikelihood of its evoking sympathy once the phony basis of the symptoms becomes apparent.

Roberto's Deception

I was retained as a consultant for a large corporation with warehouse-style stores throughout the United States. By his account, Roberto was shopping at one of the stores when he slipped on a wet surface. Other shoppers quickly turned as he called out and landed with a hard smack. Groaning and rubbing his buttocks, Roberto was rushed to a local emergency department (ED) for assessment of a possible broken hip. He spoke no words from the time of the fall onward, gesturing instead for a pad and pen. In the ED, he wrote on the pad that he was unable to speak as a result of the injury to his head. Baffled staff spoke to his wife, whom they had called, and she emerged from his ED cubicle to state that he was indeed mute. None of the doctors could fathom how a bruised bottom could result in the inability to speak.

Roberto filed suit, claiming the loss of speech as a result of an injury to his head. During the investigation, however, fellow shoppers agreed that he had never struck his head. More incriminating was the testimony of ED nurses who had heard Roberto speak to his wife in hushed tones on the day of the fall. They all stated that it was obvious that the mutism was an act in which both spouses had agreed to assume starring roles.

With this information unearthed, Roberto's lawyers quit his case. Remarkably, a new legal team summarily took over, demanding the

$1 million in damages the previous law firm had sought. The new attorneys stated that, happily enough, Roberto had recovered his ability to talk but, still insisting that he had hit his head, had simultaneously experienced the start of a persistent—and total—amnesia.

I was retained at this point. I noted that Roberto's ensuing deposition was a caricature of amnesia, with his responding, "I don't remember" and "I don't know" to every question—even when asked to say his own name. He claimed to fail to recognize his name even when it was presented to him. I noted later that the level of memory loss being malingered at that point mirrored that of end-stage Alzheimer patients. In addition, authentic amnesia patients try to minimize or hide their deficits; Roberto put them on burlesque display.

During a follow-up deposition, after the defense attorneys had again asked their questions and received the same empty replies, one had an epiphany. Noting that Roberto had been in the United States only briefly, he wondered aloud about the legality of Roberto's entry. Suddenly, Roberto became a font of information, recalling the date on which he obtained his Green Card, the names of the officials he met, and the name of the building in which the card was obtained. In his eagerness to prove that his entry was legal, Roberto exposed the true extent of his memory.

The new set of lawyers quit. Unbelievably, Roberto pursued other law firms, perhaps hoping for a token financial settlement. After all, a woman who had accidentally burned herself with McDonald's coffee had just been awarded a small fortune. His search was in vain.

To illustrate further, prisoners become malingerers when they fake medical disorders to be transferred from a prison to a hospital that has better conditions. A patient who pretends to have cancer to obtain narcotic drugs, saying they are needed to ease the pain, or who claims to have a chronic debilitating illness to be able to apply for Social Security benefits, is also malingering. The malingerer lies for purely material benefits; however, when the gains sought are emotional fulfillment, empowerment over health care providers or others, or simply the attention of caregivers or the community, the diagnosis is probably factitious disorder.

Caution is urged when attempting to differentiate between malingering and factitious disorder. Human behavior is often motivated by various conscious and unconscious objectives, and a person may feign illness to achieve more than one goal. For example, a man might pretend to have chronic pain in order both to procure narcotic pain killers and get attention from his wife. He may also unconsciously mimic a particular illness from which one of his parents suffered, thereby "sharing" their suffering. In such a case, several psychological factors are at work, thus making the patient much more than just a malingerer.

The Contrast with Conversion

Conversion disorder contrasts sharply with factitious disorder and malingering because of the patient's conviction in the former that he or she is actually ill. For example, a woman is about to strike her elderly mother when her hand suddenly falls limp and her arm becomes paralyzed. Is the woman faking paralysis to elicit sympathy as if to say, "Now look what you've done to me?" Or is the woman really physically ill, seemingly experiencing some divine retribution? The answer to both of these questions is, "no." This is a classic case of conversion disorder. The woman converts emotional paralysis (her sudden fearful discovery of her own violent impulses) into a physical paralysis as a kind of denial: Her mind uses her body to control negative impulses. The woman develops a symptom as a metaphor for unconscious emotions and actually believes that the physical problem is real.

An example of conversion on a massive scale occurred when more than 100 survivors of Cambodia's killing fields developed blindness after viewing unspeakably brutal beatings and murders at the hands of the Khmer Rouge. They experienced sudden blindness as an unconscious means of blocking out the visual horror.

Like conversion disorder, factitious disorder is a control mechanism, but in this case, patients manipulate the reactions of others by controlling their own symptoms. Just as kleptomania is often stealing for the thrill of the crime rather than for the stolen item, factitious disorder is often disease forgery for the sake of the forgery itself, coupled with the concomitant benefits of being ill (that may include nurturing, attention, sympathy, and lenience from others). Factitious disorder can occur in children, adolescents, and adults in varying degrees and, as we saw in chapter 1, often coexists with symptoms of some other psychological disorder, such as borderline personality disorder.

Brief Histories: The Origin of Munchausen Syndrome

Widely misunderstood even by health professionals, factitious disorder must be considered in a modern perspective instead of the historical view that erroneously grouped all factitious disorder patients under the extreme category of Munchausen syndrome. The term Munchausen syndrome was introduced by Dr. Richard Asher in 1951 in an article he wrote for the British medical journal, *The Lancet*, in which he described this illness as "a syndrome which most doctors have seen, but about which little has been written. Like the famous Baron von Munchausen, the persons affected have always traveled widely; and their stories, like those attributed to him, are both dramatic and untruthful. Accordingly the syndrome is respectfully dedicated to the baron, and named after him."

Munchausen syndrome is actually a misnomer. Baron Karl Friedrich Hieronymus Freiherr von Münchhausen (1720-1797) was an honorable man and a famous and colorful war hero. After his retirement from the German cavalry, he spent his time traveling around his homeland, delighting listeners with tales of his military adventures. Although he embellished some of his stories for dramatic effect, they were essentially true. Historical records bear no evidence of his having feigned illness or duped people into caring for him. However, Rudolph Erich Raspe, a thief on the run from German authorities, appropriated and anglicized the Baron's name for the title of a 1785 pamphlet of outrageous and patently false tales, *Baron Munchausen's Narrative of his Marvelous Travels and Campaigns in Russia*. That pamphlet, which was an immediate sensation in England and has prompted new editions ever since, led Asher to associate the great Baron with patients who had a syndrome characterized by itinerancy and sensational lies.

Asher noted that Munchausen syndrome is distinguished by the deliberate use by a patient of fantastic yet plausible stories to describe his or her history (called *pseudologia fantastica*), the use of self-induced dramatic symptoms to gain hospitalization, and peregrination (wandering or travel). He advised physicians to be alert to the possibility of Munchausen syndrome if a patient had 1) numerous surgical scars, usually in the abdominal area; 2) a truculent and evasive manner; 3) personal and medical histories that were fraught with acute and harrowing adventures that seemed to fall just on the wrong side of truth; and 4) a history of hospitalizations, malpractice claims, and insurance claims.

Since then, doctors have come to recognize that Munchausen patients make the simulation of disease the center of their lives; they are usually suffering from some concurrent psychological disorder; they have poor job histories and are almost always drifters; and they are relentlessly self-destructive, encouraging and submitting to countless unnecessary surgeries and dangerous diagnostic procedures over the course of their lifetimes. Their joblessness and wandering from place to place often put Munchausen patients at odds with the law in that, though generally seeking attention, they also use their symptoms to garner room and board and other types of ill-gotten gains. Many Munchausen patients also develop drug dependencies and obtain drugs illicitly. The drug abuse occurs because well-meaning doctors administer pain killers to try to relieve the alleged symptoms or because the patients have created real symptoms that require some form of chemically induced assistance. Yet another motivation for their drug-seeking behavior is the thrill of outwitting the physician. Unlike addicted malingerers, however, they are not after drugs per se.

With few exceptions in the last 50 years, the terms *factitious disorder* and *Munchausen syndrome* have been used interchangeably, but a distinction must be made between them. Not all patients who suffer from factitious disorder have Munchausen syndrome. Munchausen is the extreme and most dangerous form of the disorder, the pinnacle of a pyramid in which the benign use of illness is the base, factitious disorder is the center, and chronic and severe factitious disorder—or Munchausen syndrome—is the top.

The Beginnings of Factitious Disorder

Factitious disorder is not a discovery of modern medicine, even though Asher formally brought it into the realm of medical science and exposed it to scrutiny. As long ago as the second century A.D., Galen, the Roman equivalent of Hippocrates, reported his observations of medical signs and symptoms some people induced or feigned to simulate disease, including vomiting and rectal bleeding. Attempts to categorize this phenomenon were made in 1834 by English physician Hector Gavin; and one hundred years later, American psychiatrist Karl Menninger reported on polysurgical or doctor addiction, noting that it was marked by intense aggression against oneself and the physician, whom he believed symbolized the "perceived sadistic parent."

In 1968, Dr. H. R. Spiro took Menninger's theory a step further, proposing that the syndrome's progression is based on one's relationship with his or her parents. He observed that an early lack of parental nurturing, incomplete development of a sense of self, defects in conscience, and an inability to resolve early traumatic experiences set the stage for the factitious disorder to begin. He also noted that hospitals are a natural place for it to unfold because they are equipped to provide caretaking. He equated the wanderlust of Munchausen patients with their simultaneous search for and rejection of intimacy. He postulated that these patients turn to the medical profession as part of a masochistic ritual to transfer early hostility toward their parents to the hospital and place the job of inflicting pain in the hands of a doctor.

Over the subsequent 35 years, as the number of reported cases of factitious disorder has increased and doctors have had more opportunities to examine and observe these patients, researchers have added other predisposing factors, including significant physical illness or abuse as a child, anger against doctors for perceived mistreatment, and parents who falsified medical histories or otherwise practiced medical deceit in themselves. The very nature of our fast-paced, computerized, indifferent society is fostering factitious disorder as well. It just isn't easy to get sympathy, support, and concern in today's world.

Playing Sick Today

Researchers note that *professional patients*, one of the many informal terms that have been used by the medical community for factitious disorder patients, are men and women of above-average intelligence. With the exception of Munchausen patients, most lead productive lives when they are not in the throes of their disease portrayals. Also, people with factitious disorder tend to have more social supports than Munchausen patients, but still feel the need to seek outside nurturance. Their entire purpose is defeated if their deceptions are revealed, so they too deny their ruses, though usually less angrily. When emotional support begins to wane, the factitious disorder patient often creates a secondary crisis to generate renewed interest and additional emotional support. The patient may claim that a beloved relative has died or invoke some other personal tragedy which, when compounded with the alleged illness, mobilizes a new wave of concern.

The prevalence of factitious disorder is difficult to determine. After all, only unsuccessful deceptions are being recognized and reported. It's also difficult to track factitious disorder patients because some of them may feign illness, stop, and then return to it as stressors arise in their lives. The itinerant nature of Munchausen patients and the fear of detection experienced by all with disorders of simulation make it difficult to conduct formal studies, but a few have been completed. A consistent finding is that many factitious disorder patients work in health care settings holding such jobs as nurses, physical therapists, and nurses' aides. It is thought that for some people, the job of caregiver may be so emotionally draining that they begin to feel a desperate need for nurturance and use illness as a way of getting it. These people may also have a general fascination with medically related matters that leads them to go into medical fields in the first place.

Dr. F. Patrick McKegney, Director of Consultation-Liaison Psychiatry at Montefiore Medical Center in New York City, has reported that one percent of psychiatric consultation patients seen at his center were diagnosed by his team as having factitious disorder. That statistic is surely an underestimate of the prevalence of the illness, since patients with physical complaints alone are rarely referred to psychiatrists. Health care workers often do not recognize or suspect factitious disorder, and even when they do, they may hesitate to confront patients for fear of a vehement rebuttal. Also, because most factitious disorder patients never follow up on referrals to psychiatrists, many are never formally diagnosed.

Drs. Amanda J. Sutherland and Gary M. Rodin reported on a Toronto study in which factitious disorder was diagnosed in 10 out of 1,288 patients (or 0.8 percent) who were referred consecutively to a psychiatric consultation-liaison service. Significantly, only two factitious disorder patients agreed to ongoing psychotherapy, and one death that was attributed to factitious behavior occurred in the group. The researchers noted that although most reports of factitious disorder deal with physical symptoms, in another study 0.5 percent of admissions to a psychiatric hospital displayed only feigned psychiatric symptoms.

Drs. Sutherland and Rodin said that "since medical practitioners often do not detect psychiatric illness in patients with physical complaints, such referred cases likely represent only a small proportion of all factitious disorders." Thus, once again, the prevalence of factitious disorder is almost certainly far greater than statistics show.

In the Toronto study, factitious disorder patients ranged in age from 19 to 64, with a median age of 26 years. The average age of onset of disease simulation was 21 years. (Perhaps the onset of adulthood, with its concomitant stresses, causes certain types of people to play sick for sympathy.) When referrals were made, these patients had already undergone extensive medical diagnostic testing, including angiography (X-ray examination of the blood vessels), biopsy (removal of body tissue for examination), laparotomy (incision into the abdominal cavity), lumbar puncture (removal of cerebrospinal fluid from the lower back), and many had received medication. Several of these patients had undergone surgery, including one whose finger was removed because of a self-induced bone marrow infection. Another patient had received electroconvulsive therapy (electroshock treatments) for factitious depression. Although depression can be an underlying cause of factitious disorder, this patient faked her sadness, tearfulness, poor appetite, and other depressive indicators.

Of nine patients who had been told by their doctors that they were suspected of feigning illness, only one, the woman who had received electroconvulsive therapy, admitted to playing sick. One of the patients in the study, a woman who was legitimately ill with diabetes and had feigned several illnesses as well, denied inducing her symptoms and refused ongoing psychotherapy. She was hospitalized four months later for a condition which doctors attributed to her deliberately stopping her insulin in order to create symptoms. She died three days after her admission.

Drs. Sutherland and Rodin emphasized that factitious disorder is found in higher prevalence by researchers who specifically look for it among high-risk groups. They pointed to a study of factitious disorder among 343 patients who were referred to the National Institute for Allergy and Infectious Disease because of prolonged fever of unknown origin. Factitious disorder was diagnosed in 32 patients, or 9.3 percent. In a more recent case, 18.2 percent of patients presenting to a specialty referral center in Wisconsin with rat poison ingestion had deliberately done so as part of their factitious disorder, though the total number of patients studied was rather small.

Growing Ranks and Mounting Costs

Some attribute the swelling ranks of factitious disorder patients to greater availability of third-party payments such as those provided by insurance companies and medical assistance programs. Whether this factor contributes to the incidence of factitious disorder is uncertain, but what is clear is that feigned illness due to factitious disorder has added greatly to the cost of medical care in the developed nations. One factitious disorder patient reportedly accrued medical care costs in excess of $6 million. Modern medical care costs have skyrocketed over the past 30 years, and insurance rates have risen commensurately, forcing millions of Americans to live without health insurance. Medical care is not rendered free of charge. Someone has to pay for these highly specialized services—whether federal, state, or local governments (which means that taxpayers assume the bill), insurance companies, individuals, or hospitals that end up absorbing unpaid bills. Factitious disorder patients consume medical resources in overwhelming volume through their frequent hospitalizations, numerous surgeries, repetitive sophisticated diagnostic studies, and countless hours of care.

Dr. Dennis Donovan had a rare opportunity to observe firsthand how a single factitious disorder patient can incur a fortune in bills through feigned illness. In 1987, he wrote in the journal *Hospital and Community Psychiatry* about a woman who, over a 12-year period, had at least 52 psychiatric admissions. Her known psychiatric hospitalizations alone—which totaled 497 days—cost $20,500. She had also been hospitalized for intensive medical care on various occasions. Dr. Donovan was unable to trace some additional hospitalizations and could not obtain the patient's outpatient or prescription records to determine the cost of her outpatient care and drugs. This amount would have been significant, because, according to Dr. Donovan, the patient obtained prescriptions from as many as a dozen doctors at one time. This patient also lost 12 years of employment, and received disability pay and $15,000 in damages that she won from her employer.

The ascertainable costs of this patient's total care over a 12-year period were $104,756; conservatively adjusted, this figure is well over $2 million at 2004 rates. None of this patient's bills was paid. Dr. Donovan points out, "The extraordinary cost—both human and economic—of factitious illness might well be avoided through appropriate psychiatric intervention."

Gender and the Interface with Others

The professional literature indicates that Munchausen syndrome usually occurs among men in their twenties and thirties, while women (mostly between the ages of 20 and 50) are more often diagnosed with factitious disorder. The mainstream theory has been that the greater frequency of Munchausen syndrome in men has to do with the different ways in which men and women are socialized: The lack of roots, willful disregard for others, and edge of criminality seen among Munchausen patients ostensibly occur more often in men because society is more tolerant of these characteristics in men than women. The prevailing theory also suggests that homeless men are more likely than homeless women to travel from city to city, and thereby more likely to exhibit the wanderlust inherent in Munchausen syndrome.

As a subspecialty expert, with intensive experience over the course of more than a decade, however, I have not always concurred with the published literature. I have seen a clear female predominance among the Munchausen patients I have met. This finding may reflect a greater willingness on the part of women to seek psychiatric help. It is also possible that some women resort to drastic attention-getting behaviors to garner the attention more readily accorded men in essentially all societies. Whatever the reason, I believe that both disorders predominantly affect women.

The detective work of medical personnel doesn't always involve the factitious disorder patient alone. Sometimes the disorder is detected only through the patient's victims. For example, in the stereotypic case of *Munchausen by proxy* (MBP), in which a caregiver (usually the mother) creates symptoms in a child, the caregiver might at first seem devoted to the child—more than worthy of the praise and support of the child's health care providers and community. The parent is not discovered until the child's fake or induced illness is discovered, if it is ever uncovered at all. Similarly, in a rare variant of Munchausen by proxy called Munchausen by adult proxy, symptoms are created in one adult by another who is seeking the praiseworthy role of the selfless caregiver. Again, the victim's symptoms and their patterns provide the clues to the real pathology behind the portrayal.

Victims of factitious disorder patients are not always primary victims, as in the Munchausen by proxy cases. In fact, secondary victims are much more common and are part of every case of factitious disorder. These victims are the family, friends, medical personnel, and others who become enmeshed in the ruse and devote time and energy to support the pretender. Many of these caring people have described their experience as one of emotional rape. Duped, then disillusioned, they may need therapy themselves; as integral players, they merit my attention in their own section of this book.

The victimization of others should not necessarily be regarded as criminal, however, for the havoc factitious disorder patients create for others is more often a by-product of their own psychopathology than a deliberate goal. During the perpetration of their factitious illnesses which sometimes last years, these people live within private hells of their own creation, unable to experience the fullness and joy of life because all their experiences must revolve around sickness. What makes their plight so sad is that they honestly believe that they must go to such outrageous, desperate extremes to obtain nurturance, support, and attention in their daily lives. Hamilton and Janata suggest that some seek the self-enhancement or self-esteem that comes with the association with medical personnel and the perception of being especially complicated. Other factitious disorder patients are full of rage, and defeating caregivers is a way to express that rage, which may be displaced from people in their lives, past and present. They may be especially delighted when the physician finally becomes aware of how badly he or she has been deceived. Others feel they've lost control of their lives, and outsmarting doctors allows them to feel in control. Whatever the motive, playing sick in lieu of communicating one's real needs or emotions is unhealthy, destructive, dangerous, and almost certainly more common than we know.

3

Pseudologia Fantastica:
Lies Larger than Life

Shy and lonely, Randall was the perfect target for Fred, who befriended and drew out the young introvert with fascinating stories about his past. Randall was understandably devastated when Fred revealed that he had just been diagnosed with an aggressive cancer and had only a short time to live. This lie was only the beginning of an elaborate fantastical ruse that would eventually pull Randall into a consuming world of Internet romance, international friendships, and political intrigue: all manipulations of Fred's disturbed imagination. About one-fourth of all patients with factitious disorder —and almost all with Munchausen syndrome—exhibit what is called pseudologia fantastica, gratuitous lying about one's personal history, often with extremely dramatic and elaborate scenarios. This chapter presents three intriguing case studies that demonstrate the relationship of pseudologia fantastica to factitious disorder and how it contributes to the difficulty in making an accurate diagnosis. It also provides an unsettling picture of the chaos, confusion, and heartache suffered by family and friends who believe.

Few within arm's length of factitious disorder patients are spared entanglement in the sticky web they spin. They deliver their tales so glibly that they often rival the most silken-tongued con artist and take in all parties. Factitious disorder patients then help the hoax assume a life of its own, growing and seeking out new participants until (actually, *unless*) someone who is caught up catches on and inter-venes.

Ironically, the very nature of medical care, focused as it is on caring and curing and consumed with worries about patients' rights and malpractice claims, actually facilitates disease portrayals. The implicit obligation of the physician to his or her patient is the persistent pursuit of a definitive diagnosis and treatment, even when signs and symptoms defy logic. Vague or confusing descriptions of symptoms are not unusual in clinical practice; some patients are globally shy or inarticulate, or never developed the particular vocabulary to describe feeling-states, whether emotional or physical. However, certainly most of them want to be well and, if they can afford it, expect to see their doctors only once a year for a check-up and—they hope—a clean bill of health. Unless a person has a known history of factitious disorder, no clinician anticipates that a patient is seeking care for any reason other than a routine exam or a valid complaint.

Doctors expect their patients to be honest about their complaints and to try to verbalize them as clearly as possible so that they may be correctly treated. Generally, the more complete and accurate a patient's descriptions of symptoms, the easier it is to make a proper diagnosis. A self-aware and articulate patient is thus appreciated as an active participant in his or her own health care.

While solid information is necessary for optimal care, the old adage about too much of a good thing may apply at times. An abundance of information, including excessive drama in the presentation of symptoms and far-fetched, even extraordinary stories about the patient's life, is a cardinal feature of Munchausen syndrome. The pathological lies about past or current life events, *pseudologia fantastica*, may be unceasing, or they may revolve around the claims of illness as the moon rotates around the Earth—coming into full view at times, remaining mysteriously cloaked at others.

The following story about Fred, told from the perspective of his devoted friend Randall, demonstrates the relentless progression of pseudologia fantastica. Beginning with a credible but disturbing lie, Fred's stories soon escalate into increasingly outlandish tales that defy reason, yet Randall continues to believe. Even when faced with evidence that he has been duped, Randall's investment in the lie becomes so complete that he cannot bring himself to accept the truth. Fred literally alters Randall's reality, creating an illusory world of romance and political intrigue—all of the intimacy and adventure that is lacking in Randall's lonely and ordinary life. The psychological consequences to Randall and others like him are the most disturbing elements of pseudologia fantastica.

Randall's Encounter

About two-and-a-half years ago I went to a local car club meeting and met a guy there named Fred. He shared the same love of cars as me so we instantly became friends. He was always telling me entertaining stories about his three Navy SEAL buddies, Scott, Chris, and Lyle. They were a close knit group of guys until Lyle and Chris died in a car accident three years ago. He had TONS of incredible stories about them.

After a year-and-a-half of hanging out together things started getting kinda weird. Fred broke up with his girlfriend Julie and lost his job at the same time. I felt really really bad for him. He was constantly calling me. After awhile, he wanted to hang out everyday. I finally told him that we shouldn't spend so much time together.

A couple weeks later, I got an e-mail from Fred that said he had been diagnosed with bone cancer and he was told he had four years to live. I was stunned! I felt so bad for him. I wanted to do anything I could to be there for him. He said his dad died from bone cancer 15 years ago so he was really scared. I asked him if I could go visit him in the hospital, but he said he didn't like hospitals since the time his dad died and he just didn't want visitors.

I got really angry that he would not let me visit him and I wrote him an e-mail basically telling him off. A few minutes later, I got an e-mail back from his friend Scott, the surviving Navy SEAL. Scott basically said I needed to calm down and this was not the time to yell at Fred. Scott lives in Madrid, Spain and works at the Embassy there. Scott was in town to be with Fred and was using his laptop computer in the hospital room.

I had heard so much about Scott. We started talking until, before I knew it, we were chatting every single night.

Eventually I was introduced to Scott's wife Jessica through e-mail. She was really cool too. I knew that they appreciated everything I did for Fred. Scott wanted Fred to come to Spain to live with him so he wouldn't just die on him like his other Navy SEAL buddies. Scott figured Fred would not go to Spain unless I went too. Scott asked me to come to Spain and to talk Fred into going also.

Scott arranged for Fred and I to go visit Madrid in August, and even introduced me online to a girl, Maria Elena. Maria Elena was the best friend of Jessica. She was awesome! I found myself falling in love with her. We made so many plans together for when I came to Madrid. I knew she was the one for me.

Well, August 2001 came and it was time for the visit to Spain. I bought gifts to take for everybody. I was all packed and ready to go when I got an e-mail from Jessica. Scott's dad had committed suicide and he was too upset to have company.

I was so sad and I cried when I called Fred to relay to him the bad news. Over the next few months, I spent every single day e-mailing with Maria Elena. We talked for hours. I was so disappointed that I couldn't see her, but I figured I'd see her eventually. She told me she loved me for the first time, and I told her I loved her. We started talking about marriage and kids and everything.

In August I started to notice weird things. I could list a million red flags. The main things I noticed were that I never got e-mails from Scott, Jessica, or Maria when I was on road trips or vacations with Fred. I noticed that the word "tomorrow" was misspelled "tomarrow" by all 4 of them. Certain phrases that Fred would say, Maria would say. There were similar writing styles. But I dismissed all that because they were all such different people. There is no way anybody could have such a good imagination like that, I thought.

After the September 11 terrorist attacks in the United States, Scott feared for his family's safety so he put them and Maria Elena all on a yacht belonging to Scott's millionaire friend Ahmed. I was frustrated because I wanted to talk to Maria on the phone. Whenever Maria was in port, we were able to talk by e-mail. The same weirdness followed. I house-sat with Fred for 2 weeks and didn't get an e-mail from her until the day we stopped house-sitting. That day she picked up all my e-greetings and we chatted that night... RED FLAG that "she" was really Fred!!! But it was a red flag I couldn't see at the time.

At that time also, Fred finally got a job at a local car dealership and was working long days. Simultaneously, I wasn't able to talk to Scott or Maria that much. Supposedly they had to move around a lot because they were being chased by terrorists. Madrid did have a lot of problems with terrorism after 9/11 so I believed them. The good news was that they were all safe on the boat and they were expecting to be here in time for Christmas.

Maria and I had been talking for over 6 months now. I was very in love with her, and she was with me. She was going to be my wife, and we talked about EVERYTHING. We even started naming our kids together. I couldn't wait to see her and start my life with her. I couldn't wait to hold her after all these months. I mostly just wanted to see her so I could relieve the burden of all the suspicious things that were happening.

A few days passed and on December 22, the date they were supposed to be here, they had not arrived yet. Fred was getting worried, but he said he talked to them and they were off the coast of Mexico. On the 23rd I got a call from Fred saying he was worried and that he was going to Mexico to look for them and contact the coast guard. I lost my breath for a second. My gut told me that this was going to happen. I told him that the boat had better not sink because that's what people were assuming would happen. He acted nervous and then hung up. A few hours later, I got a call on my new cell phone. The caller ID was blocked but I answered it. "Hi Randall, this is Scott. I'm trying to reach Fred, is he with you? We're having problems with the boat." I KNEW IT WAS FRED. I realized that one year of my life, my future in a new country, a new circle of friends, a NEW WIFE, it was all a lie!!!

I knew what I had to do. I knew I needed to talk to Fred's family. I found his mother's house, went up to the door and his mom answered. I asked her if she knew his friends Scott and Jessica. She said no. I finally got the courage to ask her, "Does Fred have cancer?" She said NO. I then asked if he had been a Navy SEAL. Sickeningly, she again said NO. EVERYTHING WAS A LIE. I felt totally betrayed. I called Fred, and he of course denied everything. I was calm when I told him to never contact me again and to NEVER run into me in the street because I might do something bad to him.

I had a lot of red flags that I should have paid more attention to, but I was thinking with my heart instead of my head. My best friend of two-and-a-half years betrayed me and now I feel like I've lost 4 of my best friends. It was only one person though, and that is what is making me so insane. I feel like Fred, Scott, Jessica, and my soul mate Maria Elena all died at once. I was chasing a hopeless dream though. Even with all the overwhelming evidence, I'm still having a hard time letting go. I re-read all the e-mails, over and over and over again, trying to figure out how this guy could have pulled this off. I'm so angry at myself for letting this happen to me...for being so naive.

Randall's emotional health was seriously compromised by events that robbed him of the friendships, the family, and the future that he thought were already his. Enduring depression and anxiety eventually led Randall to seek mental health counseling. With the help of a therapist, Randall learned to be more circumspect. In time, he began taking more responsibility for his social life. Instead of retreating to the safety of the computer screen, Randall is now overcoming his innate shyness by developing outside relationships through church and a singles group.

Though Randall's relative isolation and gullibility made him ideal fodder for pseudologia fantastica, few individuals will ever encounter an individual as predatory and merciless as Fred—and one as resilient, as Fred swiftly and masterfully regrouped each time his lies threatened to collapse under their own weight. Randall is now unmistakably, unshakably, and admirably coming to terms with the complex emotional issues arising from this life-altering experience.

Pseudologia Fantastica, Both Past and Present

Pseudologia fantastica is one of the most intriguing elements of factitious disorder and especially Munchausen syndrome. Also known as *mythomania*, pseudologia fantastica has such well-defined characteristics that some researchers believe it is a sickness unto itself, deserving of further specific study. Typified by enduring stories that are often built upon some element of truth and that become self-aggrandizing, pseudologia fantastica is seldom used for profit or material gain, but for the kind of intangible benefits that underlie Munchausen syndrome. These facts make it a unique subset of pathological lying, which more commonly is used for material gain and/or has utterly no basis in fact.

Tellers of these tales believe their own lies only to the extent that they need to in order to be totally convincing. Upon confrontation they will acknowledge, at least in part, what they have lied about. Delusional patients, on the other hand, hold fast to their beliefs no matter what evidence to the contrary is presented. Since before the turn of the century— well prior to Richard Asher's creation of the term Munchausen syndrome—pseudologia fantastica was recognized as a distinctive disorder. People who employed it were dubbed *pseudologues*. A medical paper written in 1909 by Dr. E. Dupre itemized three cardinal criteria for pseudologia fantastica: The story must be probable and maintain a reference to reality; the fanciful adventures must nevertheless not strike the listener as ridiculous; and while the theme of the adventures may vary, the distinctive role of hero, heroine, or victim is almost always reserved for the storyteller. Viewed within its broader historical definition and not just from the limited perch of its modern association with Munchausen syndrome, it has several other, less classic features. It usually begins during adolescence; the ranks are evenly distributed between men and women; pseudologues often manifest frequent career or job changes, vanity, and facile and eloquent use of language; and they have a low tolerance for frustration. One-fourth of all pseudologues, male and female, simulate illness in addition to lying, and one-fifth of them not only feign sickness, but also take it on the road (as in Munchausen syndrome). In some Munchausen patients, pseudologia fantastica may be the primary disorder with disease simulation but a secondary behavioral manifestation.

The "Successful" Liar

The next case, that of Miranda, makes one wonder how she was able to convince so many people that her fantastic stories were genuine. People like Miranda and Fred—those with pseudologia fantastica—are usually very facile verbally, while the members of the audience are comparatively passive. Pseudologia fantastica patients talk and sound and act so believable that other persons just soak it up.

Pseudologia fantastica is not part of every factitious illness. Most factitious disorder patients tell only those lies that are essential to get their illness portrayal going and to give it a boost if sympathy starts to fade. Miranda's far-fetched stories, on the other hand, went well beyond the illness ruse as she concocted one tragic tale after another. Some theorists would argue that Miranda's lies were a defense mechanism against unacceptable impulses. For example, consider the sexual elements as you read Miranda's stories—rape, pregnancy, miscarriage, hysterectomy, and uterine transplant. This predominance of sexual themes could very well have indicated serious anxiety surrounding her budding sexuality—a denial of urges that she may have found frightening and forbidden. All of Miranda's stories were disaster-focused, placing her in the role of victim, but individuals exhibiting pseudologia fantastica are just as likely to re-invent themselves as athletic heroes, brilliant scholars, fearless adventurers, or unblinking stoics under adversity.

Miranda's Story

Miranda had not been an easy child. Even as a little girl she had exhibited many troubling behaviors. For example, every time her mother left her to run short errands, Miranda became extremely anxious. Her mother recalls that Miranda was only about five years old when she threw herself down the stairs in an attempt to prevent her mother from leaving her with a babysitter. Miranda had an especially difficult time adjusting to school because separation from her mother was intolerable. It was difficult for her parents to determine how much of her behavior was developmentally normal. They did not realize how serious their daughter's problems were until she entered middle school. Miranda was just on the cusp of her teens when her parents learned that she had been spreading horrific lies about herself around school.

Miranda told her teachers that she had been diagnosed with a brain tumor and was expected to live less than six months. She wrote goodbye letters to favorite teachers, asking them to pray for her and to please keep her story confidential. She produced a written account of how her funeral should be conducted and made a tape of musical selections to be played at the viewing. At the church she attended, Miranda was placed on the congregational prayer list. Her parents found out when the lie spiraled out of control and Miranda's closest friends became concerned. When the lie was discovered, Miranda entered into weekly therapy sessions.

After one year, Miranda was discharged from therapy with a positive prognosis and the assurance that she was doing well. Her parents were cautious but hopeful. Miranda entered high school and the behaviors promptly resurfaced at a new logic-defying level. Although she was an only child, Miranda claimed that she and her twin sister had been abducted and raped and that Miranda had become pregnant as a result of that assault. After escaping from their captor, Miranda and her sister were in a devastating car accident that took her sister's life and caused Miranda to miscarry. She claimed to have been taken out of school early that year so that she could undergo a hysterectomy which became necessary after the accident. Her mother stated that it was true that Miranda had been taken out of school early, but this was so that she could go to Europe with her parents. At school, Miranda stated that she went to Europe to attend memorial services for her twin sister. She also claimed that she nursed a close friend until he passed away from cancer. Her bereavement over her losses appeared genuine. She had seemingly lost a sister and a best friend following multiple personal traumas.

As time went on, Miranda's lies escalated to the point of absurdity. When she told a teacher that she had undergone a uterine transplant and was again pregnant, the teacher became suspicious and helped to expose her ruse. Miranda reentered therapy to help uncover her motivations and to control a depression that was now evident. Her mother noted that though Miranda had never practiced self-harming behaviors, within a short period of time she had lost 10 pounds and was gouging the pimples on her face, creating deep wounds.

Within 8 weeks, medication worked wonders in elevating Miranda's mood and ending her absorption with her death, her weight loss, and her self-mutilation—all symptoms of a smoldering depression that had finally become unmistakable. However, the pseudologia fantastica had predated her depression and, unfortunately, postdated it as well. Because, as an adolescent, she still lived in an insular world, her therapist advised her mother to check routinely with teachers, pastors, church congregants, and others about the tales Miranda was telling and bring any falsehoods to a crashing halt. Her friends generally refused to cooperate out of loyalty (an age-appropriate resistance to authority), but Miranda knew that she would inevitably be called to account for the houses of cards she erected almost everywhere she went, and she reduced her lying. Her parents realize, though, that their control over her woeful stories, and their ability to ensure that she complies with her antidepressant medication, will largely evaporate once she leaves their home for college or a job, as she has promised to do "as soon as I have the means to escape this KGB [her parents]."

Though Miranda was healthy, some individuals with pseudologia fantastica have, or used to have, authentic physical ailments upon which they elaborate, making their tales of hardship or derring-do even more compelling to doctors as well as the medically naïve. Sometimes, though, these apparent ailments are simply physiologic oddities of no medical consequence. For instance, 30 to 40 percent of people without any back pain or other relevant symptoms have significant abnormalities of the spine on radiographic examination. Those who are aware of these incidental findings can impute fake symptoms, including complete disability, to them. The following case, involving a more curious medical sign and first reported by Dr. Charles Ford, is illustrative.

Luis' Routine

Luis was born with *nystagmus*, rhythmic involuntary eye movements. This condition neither hinders vision nor was it a symptom of an underlying neurologic problem in his case. As part of his disease simulation, Luis would travel to emergency departments and say that he had just been in an accident in which he had hit his head and had become unconscious. A neurologic examination would inevitably follow, and doctors would notice the nystagmus, believe it to be a new symptom, and immediately admit him to the hospital for a possible brain stem contusion (or bruise). Knowing that his real but innocuous condition could be construed as something more serious under the right circumstances, Luis used his nystagmus as his key to the hospital doorway, and further exaggerated his situation with tall tales about his professional and social life in Miami, where he claimed falsely to live.

His medical condition appeared so interesting that his physicians presented him to their peers at a neurology conference. To Luis' dismay, one doctor attending the conference recognized him as having been at another local hospital only weeks before, where he had received the benign diagnosis and had been discharged.

This spontaneous discovery led to his being referred for psychiatric evaluation. Perhaps growing weary of the game or fearing further public embarrassment, Luis admitted to the psychiatrist that he had not only been faking illness but inventing his background as well—he was a local resident who had never even visited Florida.

The ability to lie convincingly is a major part of every successful presentation of a factitious disorder and one of the reasons why so many medical professionals have been duped by factitious disorder patients. Even when test results are negative, when physical appearance belies the presence of illness, and when there is no concrete information to back up claims of past illnesses and trauma, doctors are so taken in by these patients that they perform gratuitous tests and unneeded surgery (including the removal of healthy organs), and prescribe unnecessary medications. However, as suggested, relatively few factitious disorder patients feel the need to spin the yarns of pseudologia fantastica.

4

Invading the Body:
The Enemy Within

This chapter begins with the case of Flora, who was enacting one of the most dramatic and deadliest forms of factitious disorder: self-induced bleeding. It presents the confounding dilemmas faced by medical staff in caring for people who repeatedly take themselves to the point of death through compulsive blood-letting, admit themselves to a hospital, and then either refuse treatment or use up costly blood supplies in accepting transfusions. Many self-bleeders have jobs in medical settings and are skilled in obtaining the equipment—needles, needle casings, syringes—to covertly drain their own blood. (A search of one patient's room even revealed a copy of Transfusion magazine.) This chapter discusses the many manifestations of this type of factitious disorder, including various precipitating factors such as pregnancy. The chapter also emphasizes the role of physicians as detectives in tuning in to behaviors and medical histories that point to the possibility of factitious disorder.

Willing patients with factitious disorder can be treated in many instances with favorable results. But what about factitious disorder patients who refuse treatment? What happens to those patients who push their bodies beyond their limits and actually create dangerous, even deadly illnesses in themselves, then refuse to let doctors help them? Or to those who continue their self-destructive behaviors in spite of therapeutic efforts to save them?

Flora's Secret

I encountered one such patient, a 26-year-old laboratory technician, early in my career. With her ashen skin and alarmingly thin frame, Flora cut a ghastly figure. She was hesitant and timid when she entered the clinic of the prominent hospital at which she worked and, in an almost inaudible voice, complained of dizziness and weakness. Because of her appearance and symptoms, I ordered emergency tests on a sample of her blood. Meanwhile, I obtained a medical history from Flora, who insisted that she couldn't offer any reason for her condition. She said that she had been working effectively and that she had come to the clinic only because she had some free time and wanted to talk to someone about how poorly she had been feeling.

Although Flora offered little useful data, I was stunned by her blood test results. Her blood count was so low that I would have thought it was incompatible with life. I performed some additional tests including one to see if she was losing blood through her intestines, but every test was negative.

Flora's unresponsiveness to the news of her grave condition was abnormal. She asked no questions and showed no alarm or even concern. Here she was with a blood count so low that her life was in serious jeopardy, yet she could scarcely have been less interested. I doubted her truthfulness when she said that she had no clue as to how her condition had developed.

Flora's anemia was so critical that I wanted to give her an immediate blood transfusion, but she would only agree to accept an injection of iron. While waiting for the injection, she became restless and as she fidgeted, she told me, "Maybe this was a mistake. I just want to leave." Other doctors who were there with me pressed her for more information, and finally she confessed that when she felt upset she drew her own blood until she felt "satisfied" that she had drawn enough. With ready access to syringes obtained from the lab in which she worked, her bloodletting (also called self-induced phlebotomy or autophlebotomy) was easily carried out.

After owning up to her bloodletting and receiving the injection of iron, Flora bolted from the examining room with me in reckless pursuit. Instead of catching up to this patient, who disappeared into a stairwell, I stopped short and asked myself what I could possibly do if I caught her. Though her health was obviously jeopardized, Flora had never stated that she was suicidal nor was there evidence that she had drained her blood because she intended to kill herself. Medically, she was not going to die imminently, particularly with the iron now on board; in fact, she was outrunning me when I abandoned the chase! In such situations—in which profound suicidal feelings and actions are not present and death is not likely to occur at that time—any attempt to detain her could instead amount to assault and battery on my part.

I turned back toward the clinic, thinking that at least she had accepted the iron and we had made her aware that her actions had placed her in real danger. But I felt little consolation: Sometimes, as in the case of a curable lung cancer patient who continues to smoke despite our appeals to logic, we must simply allow patients to make bad decisions about their bodies.

Bleeding and Blood in Factitious Disorder

Almost all factitious disorder patients who feign blood disorders through the use of self-bleeding or other means are medical professionals and most are women, usually nurses. These patients fall into distinct groups based on the means they use to create their symptoms. For example, some, like Flora, use a very direct route to anemia, drawing their blood and either throwing it away, ingesting it, or putting it into their urine or bladder to create medical signs. One such patient received *1,000 units* of blood over a 30-year period because of autophlebotomy. Others use less direct means to create their symptoms including injecting themselves with anticoagulants (substances that prevent clotting) or swallowing rat poison, which contains an anticoagulant as its key ingredient. When self-administered in sufficient quantity, these drugs result in easy bruising or bleeding—symptoms that look like leukemia and some other severe blood disorders. Some factitious disorder patients achieve similar results with excessive doses of aspirin.

It is difficult to comprehend behavior so unnatural that it counters our most powerful human instinct for self-preservation. What could possibly motivate a person to treat herself as if she harbored an enemy within? There is still so much that we don't know about the psychological processes underlying factitious disorder. Perhaps the commonly accompanying borderline personality disorder causes patients to feel "unreal" to such an extent that they seek a confirmation of their personhood. Borderline patients who feel merged with some part of their environment, such as another person or a place, can use bloodletting as an instantly accessible reality check. Their own blood proves beyond a doubt, "I am real. I am an individual." In these cases, this disturbed behavior is a coping strategy to calm an even more disturbed thought pattern. Other theories about the reasons for self-bleeding are discussed toward the conclusion of the chapter.

Many cases of factitious anemia through self-induced phlebotomy have been reported by researchers. The first to appear in the English language were published in *Annals of Internal Medicine* in 1963. The authors described their experiences in treating two patients, one of which I have summarized next.

The Case of Rebecca

Rebecca was a 30-year-old laboratory technician who sought medical care for heavy menstrual bleeding. Doctors found only an enlarged ovary that would not have accounted for her reported bleeding problem. One month later, she was hospitalized for weakness and fainting. Although she had no signs of vaginal or other bleeding, her blood count was drastically low. Through exploratory surgery, doctors found a ruptured ovarian cyst. This finding would indeed account for *some* bleeding, so she was treated with a blood transfusion and iron and was then sent home. Doctors diagnosed her as having iron-deficiency anemia secondary to uterine blood loss.

Over the next few months, she complained of nausea and vomiting and was re-hospitalized with a host of other signs and symptoms including muscle pain, sort throat, cough, stomach pain, nose bleeds, and a dangerously low blood count. Test after test proved negative as doctors checked every possibility for the source of her blood loss. So severe was her anemia that life-saving measures were immediately taken. Iron therapy and several units of whole blood were administered despite her having had a history of allergic reactions to transfusions. After all this, her blood count fell again and she was hospitalized for re-evaluation. While she was in the hospital, her blood count began to rise without therapy, but when doctors pointed this out, instead of being elated, she predicted that it would fall again dramatically. Within 24 hours her prediction proved true. A battery of new tests still left doctors in a quandary. They were left to consider the only other possibility: Rebecca was stealing her own blood.

Hospital personnel searched the patient's room and found a needle, needle cases, syringes, transfusion tubing, and a copy of *Transfusion* magazine. After obtaining advice from a psychiatrist, doctors confronted her and she admitted to self-bloodletting and agreed to psychotherapy. When her anemia persisted in spite of outpatient treatment, she was institutionalized. Today, enforced institutionalization in such a situation would most likely constitute a remarkable deprivation of patients' rights, but it was not unusual at the time of this report in the *Annals*.

Psychiatric evaluation showed that this woman was depressed and extremely hostile toward medical professionals, but eventually she revealed feelings that stemmed from a traumatic personal experience. Her fiancé had been in an automobile accident and died after three months of hospitalization. During that time, he had refused to see her and doctors had honored his refusal, so she had been unable to check on his condition or see him one last time before he died. Her factitious disease was probably a way of getting even with doctors by confounding them and showing them to be inept, but in so doing, she placed herself in the gravest danger.

Given this woman's background and medical knowledge and the results of early tests, self-bloodletting might have been one of her doctors' considerations, but doctors are rarely trained to think of factitious illness in confounding cases even when all the evidence points to it. Had they done so, they might have saved months of observation and expensive testing and medical care.

Factitious Disorder around the World

Some mental illnesses tend to be associated only with certain cultures and certain periods of history, but this is not true of factitious disorder, which has been reported for many decades in countries around the world. Factitious anemia is a case in point. In 1949, a 44-year-old Norwegian woman was hospitalized because her urine contained blood and excessive protein, which are signs of kidney disease. During 14 months between late 1953 and January 1955, she received 40 blood transfusions for recurrent anemia, even though she showed no external signs of blood loss and tests revealed no evidence of hemolysis (the destruction of red cells while still within the body). Doctors ultimately diagnosed her as having factitious proteinuria (excessive protein). She had caused this condition by placing egg white, a pure protein, in her bladder through a urethral catheter. She had also self-induced anemia through bloodletting. This patient denied causing her own illness and was hospitalized for psychological evaluation.

Factitious bleeding is not just a Western phenomenon. For instance, in the Middle Eastern country of Yemen, an 18-year-old girl suffering from Munchausen syndrome arrived at a hospital bleeding from several places on her body. She also presented with ulcers on her tongue and air in the skin tissues under her face, around her eyes, and on her upper chest. Her disease forgery was uncovered when she was caught injecting air under her skin and lacerating herself.

In a 2003 Japanese case, a 25-year-old anemic woman confessed to years of self-bloodletting. She was given iron supplements and accepted a referral to a psychiatrist. Not soon afterwards, she was found dead: She had inserted a syringe needle into her arm and bled herself until she fainted. While she was unconscious, the blood continued to flow and she died of shock.

Why would a person willingly submit to blood transfusions? Why would someone ravage his or her body to the extent that the hoax becomes reality? There are no easy answers to these questions because the underlying motivations and catalysts for factitious disorder are as varied as the patients themselves. Still, as with other forms of factitious illness, the main goal of bloodletting and self-induced blood disorders appears to be the assumption of the sick role and the attention and nurturance it brings.

Dahlia's Chronicle

A 29-year-old, married nurse had been seen at a major diagnostic treatment center where doctors accused her of causing a blood disease by unnecessarily taking a chemotherapy agent that kills bone marrow. Dahlia denied knowledge of the true uses for the drug (knowledge a nurse would have), saying a friend had given it to her to build up her blood.

To save her life, this woman had to be transfused with packed red cells and HLA-matched platelets, which are expensive, scarce resources. A hematologist was assigned to her case, and even before her condition stabilized, he began a battery of tests to find the cause of her grave ailment.

Dahlia reported a medical history that was rife with blood problems, including a story that at the age of 19 an appendectomy had been delayed so that she could receive a blood transfusion because of anemia. She claimed that two years later she again developed severe anemia, for which she received repetitive transfusions and, she said, at the age of 24 her spleen was removed. She claimed that by the age of 27, because of anemia and severe bleeding associated with her menstrual periods, she had received over 500 transfusions of blood products.

She also created a dramatic background for herself, reporting that she had been raised on an elegant farm where life was filled with privileges and frivolity. She said that she had been a high school honor student, had studied at a prestigious university and nursing school, and ultimately achieved the status of head nurse at a medical institution near her home in Memphis, Tennessee.

Her medical history caused her doctors' curiosity to rise, and they consulted an expert in Munchausen syndrome, Dr. Charles Ford, to assess whether her illness was self-induced. She elaborated upon her story during the psychiatric consultation, saying that she had been a graduate student and researcher at the University of California at Berkeley. Unbeknownst to her, Dr. Ford was a native of that area, but he pretended to know nothing about Berkeley and the University and questioned her about them. None of her answers was correct, which led him to agree with the other doctors that she was likely to be lying about her illness. Their suspicions were confirmed when tests showed that Dahlia's blood contained high levels of a chemotherapy agent. She did not have, nor had she ever had, cancer and she had no reason to be taking such a potent and hazardous drug.

Dahlia had self-induced a rare and deadly blood disease called aplastic anemia. In aplastic anemia, there is a simultaneous drop in the number of red and white cells and blood platelets caused by a disturbance in the development of bone marrow.

As a nurse, Dahlia would have been familiar with the uses for the drug. She was a very sick woman, not only because of her anemia, but also because of the mental illnesses leading to her behaviors, not the least of which was borderline personality disorder. Typical of patients with this disorder, she created a high degree of discord among the hospital staff, engendering angry feelings and then provoking others to express their anger on her behalf. People on the hospital staff moved into two camps and then started fighting with one another.

Her need for life-saving interventions created the greatest controversy among the nurses, attending physicians, and house staff because these treatments are costly. Some caregivers believed that such limited resources were being wasted on a factitious disorder patient. Others were far more sympathetic and argued that the woman was seriously ill, both mentally and physically, and that she couldn't help herself and should receive proper treatment.

Dahlia was not psychotic and fully understood the implications of her actions, yet she continued to engage in life-threatening behaviors. When all the doctors involved with her case confronted her, she told them that they were crazy and that she didn't know anything about the drug. But when they pointed out that her blood level of the drug contradicted what she was saying, she repeated what she had told other doctors: that someone had told her it would be good for her.

Dahlia's physicians told her husband what she was doing and that she would die if her behaviors continued, but he seemed passive. He said, "Oh, my gosh, she is? We've got to do something." Then he went into her room and talked to her, and after a while he came out and said, "Gee, all of you misunderstand her illness." She had completely convinced him that the doctors didn't know what they were talking about.

In the midst of this mayhem, Dahlia demanded additional tests from her hematologist, but he refused to order them. Then she was found to be hoarding an addictive pain medication and, because of that, she was forced to leave the hospital.

Dahlia's mother was eventually contacted and she reported that the only true part of her daughter's story was that she really was a nurse. Her mother contradicted most of the other details and painted a grim picture of her daughter's childhood, which was punctuated by her parents' divorce and a financial situation that bordered on poverty. As a girl, she had been sickly and had a reputation for being a liar in grade school. Her menstrual periods, which began earlier than most of her peers, were so heavy that her mother occasionally had to bring fresh clothes to school for her. The girl developed a preoccupation with bleeding and blood early in her life.

After she was administratively discharged from the hospital, she went to another hospital with the same disease, then telephoned the hematologist who had handled her case and mockingly told him that she had done it again and this time managed to get the additional tests that he had denied her. Because of the extent of her illness and her continued factitious behavior, Dahlia most likely did not survive long.

Dahlia's early traumatic experiences with her menstrual periods, emotional neglect and deprivation as a child, nursing training, almost fetishistic preoccupation with blood and its products, and borderline personality disorder are the best explanations that can be offered for her perverse behavior. Biology may have played a role in that, even from a very early age, Dahlia had a reputation as a liar—to some unknown degree, the tendency to lie may have been inborn, or genetic. But the explanations remain incomplete and somewhat unsatisfying. Dahlia's only hope in breaking the bonds of her compulsive behavior was to accept psychiatric treatment, but like most Munchausen patients, she slammed the door on her thoughts and feelings and refused any offers of help.

The Drama of Self-Bleeding

Factitious disorder patients want dramatic symptoms that will cause doctors to take immediate note. Blood is both dramatic and highly accessible. When a person shows up at an emergency room with a very low blood count, doctors are going to take real notice. With just a little cut to an artery, a person can drop his or her blood count in a matter of minutes.

The risk at which factitious disorder patients place themselves is lost to them in their intense quest to achieve their overall goal. They develop a kind of tunnel vision which prevents them from noticing the real dangers of the symptoms they create. As you can see, in a number of these cases people have been given transfusion after transfusion. Death can result from an allergic reaction to blood. What's more, factitious disorder patients endanger others by using blood and its by-products, all scarce resources, by deliberately creating life-threatening conditions. They receive transfusions only to bleed themselves again. Barring the patient's death, the cycle can continue until the person is either caught or confronted—in which case he or she usually flees—or is gratified by the fulfillment of the needs that drove the ruse in the first place.

Exploiting Pregnancy

Researchers note that a number of pregnant women diagnosed with Munchausen syndrome have induced bleeding in themselves. Dr. Robert C. Goodlin of Omaha, Nebraska, reported several such cases, including vaginal bleeding in a 19-year-old girl who was in her third pregnancy. The daughter of a physician, her previous pregnancies had been marked by the same bleeding problem, which had led to long hospital stays. She had an impressive knowledge of medical terms, but insisted that she knew nothing of the cause of her bleeding. While hospitalized for examination, nurses found blood on her clothing and bed linen. Another patient, not the medical staff, finally uncovered her illness portrayal by catching her rubbing her vulva with such force that skin was missing and it bled to the touch.

In another case reported by Goodlin, a 23-year-old pregnant woman who had worked as a nurse's aide went to a hospital with what appeared to be blood-stained underwear and blood running down her legs. Like the young woman just mentioned, she had had painless vaginal bleeding during her two previous pregnancies. She was admitted to the hospital and doctors used ultrasound to confirm that her six-month pregnancy was normal. She left the hospital of her own accord after two days, only to return a day later covered with what again appeared to be blood. Nurses thought that the color seemed too intense for real blood, so it was tested and found to be an exogenous red liquid (i.e., one not produced by the body). The patient was furious when this trickery was discovered and left the hospital without pressing for admission. This woman had a history of emotional problems, and her children had been placed in foster care because she had physically abused them. Some of the same stressful conditions that contribute to such abusive behavior—strife-torn marriages or the hardships of single parenthood—often foster Munchausen syndrome. Yet only with further research will we fully understand what wires a person to respond to life's stressors by taking such extreme measures.

Charlotte's Perspective

Though never abusive to any children, Charlotte, an English-woman, endured first a bitter, unsettled marriage and then single parenthood. We became friends, first over the Internet and then in person. She provided this account.

In the early 1970s, I became pregnant again. It was not an accident, but I did not care about the identity of my child's father. I had lost custody of my first child because of a wildly unsettled lifestyle. But pregnancy offered a unique type of nurturing and I craved it. Suddenly, I could command attention, even if it was only because of the child inside me. In addition, motherhood offered me a way out of my peripatetic lifestyle, which was unsuitable for a baby.

Pregnancy offered hitherto opportunities for factitious behaviour. I bloomed into it after an authentic admission for cramps and blood loss. I caught a bus from my temporary accommodation to the hospital and was admitted to the labor unit. After a night on a monitor and injections to stop the contractions, I was transferred to a ward. In the company of mothers with their new babies and women with difficult pregnancies all having care lavished upon them, I knew exactly where I wanted to stay for the remainder of my pregnancy. With some "inspired" spates of contractions and self-inflicted bleeding, I managed to avoid transfer out of the hospital. Towards the end of my pregnancy, my symptoms were almost wholly factitious. The staff knew it, and they knew I knew. Attempts to discharge me continued, but I was saved at the last by the onset of edema and a rise in blood pressure. My labor began spontaneously, and my son was delivered healthy.

Why Pregnancy?

Goodlin observes that other pregnant women feign labor pains. Enacted labor pains are very difficult to prove, especially if a woman is medically knowledgeable. The apparently high prevalence of Munchausen syndrome in pregnant women may be the result of psychological and emotional turmoil fostered by pregnancy. Some women regress psychologically during pregnancy. At odds with the physical changes in their bodies, they feel more vulnerable because of their weight and inability to maneuver well. Also, pregnancy is a time that stresses a woman's sense of identity. If demands to be self-sufficient are made upon an emotionally vulnerable pregnant woman, and if she has to run a household and take care of other children and a husband as well as her unborn baby, she may seek an outlet that will allow her to be taken care of and to receive nurturance. Thus, playing sick can be a means of taking control and of escape and denial.

Conscious, Subconscious, and Unconscious Reasons

Pregnancy certainly isn't the only life experience that taxes body and mind and creates a sense of loss of control. The seemingly ordinary challenges of a routine life can create extraordinary stress for some people. When the task of living seems insurmountable, feigned or induced illness may become a way of coping.

Individuals who use implements such as needles to induce bleeding are engaging in consciously chosen behaviors. These patients have to go through the thought processes of obtaining the implement and surreptitiously and willfully engaging in the painful, disquieting acts of self-harm. Although the behaviors are carried out with full consciousness, their reasons may be entirely unconscious. One untested theory is that they are role-playing through a repetition compulsion sexual violation they experienced earlier in life.

In another self-bleeding case, the doctors came to believe that the patient's factitious disease had been instigated by an *anniversary reaction*. They conjectured that her illness was triggered by a key date in her life that called up memories, either conscious or subconscious (barely outside her conscious mind), that intensified feelings of personal grief. They had noticed that her hospitalizations and medical emergencies coincided not only with major holidays, but also with special occasions such as her child's birthday. It was also speculated that by feigning illness, this woman had been trying to cope with unresolved grief caused by her father's death when she was two years old. Her factitious behavior intensified and led to hospitalizations when her marriage began to sour and her husband, the only adult with whom she had a close relationship, threatened her with divorce. She was unable to cope with this intense domestic anxiety and she resorted to illness as a way of eliciting sympathy from her husband and forestalling the breakup. She responded well to her physicians' caring approach, seeming to substitute complaints of headache for the bleeding. Their willingness to stick by her may itself have been instrumental in her decision to end the behavior, but they recognized that the more severe factitious symptoms might recur when she was again experiencing extreme strain in her life.

In many cases, self-bleeding appears on its surface to be a form of slow suicide. Irrespective of the form it takes, the illness of the factitious disorder patient is a cry for help. It should always be regarded as such.

5

Feverish Ploys

Of all the symptoms feigned by patients who deceive, fevers are a trade favorite. Easy to falsify and often a harbinger of serious illness, fevers receive immediate, serious attention from medical staff. This chapter discusses the methods used (such as thermometer manipulation and deliberate infection) and delves into the emotional reasons why some patients are desperate enough to fly from city to city in pursuit of a hospital admission. It details the profound emotional needs of factitious disorder patients and the poignant and often tragic personal histories that contribute to their illness.

When patients have fevers—continuously or intermittently—for more than three weeks and test results are negative, they are said to have "fever of unknown origin" (FUO). FUO can indicate a number of underlying illnesses, some of them life-threatening, others less serious but still disturbing. When diagnosis of the underlying cause can eventually be accomplished, FUO proves most commonly to be due to infections such as tuberculosis, Lyme disease, or toxoplasmosis; cancer, especially Hodgkin's lymphoma and acute leukemia; and collagen vascular diseases that often combine fever with arthritis, such as lupus. Less frequently, one from a motley array of potential ailments is the culprit. The list includes the inherited disorder called Familial Mediterranean fever and unexpected adverse reactions to medications. Importantly, 5 to 15 percent of FUO cases defy diagnosis despite exhaustive studies. It is likely that a substantial proportion of these "inexplicable" cases are attributable to deception. Fever is one of the most popular factitious symptoms all over the world because, along with pain, it is among the easiest to feign.

As noted in chapter 2, in a study of 347 patients with prolonged FUO conducted by the National Institute for Allergy and Infectious Disease, more than 9 percent were diagnosed with factitious disorder. Short-term fever may not sound like a big deal, and in most patients it isn't; instead, it tends to be a sign of a minor viral infection and requires minimal treatment. But early in their training, doctors are taught to take careful histories, perform thorough physical examinations, and exercise close observation when working with febrile patients—especially those whose fevers are prolonged and mysterious. This fact makes fever an effective tool for the factitious disorder patient because it guarantees attention when presented in the proper context. Factitious disorder patients usually couple it with some other carefully chosen feature, such as joint or muscle pains. The combination is sure to bring plenty of attention and set doctors on a mad search.

Most of the factitious disorder patients who seek assistance for FUO are young women, very often in health-related professions. They generally fall into two groups: patients who manipulate thermometers and have had a bona fide febrile illness in the past, and slightly older patients who usually have serious psychiatric problems and frequently induce real disease in themselves to engage caregivers. Unless a rapid-reading electronic thermometer is used or the temperature of freshly-voided urine is determined and compared to the oral measurement, a person can easily cause the appearance of a fever simply by vigorously rubbing a thermometer on bed sheets, placing it in hot water, or drinking a hot liquid before a temperature reading is taken. Others have placed the thermometer near blazing light bulbs or switched pre-manipulated thermometers for the one they had just been given.

But maintaining apparent fever by manipulating temperature-taking devices can be difficult in a hospital where personnel are hovering about. Trained staff members will eventually observe that patients with fraudulent fever appear healthy and lack the expected increase in heart rate during febrile episodes. The patients often have unusual temperature patterns and do not improve with fever-lowering medications. Laboratory studies are typically normal. Patients have tried to circumvent these observations by creating false readings even from rectal thermometers by vigorously contracting the anal sphincter to create friction or applying a hot water bottle to their rectums in anticipation of a temperature measurement. A few take drugs such as atropine that can elevate the body's temperature. But patients who want to leave nothing to chance go for the real thing and cause authentic fevers by injecting themselves with foreign substances such as milk, dirt, or feces or by exposing themselves to bacteria in other ways.

The Story of Simone

Over a period of three years, Simone, a nurse's aide, experienced continual fevers and joint infections that defied explanation. When admitted to yet another hospital, a careful review of her medical history was performed. Doctors could confirm that she had undergone at least 15 operations without resolution of her problems. Of equal concern was that more than *180 samples* of her blood and joint tissue had been sent for culture. The intent each time was to see what bacteria or other microorganisms (such as fungi) might grow in the petri dishes over ensuing days. Any abnormal microorganisms might account for the fevers and be "showering" her joints to cause the obvious redness and swelling—while also undermining any hope of cure. A huge variety of bacteria had been cultured in the past, a finding doctors could not explain and tended to disregard.

The hospital staff carefully obtained new cultures at the times Simone's temperature would climb. They discovered not only that the cultures generally grew numerous types of microorganisms, but that most of the organisms were normally confined to the gastrointestinal tract. Such *polymicrobial* cultures—with unusual bacteria growing from tissue in the joints and from blood—raised the notion that the patient had been infecting herself, perhaps with fecal material. The staff continued to observe her keenly, ultimately leading to the recognition that Simone's intravenous lines were not falling out or malfunctioning as she claimed, but were being deliberately manipulated by her; the reasons appeared to be to contaminate her and undermine administration of antibiotics. The staff went on to conclude that she was almost certainly infecting herself with water from a dirty toilet bowl. Because her trickery was so severe and prolonged and because she had left so many hospital stays and medical/surgical procedures in her wake, she was believed to have Munchausen syndrome. The doctors even described the bacteria she used for self-infection as "Munchausen's microbes."

When Simone was confronted, she denied such outrageous behavior. However, her fevers and infections promptly stopped and did not recur over the subsequent three years of follow-up. As I will expand upon in chapter 16, some patients powerfully deny their role in the deceptions, but stop the behavior to avoid further questioning and embarrassment. Simone's outcome was a happy one despite her refusal—or, more likely, her psychological inability—to divulge the truth.

In a case with some parallels to Simone's, a 28-year-old medical technologist went to the community hospital where she was employed complaining of fevers, nausea, vomiting, cramping, and diarrhea. Her temperature at the time was 103.8 degrees. As if her problems were not already serious enough, laboratory studies showed a severe deficiency in the clotting of her blood that required her transfer to a more intensive hospital setting. Through sophisticated testing, it was finally concluded that the patient had actually induced such a high temperature and grave abdominal problems by self-administering the dangerous bacterium *Shigella*, which was available at her workplace. Like the desperate patients described in chapter 2, she simultaneously was ingesting a rodenticide to impede the normal clotting of the blood. When approached gently, she denied self-harm but did consent to psychiatric treatment. She acknowledged she had always hoped to attend medical school and also have a child, but neither goal seemed achievable. Doctors believed that these disappointments might have played some role in her factitious behavior; however, the results of her psychiatric care—if she even attended any sessions—are unknown.

How High Can You Go?

Temperatures above 105.8 degrees Fahrenheit were labeled hyperthermic fever in 1889 by French doctor Charles Richet. While a patient can experience genuine hyperthermia, ridiculously high fake fevers have been recorded by doctors since 1891 when Dr. H. Jones reported a 14-year-old patient with temperature readings of 108, 115, 135, 150, and 156 degrees Fahrenheit (the latter four are physically impossible; even the first could be tolerated by the human body only briefly). Modern researchers caution that whenever hyperthermia exists (even if someone's temperatures don't reach 156!) factitious disorder is among the diagnostic possibilities.

Allison's Ruse

Morven S. Edwards, M.D. and Karina M. Butler reported on a 15-year-old girl who was admitted to the Texas Children's Hospital with symptoms that included fever, cough, and nausea. Allison was diagnosed as having strep throat, given oral penicillin, and sent home. Despite the antibiotic, her fever and cough persisted, so she was referred to the Infectious Disease Service and hospitalized for extensive testing. Numerous diagnostic studies—including a chest X-ray, upper gastrointestinal tract study, abdominal ultrasound study, bone marrow aspirate (withdrawal of bone marrow for examination) and bronchoscopy (insertion of an instrument down the throat for examination of the trachea and bronchial system)—revealed no abnormalities. Her blood was screened for infectious agents such as hepatitis and Epstein-Barr virus, but there was no evidence that she had had any recent infection. Allison was sent home once again, but her fevers persisted.

After seven months, the teenager continued to complain of fevers and developed new problems with ankle pain. Tests for juvenile rheumatoid arthritis were negative and she was given analgesics to control the fevers. She experienced side effects to the medicine and was given different prescription drugs, but still, after 8 months, her fevers seemed to persist.

Allison claimed to be having daily temperatures of 101 to 105 degrees Fahrenheit, but when she was readmitted to the hospital, her readings were sometimes normal. This fact began to make doctors suspicious. In addition, her fever would rapidly disappear whenever she was closely scrutinized by caregivers and she lacked the sweating, hot skin, and rapid heart rate that accompany high fever. Her doctors stopped all medications and ordered that her temperatures now be taken rectally and only in the presence of a nurse. That evening Allison's temperature was 99.6, and the nurse noticed that her anus was irritated. Less than two hours later, Allison asked for her temperature to be taken again and this time it was up to 101 degrees. Her rectum was now far more irritated and extremely painful to the touch. A resident physician documented in her chart that he believed that she was using some sort of device to increase her temperature reading.

The next day, nurses tried taking Allison's temperature orally with four different thermometers, including three electronic and one mercury, but the readings were chaotic, ranging from 99.2 degrees to 105.4 degrees. They again instituted rectal readings, this time with simultaneous documentation of her heart rate, and were also instructed to check the temperature of the girl's urine if a thermometer registered a high temperature. When her principal doctor proceeded with a request for psychiatric consultation as well, the girl's fevers suddenly ended and she tried to play them down.

When she was interviewed and confronted by the psychiatrist, the teenager admitted to having faked her fevers by using a heating pad and a small water heating appliance, which accounted for the irritated and tender condition of her rectum. She confessed that her factitious behavior was initially intended to allow her to miss classes; she had previously been performing so poorly in school that she needed an excuse for not meeting the expectations of her father. Then the behavior got out of hand and she felt unable to stop.

Allison's childhood was far from idyllic and may have been a contributing factor to her factitious illness. Her parents divorced when she was six years old, and she lived with her mother for seven years until her mother's poor health forced her and her brother to move in with their father, his girlfriend, and the girlfriend's 13-year-old son. Allison had been a loner who had difficulty making friends. Her family tree was dotted with depression; indeed, one of her cousins was hospitalized for depression at the same time she had been.

Researchers have found that many adolescents respond well to confrontation and treatment, and their fraudulent fevers—termed "hyperthermia of trickery" by Edwards and Butler—may be pleas for help. In a 2000 review of 42 cases in which children or adolescents independently falsified illness of various types, Dr. Judith Libow found that 13 selected fever, making it the most popular affliction (others included diabetic complications, rashes, and infection). Younger children who engaged in the deceptive behavior universally admitted to it when confronted; the majority of adolescents did as well. Factitious disorder in general is a way of expressing dire emotional needs. Adults, however, may be more resistive to change than children and teenagers, whose frames of reference change continually as they develop. This resistance partially explains why so many adults who suffer from factitious disorder can become swept up, focusing their lives on it and dramatically altering their portrayals as needed, often incorporating apparent fever.

For example, one 35-year-old Munchausen patient feigned signs ranging from fever to bloody urine, subjecting herself to multiple exploratory surgeries for suspected peritonitis (inflammation of the membrane of the abdominal cavity). As her presentations changed, she was tested for diverse disorders including diabetes and tumors of the lymphatic system. This woman's adeptness at switching illnesses was facilitated by her employer's profession—she was the house-keeper for a doctor and drew on his textbooks and professional litera-ture to maintain the illusion of genuine illness.

Ernie's Case

Another seemingly well-read factitious disorder patient, a 24-year-old man named Ernie, initially feigned a bowel obstruction, which had resulted only in negative test results. He was referred to psychia-try for possible factitious disorder and was seen by Dr. Ford, men-tioned earlier. Ernie was admitted to the psychiatric unit of a hospital with depression and a long list of problems. He had been laid off from his job and was unable to find work because he was so sick. He had depleted his savings due to mounting medical bills and was on the verge of bankruptcy. To top it all off, he was also on probation for forging prescriptions for pain killers that he claimed to need for Crohn's disease, a serious disorder of the alimentary tract. The treat-ing physician recommended discharge and outpatient group ther-apy; Ernie agreed promptly but dropped out of the group after only two sessions. Soon thereafter, he discovered the power of fever as a medical sign when he elaborated a new claim—a report that he had Mediterranean fever—and was rushed to the hospital in an ambu-lance with a skyrocketing temperature.

The one hitch with Ernie's new portrayal was that, while he had fever in the emergency room, it vanished as soon as he was hospital-ized. After a short time, Ernie's hoax failed when tests for Mediterra-nean fever proved negative.

Ernie was in and out of the hospital several more times before doctors convinced him that his real focus should be on getting onto the psychiatric ward. The two months he spent on that ward gave the staff a chance to gather Ernie's records from other hospitals and track down his family. A conversation with Ernie's mother unlocked the heartache that was underlying Ernie's persistent disease portrayals.

Ernie was the only child of a Midwestern couple. He had suffered humiliation and ridicule as a child because of a congenital fusion of bones of the jaw. This condition made it difficult for him to eat and gave him a speech impediment that led to mockery from other children. Ernie's father, a clerk, was a kind and indulgent man, and though he was often sick with abdominal problems that kept him home from work, he took care of Ernie most of the time. Ernie's mother worked for an accountant, and would frequently leave home for jobs out of state, remaining gone for long periods. Ernie was thus subjected to two traumatic family elements: the long, severe illnesses of his father and the repetitive absences of his mother.

When Ernie was eight years old, he was placed in a home for emotionally disturbed children because of his increasingly bizarre behaviors. These odd actions included his dressing peculiarly to attract attention, telling lies, and shying away from most other children. Ernie's father died six months later, and his mother went to live in another state while Ernie remained in institutions, eventually including reform school. Ernie found his way into a foster home when he was 15 years old, but was never able to put himself on firm footing as he grew older. He barely graduated from high school and flunked out of college after only three semesters.

It is not uncommon for men and women to find themselves in love-hate relationships with one or both of their parents, especially as each new generation finds itself in conflict with the social mores and lifestyles of the preceding generation. In Ernie's case, however, the love-hate relationship with his mother was exaggerated. After years of contact limited only to an occasional gift, he relocated to Tennessee and moved in with her.

Because he was unemployed, Ernie's mother provided for his basic needs, but she was extremely critical of him, and, finally unable or unwilling to fill the emotional void in Ernie's life, tried unsuccessfully to have him permanently committed to a state institution. Despite the unpleasant relationship he had with her, Ernie experienced horrendous anxiety each time his mother went away on business: He described "unbearable loneliness, an enormous sense of emptiness and abandonment, and fear of the world." His disease portrayals were precipitated by these periods of desperate separation from his mother. Several times Ernie even flew to other states where his complaints of abdominal pain (no doubt vividly recalled and mimicked from his father) led to surgical procedures.

Even after he was admitted to a psychiatric ward, Ernie's role-playing continued. His clothes and mannerisms were perfectly suited to whatever personality he chose to portray on a particular day. One day, for example, he would dress in a three-piece suit and look like a white collar executive. On another day, he would put on tennis whites, shoes, shorts, and affect the mannerisms of a socialite walking off the court in Palm Springs. The next day he'd be outfitted in a university sweat shirt, pleated pants, and oxfords and you'd swear that he was a student at any college in the state. He was convincing to the point where he even admitted that when he assumed these different identifies he almost believed them himself.

Perhaps predictably, his mother proved uninterested in Ernie's treatment. She came to visit him once while he was hospitalized and told Dr. Ford, "I want you to take this kid, lock him up, and throw away the key." What she really meant was "throw away the kid." Recognizing Ernie's need for maternal love and responding to his endearing qualities, the staff really tried to help and get him involved in psychotherapy, but he just couldn't tolerate that kind of intimacy.

Ernie's case was followed over a period of several years because, every once in a while, he'd come back to the same hospital, but he wouldn't stay long enough to benefit from therapy. Taking the usual route of a Munchausen patient, Ernie flew around the country, getting admitted to hospitals and undergoing unwarranted surgery. After a while, the staff no longer heard from Ernie and they conjectured that he died from the complications of multiple operations. He was a sad and troubled man and none of his caregivers could remain angry with him. Everyone felt sorry for Ernie.

Ernie's story was made sadder still by the fact that he had a superior intelligence and creativity, as proved by psychological tests, yet he was only able to display them in the most ineffectual way. Although he elicited a great deal of genuine concern from the medical staff, his personality deficits rendered him unable to establish close relationships, even with his primary doctor. Unfortunately, Ernie was a Munchausen patient who was so caught up in his portrayals that, by his own admission, they eventually threatened to become his total reality.

6

Out of Control:
When the Ruse Becomes Real

*Factitious disorder is unique among mental disorders in that only by virtue
of faking illness do individuals become ill—always psychiatrically and
often physically. The story of Judith offers a prime example. Judith's childhood had been marked by a life-threatening cancer that nearly claimed her
life at the age of seven. Hospitals became her primary home to the point that
she felt truly at home only in the hospital environment. As a young adult,
Judith discovered the value of faking eating disorders as a means of gaining
access to hospitals. She studied the symptoms of anorexia nervosa until she
could fake them expertly. Over time, however, she lost her ability to control
the disorder and it began controlling her. This chapter discusses the fine line
between manipulating an illness and drifting into its domain, and how a
patient's conscious and unconscious motivations can sometimes collide.*

From childhood, we are taught that we are responsible for our own
actions and we can steer our lives along any course we choose. Over
and over again at home, in school, in song, and in prose the message
is reinforced: Go where you want to go; do what you want to do; be
what you want to be. But all too soon we learn, usually through harsh
experiences, that total control is nothing more than wishful and
poetic thinking; rather, our lives are actually directed to a large degree
by factors over which we have little or no control, such as people, cir-

cumstances, and physical and emotional health. Most of us acquire living skills as we mature that enable us to accept and cope with the perceived and real influences in our lives while maintaining whatever control we can over ourselves, our homes, and other people.

Some of us, however, are so severely affected by brutal life experiences that we do not become inured over time, but instead plummet into a tailspin when encountering a new challenge. We resort to desperate measures to exercise control over our lives and avoid collision. Feigning illness is one such desperate measure. At the conclusion of the chapter, you will better understand the quixotic control that factitious disorder can bring—and that the control it provides is an illusion.

Factitious Eating Disorders

As a control strategy, factitious disorder takes a variety of forms. A number of factitious disorder patients use eating disorders to exercise dominance over their bodies, manipulate others, and attempt to gain control over their lives. Anorexia nervosa is an eating disorder which occurs most often in adolescent girls. Persons suffering from this psychiatric illness starve themselves or use such techniques as vomiting, taking laxatives, or over-exercising to lose weight because they have a false sense of their bodies and believe that they are fat. This behavior can lead to severe weight loss and, in extreme cases, death. Bulimia nervosa, which sometimes occurs as a phase of anorexia nervosa, involves cycles of overeating, or bingeing, followed by purging. Real anorexia patients starve themselves as a compulsion, the apparent aim being the perfect body. Anorexia and bulimia are factitious (and not real) when patients consciously choose to secretly deprive themselves of nourishment (anorexia) or engage in bingeing and purging (bulimia) specifically to attract attention and exercise control over others. In the case that follows, Judith used two dangerous eating disorders—anorexia and bulimia—to try to control her life, her body, and the people around her. Judith was introduced to the power of illness when she was a very young child. A genuine bout with a life-threatening disease set the stage for the disease simulations she would carry out years later. At the age of 14, Judith began consciously and willfully feigning eating disorders.

Judith's Journey

I was diagnosed as having a cancerous tumor of the spine when I was 7 years old. The thing about having had cancer at such an early age is that I didn't really understand a lot of what was happening to me and my body. I couldn't make heads or tails of the terminology used by the doctors or what they were going to do for me, but I recognized that as soon as my parents and relatives knew that I was sick, I started getting a lot of attention.

Before my illness was diagnosed, I was having a lot of pain in my right hip. I suffered so much that at times I could hardly walk, but no one really believed that anything serious was wrong with me. They thought that I was exaggerating some minor problem or just plain faking to get attention because my parents spent so much time working and being involved with my two older sisters. I kept complaining about the pain so my mother kept taking me to the doctor, but no matter how many times we saw him, he still found nothing wrong with me. Finally, when I was almost paralyzed, the doctor did a bunch of tests and then rushed me into surgery because he found a tumor. I had spinal surgery that lasted eight hours.

My illness was pretty serious, and I almost died. I had two years of radiation therapy and two years of chemotherapy and my cancer went into remission. The cure was almost as miserable as the illness. My doctors had told me that I was going to lose my hair because of the cancer therapy, and they even tried to joke around about it, saying that I would some day get a whole new growth of hair and it might even be a different color than it had been before. Somehow I couldn't comprehend the prospect of losing my hair. When it began to happen I was dumbfounded. I cried and was horrified when my hair came out in clumps. I could remember a time when I looked and felt pretty. I was just a little girl, and I was supposed to be able to feel that way. But after all I went through, I didn't even want to look at myself in the mirror. I felt ugly and I was afraid that I was going to look like that for the rest of my life.

I missed more than a year of school during the early part of my therapy and had spent so much time in the hospital that my home became the foreign place and the hospital was the familiar, friendly place where people took care of me. The nurses and doctors and orderlies were my friends. When I was in the hospital I got lots of presents, and people doted over me day and night. It got to the point where the hospital was a haven for me and I looked forward to going there. The sick role was the only thing I knew how to do and I played it very well.

At first I didn't exaggerate any illness. I didn't need to because it was only too real, but I reached a point when I did exaggerate everything that went along with my illness. For example, sometimes I would say that I was more tired than I really was just to be able to stay in bed where I felt safe and comfortable, and to have my mother wait on me.

A year-and-a-half after I recovered from my first experience with cancer, my doctors found another tumor, this time in my lung. I was devastated by the news that I would have to go through the whole process all over again, but I did it, and eventually the cancer was brought under control. Unfortunately, I wasn't prepared to be well. Even though I had been in remission between the cancers, I never lost that label of "the sick girl" and was always treated protectively. At the age of 13 I was afraid to go to school. I was afraid not to be on chemo-therapy anymore. I was afraid to grow my hair back and to go back into the real world because I hadn't really lived there and I hadn't learned any of the social skills I needed to make it in that world. In the hospital I didn't need those skills. People sought me out to take care of me and visit me and to be nice to me. I was absolutely lost and fright-ened outside of the hospital.

When I went back to school, the kids made fun of me because I had to wear leg braces because my spinal surgery had left me with such a funny-looking limp, which made me very self-conscious and drew attention to my appearance. I was so sallow that I looked as if I had "prison pallor," which was accentuated by the faded brown rings under my eyes. They pulled my wig off and said that I was wearing a dead rat on my head. Only one or two children stuck by me. Other-wise I was isolated and excluded from all extracurricular activities. My teachers basically were either unaware or unable to deal with what I was experiencing. That reinforced my belief that the hospital environ-ment was more nurturing, supportive, and safe for me than what was outside of it.

My parents didn't know what to do for me and couldn't understand why I wasn't glad to be out of the hospital and anxious to go back to school and make friends, and lead what they considered to be a nor-mal life. They constantly lectured me about how grateful I should be that I was alive and repeatedly reminded me that they had saved my life. I had two older sisters who were healthy and attractive and neither of them understood why I was having such difficulty getting along with my parents and the other students at school. They hassled me about it and even ridiculed me. They never became the allies that I needed them to be. I had absolutely no support system at home.

My real exaggeration of illness started after my second operation, when my lung cancer went into remission and I was going through puberty and high school. By that time, being sick was like second nature to me. There were times when I lobbied to go back into the hospital and looked forward to it, even if it was just for tests or check-ups that did not require hospitalization.

When I was 14 years old many changes started happening in my life. I was trying to be popular and I didn't know how to be. I wanted to be attractive to the other sex, but I felt awkward and out of sync with the tactics that other girls used to meet boys.

That's when I started looking at how I could control my life, my body, and the way I looked, and I began my bouts of anorexia and bulimia. I deliberately created the anorexia and bulimia in myself. I was cognizant of what I was doing to the extent that I went to the library and read every book I could find on eating disorders to learn better and more unique ways of creating them. I knew everything there was to know about every eating disorder on record. I was striving for some sort of independence and control. No one in my family had ever encouraged me to be independent. They had fostered my sick role and were overprotective to the point that I wasn't even allowed to take public transportation. I finally consciously created my own independence in a negative way.

Once I started playing sick I felt as if I had taken control of my life for the very first time. It was extremely satisfying to pretend to have an illness that I could command and to deliberately do harmful things to my body because harmful things had happened to me in the past that I couldn't control. I think to some extent I became so accustomed to pain that I thought I deserved it and I missed it and felt that I couldn't live without it. I would do things that were self-destructive, like burning myself or cutting myself to make myself bleed. I wanted to feel the pain.

My actions brought immediate and constant support and nurturance from people around me. And although some of what I did brought negative attention from my parents, the bottom line was that I was still getting their attention. The more my parents fought against me, the more I fought to assert control over myself and them and to keep them in their supportive roles. I got a lot of attention when I didn't eat, and in so doing, I indirectly nurtured myself. Everyone was worried about me. I knew which strings to pull and which buttons to push, and I used them to fulfill my needs. I knew exactly what reactions I would get from playing sick.

I chose to fake eating disorders for several reasons. The primary reason was that, when I was being given chemotherapy I was nauseated all the time and whenever I ate I threw up. My mother was very conscious of my eating habits because when I got sick the second time I lost 30 pounds in one month. She was afraid that I would die if I got sick again because I couldn't afford to lose any more weight. I gained it back after the chemotherapy ended, but I deliberately started losing it again because I knew my mother would be upset. I would go into the bathroom and make myself vomit when I knew that she could hear me.

Being self conscious about my appearance because my sexuality was blooming served as another excuse for my actions. And during the 1980s eating disorders were trendy things and I was greatly influenced by what I saw in the media. There were a couple of television documentaries about anorexia and bulimia, and some books at that time, so it was easy to stay on top of things. After a while, though, the eating disorders became real, and I had trouble controlling the symptoms. I would go through long periods of depression where I would starve all day, then come home from school and eat a light dinner and go to sleep at 7 o'clock. I would do that every day and by Sunday I would be so hungry that I would binge all day. I couldn't stop eating for 24 hours and then the next day I would starve myself or try to make myself vomit.

I once overdosed on 45 Extra Strength Tylenol tablets because I had binged and wanted to vomit. I took all the tablets that were in the bottle, knowing that I was either going to get sick or not wake up the next morning. I was so depressed that I really didn't care which. Then I reached a point where anorexia and bulimia weren't good enough to control my body, and I started using drugs in addition to continuing with my eating disorders.

My mother thought she was helping me by trying to force me to eat, but that didn't work. Bribing and punishing me didn't work either. I saw several specialists in eating disorders and none of them helped me, and I became really frustrated with people trying to influence my life. I could only talk to my friends, and they were primarily the people with whom I was engaging in bad behavior.

When I was 17 I had the notion that if I signed myself into a rehabilitation hospital, I'd be able to prove that my parents were neglecting me, or something crazy like that, and I would become legally emancipated from them. But things got screwed up, and when I signed myself into such a hospital, my parents found out about my drug use and transferred me to a stricter facility. I was there for three months, and it was hell. It was such a terrible environment that I continued to starve and binge and vomit.

Two of the most nurturing and healthy environments I lived in when I was growing up were outside of my parents' home. After I was released from the rehabilitation center I went home, but nothing was working out so my parents agreed to let me stay at a therapeutic girls' home, where I was treated with a lot of respect. I didn't have that much more freedom than I had had in rehabilitation, but I really liked the people and, although I don't know why, I was quite healthy there. I signed a contract that I would not do drugs, and I didn't. I also signed a contract that I wouldn't make myself throw up, and I did that only once.

I also lived with a friend and her mother for a while, and they helped me to learn many of the living skills that I hadn't learned in the past. They taught me to do things that my mother had always done for me, and I became more independent. I learned to travel on public transportation and got a part-time job so that I could pay for some of my own things. The more real control I got over my life, the more control people outside of my family gave me, and the more I felt nurtured, comfortable, and safe, not threatened.

I can't precisely identify the point at which my life turned around. I remember that the night my parents dropped me off at college, the first thing I did was run to the nearest bathroom so I could stick my finger down my throat and make myself vomit. All during freshman year, I worked in the school's dining services. It was kind of like being offered the forbidden fruit. I was challenging myself: Put yourself around food and see if you're going to lose control.

It wasn't until the summer of my sophomore year that I finally started eating and keeping the food down. I was so busy with other things that I didn't have time to play games. If you're going to live with an eating disorder, whether it's real or not, you have to plan every minute around that disorder. I think somehow I got the feeling that it was controlling me more than I was controlling it, and I adjusted my eating habits and reintroduced food—including junk food—into my life in a normal way.

I got good grades in school because I pursued my studies with the same compulsion with which I had pursued the eating disorders. I'm still very compulsive.

I have very poor peer relationships, and I have a hard time socializing in big groups of people. Oddly enough, I'm outgoing and get along well with small groups. I like to keep a few friends rather than a lot of them. I develop stronger relationships with people who are opposites of the kind of people I tried to get along with in high school. I no longer try to be part of the popular group or a jock because to me those people are less real than people who have problems and are marginal like myself.

I'm comfortable with myself now. My limp is still fairly pronounced when I'm not wearing braces and that makes me self-conscious. But I no longer think that having a disability should be a negative thing, and I'm basically happy.

Judith's feigned anorexia and bulimia had far more complex origins than a desire for beauty, as she poignantly explained. Most people who develop anorexia and/or bulimia don't consciously plan to have these illnesses. In the beginning, Judith did not have a true eating disorder because she intentionally chose the disease. Later on, Judith's factitious behaviors became so well established that she actually developed an authentic eating disorder as she eventually lost control over her behaviors.

Judith's story demonstrates the profound implications of chronic childhood illness when the child's emotional and social needs are overlooked. Judith's young life was so closely associated with hospitals and illness that she had little opportunity to acquire normal social skills. When she was deemed healthy enough to return to school, Judith was thrown into the world of "normal" children with every expectation that she would adapt. This action only fostered her negative feelings about herself and everyone around her. A proper support system should have been in place for her, complete with counseling, so that she could have been eased into her new hospital-free environment instead of being cast into it and forced to make a go of it alone.

Judith's sense of powerlessness and vulnerability was a major catalyst behind her disease simulation and one of the main reasons that eating disorders suited her needs so well. They appeared to give her back some of the control she so desperately wanted over her body and her life, as well as some of the sympathy to which she had become accustomed.

Judith fit the profile of many factitious patients in that other psychological problems were at work, including borderline personality disorder. Her borderline personality was evident in Judith's identity crisis, unstable relationships, moodiness, manipulation of others, and self-injuring acts. (See chapter 1 for more information). Judith was depressed because she wanted to fit into what she had been told was the regular world, but her low self-esteem and other problems, such as an inability to cope effectively with anxiety and stress, prevented her from doing so.

As is the case with many factitious disorder patients, when other interests started to fill her life and meet her needs, Judith was able to abandon her factitious behavior. Also, in the demanding scholastic environment in which she had placed herself, she couldn't possibly keep up with her studies if her attention was devoted to her sick role. However, she still prefers to surround herself with people who are "marginal" like herself and with whom she does not have to feel self-conscious. She has no control over the types of people who gather comfortably in large groups, and she is still afraid of opening herself up to the kind of criticism she experienced as a young child returning to school. She continues to keep very close watch over her environment to try to protect herself.

Although Judith dropped her factitious behavior, she never received therapy that would have taught her the skills she needed to cope with life crises so that in the future she would not feel compelled to reactivate her behavior. Her personality disorder was never appropriately treated either. These realities place her at risk for a repetition of factitious disorder if her emotional resources are again taxed to their limit.

Luther's Deceit

Luther is a young man whose deceptions began at age 14, as he sought to compete with his father—a composer of hit pop songs—for the attention and love of his mother. Intellectually gifted and medically astute, he came up with a plan: to become a sickly adolescent requiring constant care. His disease of choice was asthma, which he learned to feign perfectly. Luther spent several years being schooled at home due to his feigned asthma and other contrived illnesses. In a typical week, he was taken by ambulance to the emergency room four times because of enacted intractable wheezing. On an airplane to Denver to receive definitive treatment at a national respiratory center, he feigned such a serious asthma attack that the airliner was forced to make an emergency landing, waiting ambulances blaring. I dubbed Luther's act "liejacking," a term with which he concurred.

Years later, having finally learned about factitious disorder and Munchausen syndrome, he stated,

> I was shocked that they had a name for what I was doing. I thought that I was just evil. I thought that I had been possessed by some spirit. I didn't know it was a real disease that you could suffer from, and if you could suffer from it you could be cured. You can get better. I had no clue that there were other people in the world that suffered from this disease, and it really was shocking to me that other people had this. It was a first step towards doing something to treat it.

Luther poignantly describes the isolation he had experienced during his years of enacted illness:

> I had no friends when I was sick with Munchausen because that became your friend. Disease is your friend, it's your lover, it's your enemy, it's your mother, it's everything to you. Only after I turned my back on it did I form real friendships. Now I am utterly committed to educating others about it.

Luther insightfully compares his disease portrayal to an all-consuming relationship: one that comforts (mother and friend), destroys (enemy), and physically and emotionally dominates (lover). He correctly identifies one of the bitter ironies of factitious disorder. Intended as a strategy to gain control, factitious disorder insidiously robbed Luther of all control as his life was taken over by behaviors he could not stop.

Factitious Disorder and Degrees of Control

A question that often arises, especially after considering a case such as Judith's, is whether patients with factitious disorders can control their portrayals of illness. Is the patient aware of his or her actions? Is it out of one's personal control? Or is it premeditated?

The best answer is that an episode of factitious illness may reflect any of these possibilities. One particular patient illustrates that range. She has been carefully followed over several years and does appear to have genuine dissociative episodes in which disease deception occurs. Like a person with multiple personality disorder (MPD, formally called dissociative identity disorder), this patient will produce simulated illness (e.g., mimic epileptic convulsions) while in a trancelike state. She seems genuinely unaware of the illness productions. At other times, with full awareness, this patient will simulate illnesses such as kidney disease. Her disease simulation is so realistically portrayed that, despite normal kidneys, she has been able to obtain Social Security Disability payments for end-stage renal disease (and this degree of success in obtaining financial gains brings into question the possibility of malingering). At still other times, she repetitively, in a seemingly compulsive way, gains sympathy and support from other persons by telling them falsely that her parents have recently been killed in a car wreck.

At the same time, and for these reasons, factitious disorder has a quixotic position in the taxonomy of psychiatric ailments, the *Diagnostic and Statistical Manual of Mental Disorders*. It entered the *DSM* in 1980 in response to the sheer number of case reports and the self-defeating, often self-damaging nature of the behavior; yet, it is one of only a handful of mental disorders in which the patient usually exercises at least minimal control over the expression of his or her symptoms. Parallels from the *DSM-IV* include ignominious diagnoses such as kleptomania and pyromania (respectively defined as the failure to resist the urges to steal or set fires). In "mainstream" mental disorders such as schizophrenia, depression, bipolar disorder, and panic disorder, the expression of symptoms is involuntary and they are undoubtedly unwanted.

Factitious disorder is unique among mental disorders in that only by virtue of *faking* being patients do individuals *become* patients. This paradox and the varying degrees of control over the symptoms make some researchers uncomfortable. A few believe that these individuals should not be rewarded with the trophy of *DSM-IV*-endorsed patienthood by virtue of trickery. They would instead simply define factitious behavior as misbehavior, and remove it from future editions of *DSM*. Their response is that these patients are either "crocks or crooks."

I disagree strongly. I continue to laud the recognition of factitious disorder as a psychiatric illness. Only through its inclusion in *DSM* versions will factitious disorder continue to be recognized, diagnosed, treated, and subjected to scholarly scrutiny. Note that psychiatrists do not dismiss as simple misbehavior the suicidal patient's self-inflicted gunshot wound, regardless of the degree of planning and choice. Instead, we search for the underlying psychopathology that prompted the desperate, hurtful act and seek ardently to help. I see a correlate in the manipulations of individuals with factitious disorders, who call out using the only language they know. It is only when the gunshot wound or, as in Munchausen by proxy (chapters 10 and 11), illness is inflicted on *another* should we criminalize the act and use the term *perpetrator* rather than patient.

7

False Accusations and the Girl Who Cried "Wolf"

This chapter presents the other side of the coin, detailing the stories of three patients who were mistakenly diagnosed as having factitious disorder or Munchausen syndrome when they suffered from real medical complaints. The difficult-to-classify patient is especially vulnerable to such misdiagnosis. Joan Nelson had a history of excruciating abdominal pain related to menstruation, yet her internist was blatantly insensitive to her complaints and the problem (severe endometriosis) went undiagnosed for years. Her life was further complicated by a botched oral surgery that resulted in her requesting to see her medical records. Joan was shocked to find a letter from her doctor diagnosing her with Munchausen syndrome. Joan's story reveals the implications of such false accusations which, depending on regional laws, cannot always be removed from the patient's records. This chapter also examines the medical practice of blacklisting former Munchausen patients and how this affects the patient's ability to obtain critically needed health care. In the case of Wendy Scott, a patient who was the subject of articles—and an obituary—in the New York Times, *all of her previous falsifications and unnecessary surgeries led to physicians' ignoring her pleas for care when she finally developed cancer that eventually claimed her life.*

Once a factitious disorder patient has gained a reputation at a medical institution, the chances of his or her receiving proper medical attention are diminished. Although this reaction by the medical staff is understandable, it is not appropriate, because virtually all human beings legitimately need medical attention at some time in their lives. Thus, like the boy who cried "Wolf!" just to manipulate others, factitious disorder patients might have a legitimate need for medical services, only to find themselves blackballed and unable to find anyone who will help.

What happens to someone who is legitimately sick but is suspected of having factitious disorder? I will share three such unsettling cases in this chapter, as well as the lessons to be learned.

William's Ill Fortune

I worked at a hospital where staff members who were assigned to a ward for difficult-to-diagnose patients were given a weekly opportunity to discuss their patients and any special problems they might be having as caregivers. During one of the group sessions I attended, the nurses complained vehemently about a patient whom they believed was faking his illness.

They said that this man, William, had been admitted to the hospital with complaints of crippling pains all over his body, fever, headaches, and weakness. When the nurses went into his room to treat him, he could hardly move, and even the simplest procedures became quite difficult to carry out. The nurses had to shift his body from one side of the bed to the other to change the linen, and he generally couldn't even feed himself. Yet, the nurses said, it seemed that when he wanted his cigarettes, he rarely had any particular trouble reaching for them, lighting one, and smoking it. Tests were being conducted to determine the cause of his complaints, but several of the nurses resented his presence because they felt that costly medical resources were being wasted when they could better serve someone who was genuinely sick. They felt strongly about this matter because they had some very sick patients under their care.

The office in which we held these sessions was directly across from William's room, and the nurses voiced their objections in barely audible whispers so that he wouldn't hear them. The doctors knew about their suspicions and, as a result of the meeting, the staff concurred that they had to do whatever was necessary to make William comfortable, to follow his doctors' instructions, and to maintain their professional attitude while a conclusive diagnosis was being established.

This bitter staff was extremely shaken when the patient suddenly died on the fifth day of his hospitalization. Some people cried, and everyone on the ward felt guilty about not having believed him. Some of the nurses felt they had been gruff with him, and some had given priority to other patients who seemed more clearly ill when they had to choose among patients to respond to first. The staff was devastated by the experience, and they were relieved that William's doctors had forestalled accusing him of a factitious disorder. Although I reminded them that they had done everything that was expected of them professionally, it was an event that none of them would ever forget. It would certainly color their actions in the future, and they would be far less willing to accuse someone of faking an illness, even when that really was the case.

An autopsy revealed that this patient had suffered and died from meningitis, an inflammation of the membranes lining the skull, vertebral column, and brain that causes a variety of symptoms including headaches, fever, and stiffening of the muscles. His death raised questions about whether malpractice had been involved in his treatment because his illness had not been taken seriously by some caregivers. His medical records, however, indicated that doctors had followed an acceptable course toward diagnosis, though they had failed to pinpoint the nature of his illness before it claimed his life. Had the staff openly accused him of faking, or withdrawn care, other more disturbing legal questions might have arisen—especially once he and his family realized that suspicions of factitious disorder had become a part of his medical record.

Joan's Saga

Joan Nelson of London, England, knows first hand what it's like to be unjustly accused of fakery and then to suffer the consequences. Joan is a registered nurse whose years as a young bride and mother were spent traveling with her husband during his service in the Royal Air Force. After his discharge, they settled down to family life in a quiet London suburb, and Joan found herself well-suited to her roles as wife, mother, and nurse, working for a doctor in general practice. An easy-going woman with an even temperament and gentle manner, Joan had struggled through her teenage years with difficult menstrual periods which were precursors of serious legitimate health problems she would have later in life. Here, in her own words, is her account of how she came to be falsely accused of having Munchausen syndrome:

I'd been a particularly healthy child until my periods began when I was 13. I had problems with menstruation right from the start, and my periods were not as much heavy as they were excruciatingly painful. I was told by our family doctor that what I was experiencing was normal and to get on with life.

I had my first baby at the age of 23 by Caesarean section and that first birth was a horror story. I had a hemorrhage when I was almost eight months pregnant and was rushed to a hospital, but doctors waited a week before they delivered the baby, even though I had lost all the fluid. I had a dry Caesarean birth, which was followed by a quite severe uterine infection. The wound had a lot of problems healing up and I was ill for some time. A couple of years later I became pregnant again and had another baby, who was also delivered by Caesarean because my uterus actually burst open where the scar from my first pregnancy was. The doctors who delivered this baby said that my insides were "falling to pieces."

The wound from my second birth required constant care because it kept breaking down. I also had year after year of horrendous period problems, which worsened with time.

I was 27 at that time and kept going back to our general practitioner about the problems that I was having after my second son's birth. I couldn't change doctors or see a specialist without a referral because of the restrictions in England's national health care plan. The doctor wouldn't make a referral even though I couldn't even walk the length of our driveway without being in severe pain. My doctor just said that the pain was caused by the scar stretching and curtly added that all women have period problems and I just had to put up with it.

Finally, when I was 39 years old, this doctor sent me to the hospital to have a scraping of the inside of my uterus. The doctor who performed it said they found nothing abnormal. But by that time I was really feeling quite poorly and was in so much pain that I wasn't sleeping well. I was working for a different general practitioner as a nurse, and he could see how ill I was. He said, "You can't carry on like this. I'll ring your doctor and see if he'll consider sending you elsewhere for a second opinion."

Knowing full well that I was in the office with the doctor for whom I worked, my doctor told him bluntly, "I don't consider that there's anything wrong with her, and she won't be happy until she's had a hysterectomy anyway. If you want to refer her you can." My employer referred me to a gynecologist in another area, and I was seen within a week. By then I was 40 years old.

The gynecologist said he thought that he knew what was wrong with me and said I was going to have to have a hysterectomy. I had the operation, which took more than four hours. Because of all the scar tissue, the doctor was only able to do a partial hysterectomy.

I came home feeling reasonable straight away, but within a few weeks, I was having heavy periods again with clotting. I returned to the gynecologist and he then told me that he'd found endometriosis; that's when he explained it all to me and how bad things were. [Endometriosis is a disease in which tissue similar to the mucous membrane that lines the uterus grows elsewhere in the pelvic area, causing pain, especially during menstruation.] When I was sent back to my general practitioner, he still decided that there was nothing wrong with me but I remained unable to change doctors.

In the middle of all this, I had to go into the hospital to have an impacted wisdom tooth removed, and during the oral surgery, the dentist dislocated my jaw, and I had a lot of bleeding afterwards. Subsequently, I got an infected hematoma on the side of my mouth from which my tooth had been removed, which ended up damaging both temporomandibular joints (the hinge joints of the jaw). After a number of visits with my general practitioner, I was finally sent to a specialist who wired my jaw to give the joints a rest, and I could only drink through a straw. Eventually, five and a half hours of microsurgery were required to repair my temporomandibular joints. Although I still have restricted movement I can eat and talk now.

Reports on these findings had been sent to my general practitioner to be included in my permanent medical records. I also began having problems with other organs due to endometriosis or adhesions. I asked my general practitioner to refer me to a gastroenterologist and, not long afterwards, I was also advised by a friend that I should seek compensation for the damage that had been done to my jaw.

This is how I ended up seeing my medical records. My lawyer asked the hospital for copies of the notes pertaining to my jaw. When he received those records, the referral letter from my general practitioner to the gastroenterologist was inadvertently amongst them. My lawyer asked if I had seen that letter. I hadn't. The letter stated that I had manipulated my way into getting a hysterectomy against medical advice, which led to my opening a Pandora's Box of problems and consequently, of course, I was having other organ problems. At the bottom he had written, 'In my opinion, this woman suffers with Munchausen syndrome.'

When I saw this in my medical records I felt, to put it bluntly, gut-struck. I just couldn't believe that he had written this about me. There was no reason for my general practitioner to write in my medical records that I had Munchausen syndrome. Sadly, there is no possible way to get it removed.

By the time I learned of the letter, I knew more about endometriosis. I'd contacted the endometriosis society in desperate need of help, and they supported me through a lot. But nobody can support you through something like being accused of faking serious illness by a doctor whom you trusted for years.

I'm very sympathetic toward people who are ill, probably because I have suffered so much myself. I feel that anybody who comes to a doctor or nurse with a problem or perceived problem needs help. Even if somebody's suffering with true Munchausen syndrome, he or she needs help. I've had the feeling at times during my career that some patients' ailments weren't legitimate, but if you talk to them and talk around things, you find that they quite often have another worry. They've come to you saying they've got a pain somewhere, when in fact their problems are probably something quite different and they're just looking for support and maybe some guidance and answers. Loneliness has a lot to do with this sort of thing. If they know you've got a sympathetic ear, they will come to you, and I always thought that was part of the caring profession—to listen.

False accusations can also be leveled at patients who once suffered with factitious disorder, or even Munchausen syndrome, but who have been able to recover. I will describe a patient of mine who also became a dear friend. She had recovered from Munchausen syndrome 20 years before I met her face-to-face. But she found she could not escape her past.

Memories of Wendy

Wendy Scott was perhaps the most prolific Munchausen patient in history. Growing up in a working-class town in Scotland, Wendy was repeatedly sexually abused by her stepfather, who entered her life when she was 8 years old. She ran away each time, which resulted in her eventually being confined to an institution for wayward girls. When she was old enough, she left that community entirely and embarked on a few low-paying, low-level jobs before developing authentic appendicitis. During that time she was working as a chambermaid who was essentially ignored by the guests and staff. When hospitalized for the appendectomy, she discovered that the hospital offered a magnificent respite from the daily grind. From that first encounter with the medical setting, Wendy lived the life of a "hospital hobo," traveling from town to town, then country to country, in pursuit of new hospitals. She ate at soup kitchens, slept in the streets, or squatted in empty buildings—momentary immobility as she traversed much of Europe and Scandinavia, including countries where English is not commonly spoken. Throughout she favored rural hospitals, hoping to find less sophisticated diagnosticians who would unwittingly let her prolong her stay, but was seen at hospitals as famous as Charing Cross in London, where her doctor in 1974 still remembers her though she stayed only hours before escaping back to the streets in response to staff suspicions. As she put it when she explained her story to me and became my patient, "Everyone understands the universal language of 'ouch'," and thus she readily garnered 800 hospitalizations in 650 different hospitals over a 12-year period.

In 1997, she sheepishly shared her story —which now included 20 years of recovery—in an e-mail to me. Wendy had found recovery in the most unlikely of settings: a hostel for the homeless. Here, Wendy felt supported by caring staff and made friends with other residents who shared a lifestyle much like hers on the fringe of society. For the first time, she established strong social bonds, something that had been an aching void in her life. Also, she befriended a stray kitten, as lost as the human occupants of the shelter, who tugged at her heart. Wendy took over the care of "Tiggy." Soon, though, she realized that if she were re-hospitalized, Tiggy would be left to fend for herself. Wendy now had real motivation for staying well: a kitten whose survival depended upon her, and real friends who cared about her. In this way, Wendy began to make her slow recovery. She went on to take the shaky step of looking for work and eventually found it at the London Zoo, the perfect setting for an animal lover whose personal family of strays grew to several cats and dogs. Wendy went even further: She became a source of inspiration to other Munchausen patients because of her definitive recovery. She is credited with developing the first

Munchausen telephone-based support group in the United Kingdom, and later established an e-mail exchange with others who were engaged in disease portrayals and trying to stop. Her story was featured in newspapers and in a television documentary and she generously donated time each year to an area medical school where students had to question her to try to guess that she had been an active Munchausen patient. She was forced to retire from the Zoo due to emphysema from a lifetime of chain smoking, but lived quietly and happily in her own flat as a medical pensioner. She even found a life partner through the Internet whom she occasionally visited in the United States.

In early 1998, the tenor of her e-mails to me changed abruptly. She spoke of abdominal pain and the feeling of a mass in her side. Her e-mails became less frequent as the symptoms increased, and she asked for nothing from me other than my prayers. She pursued doctors' visits, but was always dismissed summarily as an obvious Munchausen patient once they saw her abdomen, which showed the scars of more than 40 unnecessary surgical procedures. In addition, her arms and legs were roadmaps of staff members' efforts to find veins destroyed through overuse in blood-drawing. Through fortuitous circumstances that Wendy could not have foreseen, she wound up at my hospital in Alabama. With her abdomen a tell-tale roadmap of scars, my emergency department colleagues promptly called to protest that she was "a classic Munchausen," one complaining to me that "It looks like she was in a duel with Zorro and lost. Why are you wasting our time?" With my reminder about the standard of care that governs all doctors, an MRI of her abdomen and other tests were performed, proving within a few hours that she had colon cancer. The best surgeons could do was reduce the bulk of the tumor so that it caused slightly less pain. Some of the tests performed in America had been performed in the United Kingdom but were given appallingly little credence. Clearly, British physicians had seen the mass that was now bulging up in her belly—one had commented to Wendy about it, and another drew a picture of it in her medical chart—but they were too wary of her past (well-detailed in the "Munch Bunch" black books that are commonplace in British hospitals) to believe their own eyes.

At my hospital, Wendy spent four months receiving surgery, chemotherapy, and radiation therapy to little avail. The focus of these interventions and the heavy narcotics she received was on controlling Wendy's horrific pain, but the results were mixed at best; her cigarettes seemed to provide her with more comfort, and there was no point in trying to dissuade her from her nicotine addiction. Certainly, no one, except perhaps Wendy herself, had any hope of remission, let alone cure. Wendy was eager to share her experiences with anyone who would listen and, appearing on television and radio programs, she now sought an audience who could understand that even Munchausen patients can become truly ill. Although she was discharged back to England with a prognosis of 20 months and remained as feisty as ever, she passed away in less than one month. Her ashes were scattered on a street that held meaning for her and those she loved. First her fascinating life story and then her obituary appeared in *The New York Times*, serving as profound cautionary messages to the world.

Since Wendy's death, I have retraced her route within England, met with doctors who still remembered her from her earliest days as a peripatetic patient, corresponded with her family and with the last doctor to see her alive, and met with her partner during her last years. Her partner spoke memorably about Wendy's blacklisting in this way:

> When Wendy got ill [with what proved to be cancer], the doctor down the road did not want to give her enough pain medicine. At that point, Wendy was really starting to hurt. Wendy had to use all her skills to get enough pain medicine because she was on this Munchausen blacklist. Once you get on a blacklist, you don't get off of it. And it's pretty bad then when you do get sick. They don't pay any attention to you. Since there are long waiting lists in a free medical system such as England's, it was very easy to put her at the end of a long line and not tend to her at all. Don't they send criminals on Death Row for routine medical treatment if they need it?

These cases point to the complexity of issues surrounding factitious disorder, especially as they affect the wrongly accused. But such issues strongly affect medical professionals too, whose mission is to care for and cure the patients they serve. Although most clinicians err in the reverse (overly treating false illnesses), there have been times, as demonstrated above, when clinicians have failed to treat legitimately ill patients whom they've suspected of disease portrayals.

Health professionals, and especially physicians, have a delicate line to walk when suspicious about apparent disease. Ensuring the well being of the patient, whatever the illness, must always come first. Yet, as medical costs soar and resources become scarcer, physicians are being held increasingly accountable by both corporate and legal standards for their treatment decisions. That is, they are expected to have as much enthusiasm for saving money as for saving lives. Chapter 14 will explore more fully the legal and ethical issues surrounding factitious disorder.

8

Drawing Back the Curtains:
The Motives Behind the Madness

This chapter probes the underlying motivations for playing sick, opening with a patient's personal insights as to why she had feigned multiple sclerosis, deafmutism, and multiple personality disorder. With surprising forthrightness, Melissa explains that she is attracted to the intellectual thrill of outwitting doctors, "the most highly trained and intelligent people" she knows. She also takes satisfaction from transgressing her "goody-goody" persona and finds a release from her anxiety, isolation, and boredom. Many patients also have a positive regard for their own self-inflicted pain as proof of their boundaries and selfhood. The unnecessary disfigurement that occurs in many cases is often the result of a psychic conflict turned outward: a way of expressing abuse and taking control. Patients commonly exhibit a dazzling degree of endurance and enthusiasm for physical suffering. This chapter contains a summary of the motivational theories that have been offered. It further illustrates the complex interplay of background and motivation by concluding with case histories in which individuals feigned or produced hormonal ailments.

Identifying the motivations behind disease portrayals can help to answer questions about the types of people apt to carry out such hoaxes. The most recent iteration of the *Diagnostic and Statistical Manual of Mental Disorders* points to several possible predisposing factors and causes. These include the presence of other mental disorders or general medical conditions during childhood or adolescence that led to extensive medical treatment and hospitalization; family disruption or emotional and/or physical abuse in childhood; a grudge against the medical profession; employment in a medically-related position; and, as mentioned before, the presence of a severe personality disorder. These features, however, only hint at the panoply of personal reasons for factitious disorder and Munchausen syndrome.

Adventuresome psychiatrists, psychologists, and sociologists have offered a potpourri of theories to explain the phenomenon of factitious disorder, but one patient I came to know provided us all with insight by listing the reasons, as she saw them, in her own case. Forty-one-year-old Melissa, who traveled from her home in another country to meet with me, had successfully feigned multiple sclerosis, deafmutism, multiple personality disorder, and numerous other maladies. She offers this thoughtful and thorough self-analysis of her motives.

Melissa's Perspective

What are the reasons for my behavior? I'm going to list them as I know them as of today.

First, I play an intellectual game with the most highly trained and intelligent group of people I know: doctors. In this game, I fool the doctor by presenting false symptoms, faking them so well as to be believable. I feel like I do when I watch really good performers act out a live play or excellent musicians perform. I empathize with doctors so that I can feel the challenge, the frustration, the urgency and the satisfaction—and eventually the anger and the hurt. I want to be challenged in this way, to be pushed to my best with a great reward at the end in most cases. I try to choose a doctor who will continue to play the game with me, allowing me to take up a great deal of his time and interest. I enjoy challenging him with the treatment of my condition. In this case, it does not matter when I have tests and pain is being inflicted on me. I am so wrapped up in the scenario, the emotions of the professionals, that I feel the pain is worth it. I do not feel superior to the doctors but do derive satisfaction out of knowing what is going through their heads and being able to manipulate their actions.

Second, I have always been a goody-goody. Now I am going against my own strong moral beliefs, against society's, and against my parents'. I am totally contrary to the "me" I had always portrayed. Even the normal rebellion in adolescence evaded me. The only thing I did was lie (and no one knew it). I have done this as long as I can remember. I used it to portray that perfect image of myself to the world. But internally, I was in severe distress about my lying. In my later high school years, I started lying much, much more. Not only did I lie to keep that perfect image of me in my family's mind, but also to make me sound more interesting to others. I wanted to see a counselor, but I felt that my problem was too weird and embarrassing.

Third, when I am acting (especially when I am faking multiple personalities in a psychiatric hospital), I am very popular with the doctors, nurses, and patients for a while. I thrive on their concern. Some doctors have obviously been taken by me and gone out of their way to help me. Patients take to me especially in a helping way. I have studied and portrayed psychosis and schizophrenia and feel kindred with those suffering from those disorders.

Fourth, I get relief from extreme anxiety. Upon entering the hospital, I feel the pressure of anxiety relieved like after sex. The anxiety builds up over time so that I feel I need a great release or I will become completely nonfunctioning, become psychotic, or kill myself. This alone accounts for much of the timing of my acts.

Fifth, it is something to fill extra time. It is, pure and simple, intense intellectual stimulation for a bored mind. I have not developed the effective planning of leisure activities for myself, including social activities. Often, I think of what would be enjoyable—and behold! An act in a hospital springs to mind. At this point, I have either pursued that activity or have to fight to keep it from popping into my head at every opportunity as long as I have free time on my hands. This alone decreases my enjoyment of other leisure activities, sometimes only endured as a distraction from my obsession.

Sixth is correlation to my menstrual cycles. I know that no one has studied this possibility as having a role in factitious disorder, but my estimate is that 80 percent of my factitious admissions to hospitals have been on the Friday just before the start of my period.

Seventh is fame and recognition, even though it is negative. I love the attention generated by the oddities of my behavior and psychopathology. I enjoy being the subject of case conferences and would love to write a book about my adventures.

Eighth is control over my environment. I enjoy the sense of control I have when I am running the show.

Ninth is escapism, withdrawal, and regression. I have a poor set of coping skills for stress in some situations, and just the extreme dread of stress can set me off. These situations can include having to do too much in too little time (especially if it is physical work like house-cleaning); having to be alone or with someone not important to me for a long time (like a whole weekend); or having to entertain or be with others who have certain expectations of me. Sometimes my need to escape responsibility has resulted in my regressing to the point of others completely looking after me, both physically and emotionally (as in when I acted completely paralyzed with Guillain-Barré syn-drome while acting schizophrenic—in effect, I could not move or make decisions).

These motivations, or subsets of them, hold true for many patients. But motivations can be multifold and vary from case to case, so it is difficult to make generalizations about all factitious disorder patients. Doctors are trained to follow specific paths toward diagnosis and to scrutinize small pieces of information in reaching conclusions. But when dealing with factitious disorder, medical professionals must look at these patients in the broadest terms. They must overlook nothing, no matter how far-fetched it may seem, that might contri-bute to answering the questions: "Who would do something like this, and why?"

The Motives and the Challenges of Uncovering Them

While borderline personality disorder is characterized by self-muti-lation which the patient acknowledges, factitious behavior involves concealing the volition underpinning the self-abuse. Both can occur at the same time, or alternate in ways we can rarely predict. The case histories already presented demonstrate to a dazzling degree that the endurance of pain—often extreme in quality—is common to both borderline personality disorder and factitious disorder. Paradoxically, many patients with borderline personality and/or factitious disorder regard self-inflicted pain as positive, particularly pain that results from having misled physicians to perform complex surgical operations. The distorted thought processes of these patients are evident even in the way they speak about pain. One woman, after injecting herself with bacteria, created a horrendously painful bacterial infection in her spine. When recounting the ordeal which nearly claimed her life, she referred to her pain as *delicious*.

Since borderline and factitious disorder patients find that pain reminds them that they are real, pain has the effect of organizing them. They immediately become patients and there is no more ambiguity about the role they are to fulfill and who they are. It helps them define the boundaries of where they end and the world begins.

In many cases, borderline and factitious patients externalize their psychic struggles by producing scars or other tangible evidence of their internal conflict. This dynamic explains the horrifying and ultimately unnecessary disfigurement factitious patients are willing to undergo. Wendy Scott's arms, legs, and abdomen were grossly deformed by scarring so severe that experienced surgeons found themselves dumbfounded and appalled. Interestingly, in enduring pain some patients feel a primitive honor that is reminiscent of some tribal cultures. Many cultures admire and celebrate individuals who demonstrate stoicism while bearing great pain. In some tribal societies, rites of passage are based on endurance of extreme pain and even scarification (the creation of permanent scars that can cover the individual virtually from head to toe). Modern societies have their own version of delivering this message. Consider the recruiting commercials for the military that depict the pain-contorted faces of new recruits as eliminating weakness.

Those who continually feel bad about themselves, as borderline and factitious disorder patients generally do, believe not only that they deserve punishment but seek it with the avidity of the ancient ascetics (who carried pebbles in their shoes) and self-flagellants (who flogged themselves in service to God). Though not a conscious motivation for Melissa, this recognition means that some people continue to believe that pain has spiritually redeeming qualities. Doctors are missing this moral component in some cases because, though we try not to, we always approach patients with preconceptions, one of which is that people would never want to be in pain.

I am reminded of a woman who plunged a knife into her chest, barely missing her heart. She claimed to be a member of a religious group which didn't believe in any demarcation between life and death, so she couldn't understand why the doctors were anxious about her well-being and why we were talking about protracted hospitalization for psychiatric care. She really believed that her action was insignificant, and yet we were dismayed as a group of professionals. Even if patients earnestly say things like, "suffering is good for the soul," most doctors would dismiss that explanation instantly. Yet piety for tolerating pain may be an unconscious factor in some cases of factitious disorder. People do things all the time for reasons of which they are not aware, and their actions may be highly influenced by spiritual beliefs, even unconventional and subconscious ones.

Given sufficient time with a factitious disorder patient, which is rare because these patients typically flee, doctors may be able to pinpoint individual motivation, even if a person is unaware of the forces driving his or her false illness for instance, protective environments, such as hospitals, are hard to give up if a person is not used to feeling safe in life.

Some disease portrayals are fraught with elements of sadomasochism. In a sadomasochistic relationship, the abused person identifies with the abuser and the relationship becomes symbiotic. In kidnapping and prisoners-of-war cases there can also be an identification that occurs between captive and captor called the Stockholm syndrome. In 1974, four Swedes held in a bank vault for six days during a robbery became attached to their captors. According to psychologists, the abused bond to their abusers as a means to endure violence and fear. Similarly, adults with factitious disorder may identify with their childhood abusers and perpetuate through self-induced illness the physical abuse that they experienced as children. They may accept the idea that abuse is a normal part of living.

For patients who have suffered childhood abuse, control is a huge issue. They were not strong or powerful enough as children to control what was happening to them. As adults, they have unresolved rage that displays itself in highly controlling behaviors. For example, they may engineer for doctors to contribute to their abuse through unnecessary tests and surgeries. Even though it harms them, the patient may feel in control through this behavior. In childhood there was nothing this person could do about the physical punishment; now the patient can intensify or curtail it at whim.

Sexual abuse also provides a foundation for self-inflicted physical disorders. Much more research is needed in this area, but consider the case of a young girl who stuck her eyes with pins to escape continual rape by her father. Once she was seriously wounded, she was extricated from her painful environment. That was obviously an extraordinarily desperate way of ending the abuse.

Sometimes feigned illnesses have symbolic aspects that also suggest a background of sexual violation. Munchausen by proxy, for example, has some sexual overtones since instrumentation being applied to the body in some ways is a sexual act. And tampering with and handling another person's genitals, urine, and feces, and injecting substances into the body, all have sexual connotations.

The Range of Approaches

The kinds of *psychodynamic* or *psychoanalytic* hypotheses illustrated above are extremely useful in many cases and have a rich history. For those reasons, I have given them a lot of attention. However, they necessarily involve some conjecture about an individual's unconscious drives and are therefore difficult to prove.

In contrast, *behavioral* theories focus on observable responses rather than impute actions to unconscious impulses, conflicts, and defense mechanisms. Behaviorists often focus on the fact that many patients with factitious disorder have experienced a critical illness as children or had a relative who was seriously ill. These children may find it rewarding to experience or witness the sympathy, attention, encouragement, and affection that is accorded occupants of the "sick role." They may also be gratified that illness permits an avoidance of responsibilities and duties. Behavioral approaches conclude that this past social learning and reinforcement can influence children as they grow up and are expressed through illness deception. Behavioral perspectives contribute to our understanding of factitious illness behavior, but do not explain why most children with such backgrounds do not become high utilizers of health care.

Faulty cognitive processing is another theory. In this view, the patient perceives bodily sensations abnormally, misinterpreting normal physiological functions as alarming or dangerous. By frequently visiting physicians and undergoing physical examinations and procedures, the patient is reassured, albeit temporarily, that no health problems exist. A serious problem with the cognitive processing model is that it assumes that factitious disorder is ultimately guided by the patient's authentic worry about his or her health. In reality, disease forgers deliberately feign or produce signs and symptoms; they do not simply misperceive or misinterpret them.

A *biological/organic view* suggests that *abnormal brain anatomy and/or function* is at the root of some cases. This neuropsychiatric approach to feigned or induced illness is in its infancy, and testing is constrained by the shortage of research funds. In addition, there are ethical reasons not to subject patients to batteries of brain and other tests when continual testing is one of the problems that treatment seeks to overcome. There have been no genetic studies of medical deception. Brain imaging, specialized psychological testing, and brain-wave studies of these patients have been small in scale, and abnormalities observed in a minority of the patients are nonspecific—that is, these same findings appear in a wide range of conditions that have nothing to do with disease simulation or induction.

Social psychologist James C. Hamilton has advanced the so-called *self-enhancement hypothesis*. He and his colleagues have shown in several experiments that, curiously, some individuals made to believe that they have an unusual, if rather inconsequential, medical ano-maly experience increased self-esteem as a result. They feel special and can even covet the prospect of being evaluated and treated by high-status physicians—people whom they might not otherwise meet. The creation of research settings in which to study subjects' thoughts and feelings represents an extraordinary advance in the field and holds great promise.

Motives in Action: Playing with Hormones

Being knowledgeable about factitious disorder in general and the various motivations behind it is central to any hope of treating these patients. The keen detective work and sensitivity about which I spoke earlier—perseverance and the ability to approach a patient correctly once feigned illness is suspected—are essential because factitious dis-order patients are so very good at what they do.

This fact is well illustrated by cases of factitious endocrine disor-ders (such as feigned diabetes and thyroid disease) that occur with alarming frequency. Persons who feign endocrine disorders may be actual diabetics who purposely stop taking their insulin to raise their blood sugars, or non-diabetics who take insulin to lower their blood sugars. Either way, such dangerous behaviors can result in coma. In some states, insulin can be purchased without a prescription, making it easy for patients with factitious disorder to produce erratic blood sugar readings. Where it is not easily obtained over the counter, insulin has been a coveted prize stolen by factitious disorder patients who are intent upon using this means to create a serious blood sugar condition.

The extent to which a patient will go to create this physical malady is extreme. One hospitalized patient hid the insulin in the toilet reservoir in his bathroom. Another suspended vials of insulin on a string outside the hospital room window. A nun with factitious disorder hid her insulin and syringe in the hem of her habit. These patients hoard their precious stash the way junkies hoard drugs. For these patients, the bottle of insulin becomes, in psychoanalytic terminology, a transitional object—a kind of security blanket that has a connection with comforting childhood memories. This transitional object also reflects the motivations underlying the portrayal.

For example, factitious disorder patients who feel especially vulnerable might place special value on the secrecy of their transitional object because they alone have the power to keep it concealed. They also have the power to use it in manipulating others who become thoroughly involved in the havoc wreaked by the abused substance. Similarly, self-mutilators revere and protect their own transitional objects, the tools for deliberate self-harm. Be it a comb, a piece of glass from a broken thermometer, or a strand of hair used like a saw, the value often lies more in its concealment than in its capacity for inflicting damage.

Most factitious disorder patients who feign endocrine disease are medical professionals or have other ways to access insulin, thyroid hormone, androgens, or other hormones. At least four patients have used drugs to simulate the signs and symptoms of pheochromocytoma, a rare disease in which an adrenal-cell tumor releases excessive adrenaline and associated products to cause recurrent episodes of exceptional anxiety and sweatiness, headaches, nausea, and a phenomenally rapid heart rate. A 27-year-old nurse who acknowledged that she enjoyed medical care added epinephrine (adrenaline) to her urine specimens and submitted to numerous X-rays; however, she refused to undergo exploratory surgery as her doctor recommended. Later, when real abdominal pain made her believe she actually did have the adrenal tumor she was faking, she requested surgery. Doctors operated because X-rays had indeed shown a mass, but it proved merely to be an ovarian cyst.

One 41-year-old female paramedic created the appearance of pheochromocytoma by using a drug that dilates air passages in asthma and bronchial conditions and that also stimulates the heart. A 22-year-old female medical student injected herself with a drug that raised her blood pressure. She also tampered with her urine samples and subjected herself to the surgical removal of her adrenal glands. A 35-year-old nurse had all of the classic symptoms of pheochromocytoma after injecting herself with epinephrine stolen from her veterinarian-husband's office. These women had access to drugs not available to the general public that enabled them to create extraordinarily realistic features of a specific disorder. Ultimately, it also helped their doctors to prove they were creating their symptoms, but not before two of them had both adrenal glands surgically removed. As mentioned before, factitious illness often results in real physical disorders and such was the case with these women. Removal of both adrenal glands caused them to develop an authentic illness called Addison's disease (from which President John F. Kennedy also suffered). Addison's disease is caused by a lack of hormones from the adrenal glands, and requires the use of steroids.

The 35-year-old nurse's case is of particular interest. She eventually left her husband and moved to Washington, D.C., where she was seen for her Addison's disease at the National Institute of Health and Human Development. Doctors there found that her main problem was that she was not following physicians' instructions for the treatment of the Addison's. She continued to be her own worst enemy even while attempting to be in control. What is so troubling is that she developed an authentic medical illness as a result of the intervention for a factitious illness, then used noncompliance with treatment for that real illness to manipulate doctors even further, creating a double jeopardy. The potential exists for a malpractice suit because healthy organs were removed from her body as her doctors overlooked the possibility of factitious disorder.

Proving that a patient had access to the medication is but one step in confirming the presence of factitious disorder. Medical professionals often must also show through conclusive tests that the condition cannot be otherwise explained. In other words, one is presumed ill until proved guilty of faking. That's sound medical ethics, not to mention good legal advice. Had Joan Nelson, the Englishwoman falsely accused of having Munchausen syndrome, been in the U.S., some sharp lawyer would undoubtedly have counseled her to sue her doctor for negligence, libel, and pain and suffering. But, as Joan found, this burden of proof can be costly.

The time spent by factitious disorder patients in inducing dangerous symptoms while fending off medical detectives can result in the greatest cost of all—the loss of a human life.

Consuelo's Facade

In a 1969 case of factitious *thyroid* disease reported by Doctors Rose, Sanders, Webb, and Hines (*Annals of Internal Medicine*), a 34-year-old single woman incurred that very high cost. Her portrayals began after the death of her father. At that time she had suffered diarrhea and heat intolerance and lost 30 pounds as patients with hyperthyroidism (excess thyroid hormone) might. Years slipped by and her symptoms continued to suggest thyroid disease, yet doctors could find no organic cause for her illness. She denied that she was taking thyroid medication. Fifteen years after her first symptoms erupted, she was admitted to a hospital for an overdose of digitalis. Afterwards, when doctors examined her for reemployment, she showed signs of thyroid disease, but now she denied all of her symptoms. She was hospitalized for further tests and transferred to a psychiatric unit for three weeks of evaluation.

Searches of her belongings failed to turn up any damaging evidence, but through therapy sessions doctors learned that she had been especially close to her father. After his death, she had lapsed into depression, for which she was given electroconvulsive treatments. She lived with her mother and brother, who were both alcoholic, and apart from her job of 29 years as a clerical supervisor, her life was empty. Loath to tolerate personal weakness, she set high standards and was extremely hard on herself. She put up a good front, but beneath the pleasantries were anger and denial of her hardships. She handled her feelings by keeping busy. In her case this meant being hospitalized, having tests run, and engaging doctors and caregivers. She eventually returned to work and nine months later was found dead in her bed, the victim of a probable barbiturate overdose.

Unable to prove that she had taken thyroid medication to cause her own symptoms, her doctors diagnosed her as having "occult" thyrotoxicosis, a term used when indisputable evidence of factitious thyroid disease cannot be uncovered. Doctors noted that she was excessively emotional and attention-seeking, immature, and dependent. She was secretive about her feelings and background, which is characteristic of factitious disorder patients, and denied taking thyroid medication though it seems certain that she did. The increased energy she derived from thyroid pills (which can act as a stimulant) may actually have facilitated the ruse, jolting her from her depression and motivating her continued usage of the medication. Thyroid medication appeared to be her means of coping.

Doctors Rose, Sanders, Webb, and Hines note that factitious disorder patients who abuse thyroid medications "have a serious psychiatric problem, often underlying depression, requiring definitive treatment. They should be carried in a supportive relationship until they will accept full psychiatric therapy. They should be treated as in suicidal attempts, watched for continued use of thyroid medication, worsening of depression, or suicidal gestures." They warn that in such cases, confrontation between patient and doctor is not as important as a supportive relationship. If confrontation becomes necessary, it should be carried out only after the doctor/patient relationship has been established and affirmed.

Although feigned thyroid disease makes for fascinating and unusual case histories, the most common form of factitious endocrine disease is one with which we opened this section: the surreptitious injection of hypoglycemic agents such as insulin. What ensues after patients inject themselves—the coma and other symptoms—is no longer a simulation, but a real, life-threatening condition. The first case of factitious hypoglycemia was reported in 1946. Since then, it has become one of the diseases of choice among factitious disorder patients. Some researchers have speculated that the number of cases of factitious hypoglycemia in the U.S. is equal to the number of authentic cases of insulinoma (an insulin secreting tumor). Because insulin is so effective at getting quick, dramatic results, patients can induce symptoms right away and use them as leverage against caregivers, constituting a form of blackmail.

Deirdre's Case

Deirdre was a factitious disorder patient and a genuine diabetic who was hospitalized 15 times in five cities from January 1967 to July 1969 for hypoglycemic episodes and coma. Motivated by her desire to be cared for, this 18-year-old girl repeatedly induced coma by injecting herself with insulin. When she stabilized and her doctors tried to discharge her, she injected herself again, so that she could not be sent home.

When doctors were convinced that this patient had factitious hypoglycemia, they searched her hospital room in her absence and found six vials of insulin, syringes, needles, and alcohol swabs in her purse. Because of her past denials that she was injecting herself with insulin, doctors surreptitiously added a radioactive chemical to each bottle of insulin. That evening she had a serious hypoglycemic reaction, and the next day she was taken to a low level irradiation laboratory where tests proved that she had injected some of the radioactive insulin. Her caregivers also discovered that the fluid level of insulin in one of her hidden vials had dropped. (The searches and exposure to radiation that occurred in this case would be illegal today unless the patient had agreed to give the doctors *carte blanche* as a precondition to admission.)

Before bringing their findings to the patient, doctors consulted a psychiatrist who urged them to talk to her in a nonaccusatory way and to propose that she allow them to help her manage her diabetes. Deirdre admitted her deception and although she couldn't offer an explanation for her actions, she agreed to psychiatric evaluation and treatment and to regulation of her insulin dosage by her doctors. Her diet and insulin intake were ultimately controlled and she was followed for several years with no relapses of her illness portrayal.

Therapists learned that this girl was racked with self-pity and frustration after she found out that she had diabetes. She came from a dysfunctional family, where her father worked away from home during the week, and on weekends ruled their home as a dictator. Her mother had surrendered to this unhappy life and did nothing to try to change it. Of four children in the family, Deirdre and one of her younger brothers were the central objects of their father's rules and restrictions. She wasn't allowed to date, and her feelings of being trapped turned into anger and tension that had to be suppressed lest she incur more of her father's wrath. Doctors hypothesized that her factitious disorder was an unconscious way of striking back at her parents for the life they had imposed on her and at her health care professionals for not being able to treat her whole problem. She took pleasure in keeping them confounded over her illness and spending time in the hospital away from home.

The extremes to which some of these patients will go are unbelievable, and patients who were self-injecting insulin have even allowed the removal of their pancreas in the search for a supposed insulin-producing tumor. Sometimes when doctors become suspicious and patients fear discovery and abandonment, they put themselves at the threshold of death, as in Deirdre's case. The doctors then end up having to take care of them rather than letting them die.

The Diabetes branch of the National Institute of Diabetes and Digestive and Kidney Disease in Bethesda, Maryland, tracked ten patients with factitious hypoglycemia for an average of five years, but some were followed for as long as 15 years. Two patients committed suicide, and only three of the patients abandoned their hoaxes and went on to lead lives that did not center on fraudulent illness.

Another group of doctors who studied 12 cases of factitious hypoglycemia found that the average age of the patients was 26 years. Six of the patients worked in medical or paramedical fields, which gave them easy access to insulin. Nine of the patients genuinely had diabetes mellitus.

Nearly all of the patients reported to have feigned or induced hypoglycemia have been women, quite a few of whom were nurses, doctors' wives, health care workers, and/or actual diabetics. Many of them had personality problems and troubled sexual relationships, and they all had symptoms of other mental disorders, such as depression. Like factitious disorder patients in general, they were familiar with and had access to medications that would create their symptoms; they had a keen interest in medicine and doctors; and many of them witnessed illness in friends and relatives and used them as models. Also, a significant number of them had been deprived of parental love and support through the death of parents or through their parents' indifference and/or immaturity.

I underscore the fact that health care professionals make up a large percentage of all factitious disorder patients, perhaps a third to a half of them. Others acquire their knowledge by reading articles or books, or by scouring the Internet. Many factitious disorder patients have spent their entire lives studying every possible aspect of their chosen disease and have become experts in their specialization, often exhibiting far greater knowledge about their disease than the trained clinicians who end up caring for them.

9

Mental Masquerades

Feigned illnesses are not always physical in nature. This chapter explores the wide range of mental illnesses that patients simulate in the interest of gaining attention and nurturance. Shondra, a 14-year-old, successfully mimicked schizophrenia and was hospitalized numerous times for psychotic episodes. Her home life of deprivation and abuse led her to seek refuge in a psychiatric hospital during dangerous periods of intolerable stress. Other feigned mental illnesses include multiple personality disorder, post-traumatic stress disorder, drug abuse, and dementia. It has been recognized recently that there is a continuum of mental masquerades that includes embellishing one's identity. Examples include false heroism, victimization, and personal crises such as bereavement. This forme fruste of the disorders of simulation is among the most easily enacted ploys. Both feigned heroism and invented victimization garnered national attention after the September 11, 2001 World Trade Center tragedy. This chapter examines some of the ways that clinicians identify fabricated psychiatric symptoms and/or identities and expose the ruses.

Playing the Madman

Physical illnesses that are created or conjured comprise the largest number of factitious disorder cases, but some persons with factitious disorder prefer instead to mimic psychological illnesses. In this variant, a person pretends to have an emotional problem such as grief, or a major mental illness such as depression or obsessive-compulsive disorder. It is one of the greatest ironies in all of medicine that a real mental disorder, factitious disorder, can be diagnosed when a person without a mental illness deceives others into believing that he or she has one.

Although reports of factitious disorder with psychological symptoms alone are infrequent, when such cases do arise, the traits that are manifested typically resemble those seen in Munchausen syndrome. Those traits include itinerancy, lawlessness, self-destructiveness, problems with developing and maintaining relationships, difficulties with sexual intimacy, open hostility, a worsening of symptoms during observation, and pseudologia fantastica. The prognosis for recovery is guarded. The diagnostic criteria for factitious disorder with psychological symptoms are identical to the criteria for factitious disorder with physical symptoms, except that the symptoms must be only emotional or behavioral.

Shondra's Refuge

In the journal *Hospital and Community Psychiatry*, Dr. David Greenfeld reported on a 14-year-old New England girl who was eight-and-a-half months pregnant and nearly mute when she was admitted to a psychiatric hospital for seclusiveness and severe confusion. Shondra had been in psychiatric institutions twice before for those symptoms as well as hallucinations in which voices told her to kill herself. During her first hospitalization, she was diagnosed with schizophreniform disorder (early schizophrenia) and discharged after three weeks. During her second hospitalization, she was said to have full-blown schizophrenia. Antipsychotic medications were prescribed for her, but she never returned for follow-up treatment.

Shondra had been abandoned by her father in infancy. She was raised by a mother who was unemployed and supported five foster children and four natural children through public assistance programs. Following an investigation of the home, a social worker for a state agency placed the foster children in other homes and referred Shondra for her current hospitalization, during which she gave birth to a baby girl who was to be placed quickly in foster care. When Shondra realized that she would lose her child, she made a startling recovery and declared that nothing had ever been wrong with her. She confessed to her doctors that she had learned to mimic psychosis by watching her cousin who suffered from real psychiatric illness. She feigned symptoms whenever her situation at home became intolerable and she resorted to withdrawal, in the form of silence and staying in bed, as her means of escape.

Her worsening symptoms, such as hearing voices, and her first two hospitalizations coincided with family problems such as sexual harassment from her mother's alcoholic boyfriend. She admitted to doctors that she had pressed for her third admission so that her baby would be born under the best possible conditions; this behavior represented an act of desperation as well as an ingenious survival tactic. She asked her doctors to help make it possible for her and her child to stay with the baby's father.

Psychological tests proved that Shondra wasn't psychotic, and she and her baby went to live with the child's father and his family. Doctors thought that she had carefully selected the man who fathered her child because he lived in a more secure and nurturing environment than her own, a belief that was substantiated by follow-up. Two years later, mother and daughter were thriving and Shondra had had no further psychiatric hospitalizations.

Dr. Greenfeld notes that feigned psychosis may be common among extremely poor and homeless youngsters and adults, who could view feigned mental illness and psychiatric hospitalization as a way of relieving their physical and emotional agony. In that regard, there is marked overlap among factitious disorder, malingering, and genuine environmental chaos.

Fictitious Factitious Disorders?

Some researchers believe that because the motivation is often unknown or uncertain, the diagnostic legitimacy of factitious disorder with psychological symptoms is compromised. In a 1989 paper published in the *American Journal of Psychiatry*, Dr. Richard Rogers proposes that the difficulty in determining whether psychological symptoms are intentional suggests that the diagnosis of factitious disorder with psychological symptoms should be abandoned altogether. Rogers and others believe that patients who are diagnosed with factitious psychosis (pseudopsychosis) tend to have family histories of mental illness and that they often seem over time to develop true, undeniable psychoses such as schizophrenia. There is support for this assertion. One researcher reported on six patients who were thought to be feigning schizophrenic psychosis, but only one ultimately proved to be factitious. He suggested that what we're diagnosing as factitious disorder with psychological symptoms is actually the initial warning sign of what is going to emerge as an authentic psychosis, and that we may be doing most of these patients a disservice by giving them a factitious disorder label.

Bart's Tale

One patient who *did* clearly have factitious schizophrenia was named Bart. He came to the hospital late at night with the story that he had been diagnosed as having schizophrenia at another institution and that his main symptoms were bizarre delusions of people following and looking at him. Then he described hallucinations in which voices were telling him to do things like injure or kill his family (called *command hallucinations*). One common sign in schizophrenia is an alteration in emotions with patients showing blunted or inappropriate emotional responses. There's an incongruity between the emotions being expressed and the words the patient is saying. Also, the answers the patient gives are odd, and the interviewer can't quite follow the thought processes behind the answers. When you've finished talking to a person with acute schizophrenia, you get the strange feeling that you didn't quite make contact. You're always left wondering what's really going on inside that person's mind.

When the more experienced staff on the ward talked with Bart, they found that his thoughts were just too well organized and well directed for schizophrenia, and so he received psychological testing. Even though he endorsed some of the obviously psychotic items such as answering "yes" when asked if he heard voices, the psychological testing suggested an antisocial personality disorder rather than a thought disorder or psychosis. He was not able to fake the more subtle items within the psychological tests that would indicate real distortions in perception and the way he thought.

Multiple Identities

Among the most fascinating forms of factitious psychological disorder are cases involving claims of multiple personality disorder (MPD). The following case, reported in the journal *Psychotherapy*, is complex but also classic.

Elaine's Portrayal

Fifteen-year-old Elaine began having problems as early as elementary school. There, she had had poor relationships and had been considered a pathological liar. She displayed signs of self-mutilation and once blamed her innocent father for burning her with cigarettes. During an early hospitalization, Elaine described four other personalities in addition to her own, including three girls—ages four, eight, and twelve—and a ten-year-old boy. Later on, before beginning therapy, she presented two others: a 78-year-old woman and another young boy.

This girl's portrayal was so convincing that she was diagnosed as having MPD and referred for hospitalization and then outpatient therapy. Her hoax began to unravel during therapy when she told lies about events that had never occurred and that seemed designed to get attention from adults. The other red flag was the detailed biography Elaine provided about her 78-year-old personality, which was totally out of character for even the most creative MPD patient.

Instead of confronting the patient, therapy was continued and caregivers learned that Elaine had previously read all she could about sexual abuse after meeting a girl who had undergone this trauma (such abuse is said to be a contributor to MPD). She read the book *Sybil*, saw the movie of the same title, and even mimicked some of the sketches that Sybil drew. After weeks of treatment, the patient told her therapist that she kept a journal and was asked to bring it to her next session. By that time, another personality had emerged, this one a paraplegic who turned up on the floor outside the therapist's office, crawled inside, and presented the therapist with the journal. Entries intimated that the patient was feigning MPD. When confronted by her therapist, Elaine seemed relieved that the truth was finally known, and after a further year of therapy, she no longer showed signs of MPD—and therefore of factitious disorder.

Combining the Types

Although most of the published cases of factitious disorder involve only physical symptoms, enough of the remaining cases mix both physical and psychological symptoms to be classified officially as factitious disorder with combined psychological and physical signs and symptoms, which the following case demonstrates. Gigi has created the ruse of having multiple personality disorder *and* secretly fails to take medications intended to prevent medical crises.

Gigi's Narrative

I am a 50-year-old woman and I have a factitious disorder. This is the first time I have admitted this reality to anyone.

I have a long psychiatric history of numerous doctors, therapists, and hospitalizations, but have not been honest enough to get much benefit. I now have severe hypertension, which is enough to get me into the hospital whenever I decide to stop my medication.

The first time I saw a therapist, I don't know why but I began to act out having MPD. This continues on a major scale, involving 12 different personalities who have names, ages, lifestyles, and experiences that are totally different from my own. At first, I used this as a way to talk about the abuse I suffered as a child and teenager and couldn't communicate in any other way. But it has gotten way out of hand. It has become so complex that I don't know how to pull back.

I was sent to a specialist in MPD and it is the entire focus of my treatment. I generally have had my therapist worried to death about me because of the stories I invent. I never keep up with my blood pressure medications, using the 'dissociation' from personality to personality as an excuse for not remembering to take it. I realize that I could get very sick as a result—but I am not ready to make a change toward being healed.

Factitious disorder and Munchausen syndrome have also been recorded as existing simultaneously with apparently *authentic* multiple personality disorder. Dr. Ellen Toth and therapist Andrea Baggaley of Alberta, Canada, reported in the journal *Psychiatry* on a girl who developed five different personalities as a way of dealing with years of parental indifference and sexual abuse by her brother and a male baby sitter. In addition to psychiatric treatment for MPD, she had 58 non-psychiatric hospitalizations for symptoms that included shortness of breath, head injuries, nose bleeds, chronic anemia, blood clots, gastrointestinal bleeding, urinary tract problems, and self-induced hypoglycemia. She also reported fever and vomiting, but these signs were never documented by caregivers. Through disease portrayals, she subjected herself to 13 operations and received 76 units of packed red blood cells. She was officially diagnosed as having

Munchausen syndrome after a syringe and a vial of suspected fecal material were found in her hospital room. This patient still seeks and gains hospitalization, and discharges herself whenever she hears talk of factitious disorder among her caregivers, but her multiple personality disorder continues to be an apparently valid psychiatric condition.

As I pointed out earlier, some psychiatric professionals insist that factitious disorder with psychological symptoms does not exist, even in the face of cases such as Bart's and Gigi's. Actually, it is easier to deceive using a psychological illness than most physical illnesses because psychological symptoms are harder to disconfirm. My contention is that factitious disorder with psychological symptoms is a valid diagnosis. I consider the manifestations of factitious disorder—whether they involve psychological symptoms, physical symptoms, or both—to have the same underlying psychodynamic issues: the need for nurturance, sympathy, control, or the expression of rage.

A study in England revealed that out of 775 patients under the age of 65 who were admitted to a psychiatric hospital, four had Munchausen syndrome. Researchers said that they believed that figure was an underestimate because it may have been overlooked in a number of cases. One of the confirmed Munchausen patients, a 28-year-old man, was admitted after supposedly taking an overdose of drugs because he was suicidal over having been diagnosed with AIDS. Blood tests for the AIDS virus, however, were negative. He told doctors that he was alcoholic and a homosexual prostitute. Although he denied having had psychological problems in the past, his caregivers learned that he had received psychiatric treatment in England, Scotland, and elsewhere in Europe for a variety of diagnoses, including personality disorder, alcohol abuse, depression, sexual deviancy, and Munchausen syndrome. The oldest of eight children of alcoholic parents, he was raised in foster care. By the time he was 20 years old, he was facing an 18-month prison term for gross indecency. Like other Munchausen patients, he did not stay in any place long enough to benefit from therapy, and he continued his behavior. Though his depression and HIV status were falsified, other elements of his story may have been true.

The Role of Drugs and Alcohol

Misuse of drugs and/or alcohol is common among factitious disorder patients with psychological symptoms. They may secretly use psychoactive substances to produce signs that suggest a mental disorder. Stimulants such as amphetamines, cocaine, or caffeine may be used to produce restlessness or insomnia. Illegal drugs such as LSD (lysergic acid diethylamide), mescaline, and marijuana might be used to induce altered levels of consciousness and perception. Heroin and morphine, which are pain killers, may be employed to induce euphoria (Heroin is legal in the U.K. but not the U.S.). Hypnotics such as barbiturates can be used to create lethargy. Combinations of these substances often produce extraordinarily bizarre presentations. The main difference between factitious and actual drug abusers is that the factitious disorder patient induces an altered state not as an end in itself, but as a way to mislead caregivers and others. For them, the issue is not whether they have truly become addicted, but whether they can get the drugs under false pretenses and stay connected with health care professionals.

Psychological Manifestations

Psychiatrists frequently see people who fake illness simply to dodge the law or avoid court appearances—classic cases of malingering. They generally ask for a statement on official letterhead because they were supposed to go to court on a specific day and couldn't because they were hospitalized. They act as if the schedules collided through sheer coincidence and the supposed illness wasn't related to the court date at all.

As I have mentioned elsewhere in this chapter, malingering and factitious disorder sometimes overlap and doctors may have difficulty determining which diagnosis applies in a given case. If you can identify an external motivation, then it becomes malingering, and if you can't, it's factitious. But those are pretty soft territories and a lot of cases fall right in the middle, particularly when factitious psychological disorders are involved.

Amnesia and Dementia

Amnesia and dementia are easy to feign but the truth is likely to emerge if the doctor has sustained access to the patient. Dementia is caused by organic factors and is marked most prominently by short- and long-term memory loss. Memory deficits are easy to fake during brief personal exchanges because this form of deception simply requires the withholding of information. Dismissive and inconsistent responses, with blithe and ready responses of "I don't know" and "I have no idea," are characteristic of feigned amnesia and dementia. Patients with authentic memory limitations tend to be embarrassed by their deficits, demonstrate consistency in their memory problems, and struggle to remember rather than dismiss questions out-of-hand. They also have little or nothing to gain through their memory deficits. Another clear sign that someone is probably feigning amnesia or dementia is when he or she remembers what you said near the beginning of the interview and later incorporates it into the conversation where it is pertinent. The memory of a person with genuine dementia wouldn't be that accurate. Comic examples of persons who have feigned memory disorders include a woman who was asked a number of questions by a resident doctor and repeatedly exhibited severe memory loss. When examined the next day, she replied, "As I said yesterday, I can't remember anything."

The Element of Selection

To a large extent, the motivations underlying factitious disorder are unconscious, even though the choice of symptoms is conscious. By definition, lying is a conscious behavior. People know that they are lying, but unconscious mechanisms may drive the need to lie. Some patients who feign psychosis really do fear that they are "falling apart," but they don't have the particular disorder they are trying to feign. Since there may be some overlap between what they are really suffering from, such as depression, and what they are feigning, it takes a lot of work by mental health professionals to sort out the true illness from the fake one.

The medical literature shows that not all patients with factitious disorder who exhibit psychological symptoms are looking fearfully over their shoulders at invisible men or openly talking to themselves. Factitious disorder patients can be far more subtle than that and have, for instance, faked poor results on IQ tests and similar measures designed to determine if a person has any kind of brain impairment. On personality tests, there aren't necessarily correct and incorrect answers, but through the patterns of answers, doctors can gain a sense of whether people are minimizing or exaggerating symptoms. Certain questions are easy, and a clever patient can readily figure out what to say to appear mentally compromised. But most of the questions are much more subtle, and an average person wouldn't know how a sick person would respond. In general, though, to see if the results are being faked, a clinician must look not only at these tests, but at the whole clinical picture.

Rather than feigning formal psychiatric ailments, some individuals embellish their identities. They transmogrify themselves from anonymity to public notice by claiming to be heroes, victims, or simply everyday folks with decidedly heavy burdens to bear. In such cases, the focus is on standing in the spotlight, as in the cases of invented disease. Certainly one of the heaviest burdens anyone can bear is that of having lost a loved one. Most of us empathize deeply with the recently bereaved; as witnesses to their sorrow, we are reminded of our own mortality and that of the people we love.

Bereavement

The symptoms most commonly associated with factitious disorder with psychological symptoms—such as depression, visual and auditory hallucinations, memory loss, dissociative and conversion symptoms, and suicidal thinking—are frequently tied into claims of bereavement. While bereavement is not a mental disorder, we naturally empathize when we encounter bereaved people. In an article in the *American Journal of Psychiatry*, Dr. M. R. Phillips and colleagues reported on 20 factitious disorder patients who faked the deaths of loved ones to assume the sick role. In addition to exhibiting psychological symptoms that included threats of self-destruction, 15 of them had also feigned physical symptoms at one time or another. My own experiences with patients who fake or exaggerate emotional symptoms due to bereavement suggest that these people often claim that numerous family members have died; however, when doctors check out their stories, they find that nobody close to them has passed away at all.

In the following case, a woman's factitious physical ailments began in adolescence. She unaccountably switched to feigned bereavement as a young adult, and then carried out her ruses almost compulsively for many years. However, the shame from repeated discovery of the falsehoods, combined with the glow of success in her professional and personal lives, helped her end the behavior at age 25. She is now a wife, mother, and employee, albeit one still perplexed by her own past deceptions.

Molly's Story

I did the things most kids do—pretended I was ill when I wasn't to get a day off from school now and then. But things took a more sinister turn after an accident at school when I was 11. I had a bad fall while running on the playground and had a concussion. I ended up in the hospital for two days. Over the next few years, I pretended on at least two other occasions to have concussions. Later, after leaving home, I pretended to have broken arms and wrists, to the same end: It all was to get the attention of family and friends.

When I was 19 and working in my first job, I pretended that someone in my family had died. I sat at my desk and almost coldly decided to tell my co-workers that I had just had a phone call to say that my brother had killed himself. I could play a role and be very brave. After a week off for the "funeral," I came back. Over the next few months I developed it further and further. I gradually "killed off" the rest of my family. I pretended that my mother died of Hodgkin's disease, that my father had a heart attack as a result of the trauma, and that my last remaining brother (who didn't actually exist) then hanged himself. A major bonus in all this was attention from my boss; I enjoyed his attention and care. I was found out when my father phoned my office about something. My boss confronted me and I denied everything, resigned, and ran away.

Five months later I got another job. After a few months, I started the same pattern. I got a friend from America to post a letter to my boss—a letter that I had secretly written. The letter said that, in the past, I had been involved in a shooting in a store in which my parents had been killed. I liked the attention that resulted from that letter, especially that of my male co-workers. Of course, it took only about two weeks for the boss to find out that this was all nonsense and I was dismissed.

I was now 21 years old, found a new job, and did well for two years. Then, for reasons I don't know, I pretended to be pregnant and, later, to suffer a miscarriage, returning to work "bravely" the following day. Still, my work had always been excellent and I was promoted. Within weeks of starting, I again claimed that I was pregnant—this time with twins—and later said I lost the twins in a car accident. Someone from my first job tipped off my boss and I was found out within a very short time and confronted.

I did not admit that the pregnancy was a lie. I admitted that I had lied about having a husband. I continued the lies, but also found a way to admit to at least one lie whilst saving face. Although they had every right to do so, they did not sack me. They gave me another chance. And I did not run away because I now had reasons to stay and things to protect. I was at the top of my profession, had a house, a boyfriend, and just too much to lose. I stuck it out even though it was humiliating: everyone knew and talked about me, but soon it was yesterday's news.

It has been 12 years now since this episode and I have never done it again. I haven't pretended to be ill or lied about my family, or anyone dying, or anything else. I haven't wanted or needed to. And if it has ever occurred to me, however remotely, I have only had to think of the terrible feeling of discovery and the complete havoc that I wreaked on my own life.

I have been married for many years—to a doctor. Although that choice may sound suspect, I actually get less attention, not more, from him because he's so busy!

In the *British Journal of Psychiatry*, Drs. John Snowdon, Richard Solomons, and Howard Druce attempted to point out the high incidence of factitious bereavement. They report on 12 patients falsely claiming bereavement, all of whom were observed at a London teaching hospital. Six had hurt themselves or reported acts of self-destruction, one had threatened suicide, and five were admitted for feigned non-psychiatric reasons. All but one of these patients were men. Nine of them said that they were grieving for more than one dead family member.

One of the 12 patients, a 41-year-old man, was admitted after complaining that he had lost consciousness after a fall. He was transferred to a psychiatric ward when he told his caregivers that he was deeply depressed because he had lost his wife and two children in an auto accident two years earlier. When doctors contacted his private physician, they learned that this man had never been married. He discharged himself without warning.

In another of the 12 cases, a 28-year-old man sought admission to the hospital after he supposedly took an aspirin overdose. He told doctors that he had been depressed and suicidal since he witnessed the gruesome death of his mother three weeks earlier when she fell down a flight of stairs and was impaled on a metal railing. He seemed so sincere that he was admitted to the psychiatric unit, where he attacked a female patient, then discharged himself. Doctors, who were unable to substantiate his story, later learned that he had previously been admitted to three mental hospitals using aliases.

Dr. Snowdon and his associates note that the telltale signs of feigned grief include a lack of corroborating witnesses or difficulty in reaching them; transfer of these patients from non-psychiatric wards, where ingenuous medical caregivers may be sympathetic to such sad tales; and grief that is unusual in that it is delayed, inhibited, extended, or especially intense. Most of the deaths described are dramatic and especially violent and are often reported to have happened to a child or adolescent.

Joel's Case

Sending in the (Diagnostic) Troops

When looking at the broader picture to determine if a patient has factitious disorder with psychological symptoms, examiners must take social climates and world events into consideration. With AIDS being a major health concern, psychiatrists are seeing factitious AIDS cases. Likewise, with each new military conflict, we see factitious post-traumatic stress disorder (PTSD), which is characterized by symptoms—such as high anxiety and flashbacks of the traumatic situation—that emerge after shattering events such as participation in combat.

We always see cases of factitious PTSD after a military conflict in which doctors ultimately find that the individuals never even served at the time. Many cases of factitious PTSD relate to Viet Nam and, even decades later, continue to emerge out of that conflict. Regardless of the alleged site of battle, some patients have attended PTSD therapy programs for years before it is determined that they never participated in battle or even visited in the country claimed.

Researchers have noted that *genuine* PTSD related to military action or war is earmarked by a number of characteristics or actions of the patient. They include: 1) attempting to minimize the relationship between one's symptoms and the trauma experience; 2) blaming oneself; 3) having dreams about traumatic events; 4) denying the emotional impact of combat; 5) being unwilling to recount combat stories; 6) experiencing guilt over having survived; 7) avoiding environments that resemble the combat situation; and 8) feeling angry at the personal inability to overcome PTSD. Phony war heroes often fail to present this complete picture in creating their symptoms. A book (*Stolen Valor*) and at least one website are dedicated to exposing those who have claimed falsely to have served in horrific combat or to have lived in squalor for years as prisoners of war. One of the many individuals who have been exposed offered the following virtual (online) apology:

> I have represented myself as a former POW. Of course this is not true. I am a USAF veteran of the Viet Nam era but never served overseas. I make no excuse for doing this other than trying to find a reason to validate my being on this earth. I apologize to all persons that I have angered or hurt by my misrepresentations of being someone I was not. I am a coward. I will never imply nor outright lie to anyone again concerning my military service. I am 55 years old and it's time I became truthful and honest with all. I am not asking for forgiveness nor would I expect it. I only want it to be known that I am truly repentant for the claims I had made and only ask that I am believed when I tell you, "Never Again."

Factitious PTSD has also been diagnosed in people who create crises such as ostensive motor vehicle accidents and say they have flashbacks and excessive startle reactions as a result. One man in Scotland claimed that he was depressed and drinking heavily because he had killed a six-year-old child in an auto accident. He displayed symptoms of depression and PTSD. He said that he had tried to commit suicide by cutting his wrists and that he was contemplating shooting himself. Inconsistent details of the accident weakened his story. He fled from the hospital under questioning by suspicious doctors, who were later told by police that they had no record of any such accident. Doctors who reported this case in the *Journal of Clinical Psychiatry* candidly noted that "were it not for the inconsistencies in his history and the contrast between the history and objective mental status examination, his presentation closely mimicked that expected of persons presenting after a real accident of this type."

Yet another group in which factitious PTSD or depression has been reported is comprised of patients, briefly noted earlier, who falsely claim to have been diagnosed with HIV or AIDS. In the first reported case of factitious AIDS to include physical and psychological symptoms, Drs. Steven E. Nickoloff and his co-workers described a 33-year-old man who was referred to an emergency room because of suicidal ideation. He told doctors that he had already attempted suicide by taking an overdose of antidepressants and that he was becoming increasingly depressed and angry because he had failed to end his life. Complaints that ranged from not sleeping for days at a time to rapid weight loss and pronounced mood swings gained him admission to a psychiatric ward. There, he fed doctors a dramatic psychiatric history, saying that he had bipolar disorder (a malady marked by manic and depressive episodes), had tried to commit suicide four times, and had long abused alcohol and drugs. He said that many different types of therapy had failed to help him and demanded that doctors treat him with electroconvulsive therapy. He also said that he had experienced the traumas of learning that he had tested positive for HIV and that one of his friends had died of AIDS.

In highly involved cases such as this one where pseudologia fantastica plays an important role in the hoax, patients tend to forget some of the lies they tell or details they provide. Inconsistencies lead to discovery. Such discrepancies and other questionable information, including the patient's claim that he had not slept at all for 18 days in a row before his admission to the hospital, instilled doubts in his doctors' minds. When they asked for permission to contact his family and past caregivers, he refused. When he developed lesions on his legs that he claimed were Kaposi's sarcoma (a disease of primitive vascular tissue sometimes found in AIDS patients), biopsies revealed that they had actually been caused by heat or chemicals. He signed a consent form for an HIV test, but he left the hospital before the result was available. His HIV test was negative, and his doctors never heard from him again.

Doctors Nickoloff et al. concluded that, when presented with an atypical history or lack of appropriate physical findings for any disorder, the physician should promptly obtain previous medical records and communicate with other health care providers. They added, "It is likely that our patient's true colors would have shown earlier if we had made continued hospitalization dependent on consent for release of information."

Factitious Victimization and Heroism

As I have shown through many of the cases already presented in this book, some people covet the status of victim or hero rather than patient. Over the past 10 years, as more and more such cases have come to my attention, I have formally proposed categories of *factitious victimization* and *factitious heroism*. Physical trauma and/or emotional devastation may be alleged in the victimization cases, whereas false heroes accept their ill-garnered accolades, often with mock humility. "Vanity" arsonists, for instance, tend to be volunteer firefighters hungry for the limelight. They set fires, wait until they are large enough to be of some real threat, and then either put them out or call for reinforcement. Invariably, they are then lauded for their vigilance in having been first on the scene and for their independence and fierceness in having single-handedly put out a threatening blaze. In the same way, police officers have sought to outdo their colleagues by reporting crimes that never occurred or staging crime scenes—again, which feature scenarios involving illusory attentiveness and bravery.

One Alabama case is illustrative. There was an explosion of media coverage when a novice police officer reported that, from a distance, he happened to see a woman drive onto a bridge, stop, emerge with an infant, then throw the infant into the water below. All other area police investigations ground to a halt to focus on this appalling case; a police artist's rendition of the woman was posted everywhere, and newspapers and television news shows featured little else. With time and the accumulation of dead ends, variations in the officer's story, and the discovery that he had made at least one false police report in another state, the announcement came from the Chief that the man admitted that no such crime had occurred. No explanations were offered, and no further comments were ever forthcoming. However, at least in retrospect, several warning signs very common to factitious heroism and victimization were present: the man had made other fallacious claims; he had knowledge about law enforcement; he set up a high-profile, highly unusual crime scenario that would inevitably attract widespread attention; he incorporated elements that didn't ring true (It certainly would not have been in the best interests of the alleged offender to dispose publicly of a live infant.); his descriptions of the crime wavered; and a thorough investigation only led back to him.

In another shocking but famous case, a long-serving police officer staged his own suicide to appear to be a homicide in the line of duty, thereby ensuring himself a hero's burial. Obviously, his suffering was so deep as to commit suicide; yet his vanity was such that he relished the elaborate trappings and news coverage of a formal police burial.

Lou's Scam

Predictably enough, in the wake of the September 11, 2001 terrorist attacks on New York City's World Trade Towers, fake survivors have emerged as falsely-bereaved individuals. Although most of the articles published and personal accounts posted during and after the attacks are poignant and true, some have been exposed as shams. For instance, tiny Opp, Florida hit the map when newcomer Louis Esposito courted adulation through heroism that proved to be factitious. In 2002, he let it drop at the post office that he was one of the flag-raising firefighters on a new postage stamp commemorating the rescuers. He signed autographs, had his photo taken with fans, spoke to student groups, showed off a scar from a beam that fell from the Towers, and flaunted a firefighter's badge. But everyone wanted to know why he had moved to Opp. He said that he had moved to the town to escape the tall towers of New York City and frightening memories of September 11. In reality, he was an ex-con nowhere near New York on that day. His closest brush with fire may have been when he lit cigarettes at one of the many prisons in which he had served time.

Factitious victimization claims have involved stalking, sexual harassment, emotional and physical abuse and neglect, rape, and countless other crimes. Although I believe that childhood abuse plays a role in the development and expression of many instances of factitious disorder, the fact remains that, like prototypical factitious disorder patients, individuals have invented abuse histories and adult sexual crimes to garner emotional satisfaction. When crimes such as rape are reported for external reasons such as concealing consensual activity that was discovered, retaliating against a partner, or explaining an unplanned pregnancy, malingering would be involved rather than factitious disorder.

The following cases of false adolescent sexual abuse are highly unusual. They involve both competition and enmeshment between two young women with factitious disorder that includes fallacious claims of sexual abuse. The story was told by Tara.

The Deceptions of Tara and Zoë

I am a 20-year-old vocational tech student who is the best friend of someone who suffers from factitious disorder. I am writing you, however, regarding myself, as well as behaviors that my friend and I engage in together.

My friend Zoë often fakes fainting spells and seizures, and is taken to the hospital routinely. She has recently diagnosed herself with factitious disorder and is reading up on the literature. I think she is trying to help herself.

One of the things I learned from reading one of the articles lying around is that factitious disorder doesn't always relate to medical care, hospitals, and doctors. I was surprised by this because I never considered that I could have factitious disorder. But I have some rather odd attention-seeking habits. I look very young for my age. Once, by mistake, I was picked up by the police in my hometown because they thought I was an underage runaway. Since then, I have been actively trying to fool people into believing I am indeed a teen runaway. I have made up a false identification card and do whatever it takes to be brought into child protective custody and then placed in a foster family. I have portrayed myself as having been sexually abused, and then taken advantage of the attention and the foster family placement. I lie in every way I need to, but I have never implicated a real, existing person as the perpetrator of the sexual abuse.

Zoë has recently entered into my ridiculous schemes and has begun to replace her "hospital/medical" desires with the same "being-a-child-in-need" schemes. The only difference between us is that she enjoys the attention from the police and doesn't much care about the foster family part, whereas I detest the police and covet the family concept.

My biggest concern, though, is that Zoë is very upset that I would even suggest that I fit into the factitious disorder category because I have not faked sickness and she feels I am making light of her plight by saying I think I have factitious disorder as well. I am simply trying to put a name to my problem so that I can have a focus for pursuing its solution.

The two have entered into a kind of folie à deux in which they conspire in their deceptions. Each is aware of the other's behavior but keeps it quiet. Instead, Zoë is now borrowing Tara's game plan while Tara, more helpfully, has diagnosed herself based on Zoë's research.

Zoë "doth protest too much." While she claims that Tara's accurate self-diagnosis of factitious disorder (specifically, factitious victimization) makes light of her more physically-based case, she seems to grasp her own factitious disorder as a magnificent jewel she fears will be stolen. At the very same time, she has perversely "stolen" Tara's invention of the sexually-abused, wayward teen. She also relishes the attention of the police, and appears to be a "men-in-uniform" groupie. Of the two, clearly Tara has the greater insight and the stronger self-definition. It is heartening that both apparently want to get well, but Zoë's prognosis is worse than Tara's because Zoë is elaborating new permutations of her factitious disorder. I question whether she is culling the literature to help herself or to improve her game. There is a risk that competition for the top slot could cause these two to escalate, practicing more dangerous behaviors over time.

10

Munchausen by Proxy: When Factitious Disorder Becomes Abuse

In Munchausen by proxy (MBP), individuals create symptoms of illness not in themselves, but in dependent others who serve as "proxies." The majority of MBP perpetrators are women, most often mothers, who induce illness in their children or subject them to painful medical procedures in a quest for emotional satisfaction, such as attention from and control over others. MBP is a form of maltreatment (abuse and neglect), not a mental disorder. The effect of MBP maltreatment on children who survive to adulthood is poignantly expressed in a first-person account. This narrative reveals the profound confusion experienced by adult survivors in how to respond to legitimate illness and how to overcome feelings of shame or guilt for having been unwitting participants. Not surprisingly, some MBP children grow up to develop factitious disorder.

The cruelest and deadliest phenomenon presented in this book is *Munchausen by proxy* (MBP). In this disturbing behavior, instead of creating signs of illness in themselves, adults produce the appearance of illness in others—typically in children, but sometimes in other adults, the elderly, or even animals. Tragically, such actions are usually taken by a seemingly loving, caring individual, almost always without the knowledge of the spouse, partner, or other family members. MBP can be understood as health-related maltreatment manifested by physical abuse or neglect, emotional abuse or neglect, and/or sexual abuse.

MBP is not a mental illness even though the behaviors and motives are similar to factitious disorder, which is a mental illness. The critical difference is in who is harmed: oneself (factitious disorder) or someone else (MBP). An analogy might help. Barring an accident, if a person shoots herself, we can usually assume she is psychiatrically ill (probably suicidal). But, without instigation, if she shoots someone else, we can generally assume that she is not mentally ill. It is much more likely that she is homicidal. Being homicidal does not qualify as an emotional ailment. However, being suicidal does. By aiming her deceptions at her child, not herself, the MBP perpetrator unmasks herself as a perpetrator, not a patient. Her actions constitute abuse, not mental disease.

MBP maltreatment falls decisively under the criteria contained in the Federal Child Abuse Prevention and Treatment Act of 1974. This Act defines child abuse and neglect as "the physical or mental injury, sexual abuse, negligent treatment, or maltreatment of a child under the age of 18 by a person who is responsible for the child's welfare under circumstances which indicate that the child's health or welfare is harmed or threatened thereby." In other words, it is any maltreatment of a child or adolescent by a parent, guardian, or other caretaker. Acts in some states define maltreatment of the elderly in similar terms.

The main types of abuse are emotional, physical, and sexual; neglect is categorized as physical or emotional. The permutations of maltreatment are innumerable, but include nutritional neglect, intentional drugging or poisoning (apart from MBP), neglect of necessary medical care, neglect of safety, educational neglect, and MBP itself. The types and subtypes overlap and intertwine in many cases. For instance, Julie Gregory, author of the book *Sickened: The Memoir of a Munchausen by Proxy Childhood*, was undoubtedly subjected to severe MBP. It incorporated medical abuse, social deprivation, nutritional neglect, and medical neglect (The last was manifested by her mother's delaying badly needed treatment for authentic maladies.). Physical abuse in the form of beatings and emotional abuse through her mother's constantly shaming her and hurling outrageous accusations occurred as well but was usually independent of the MBP.

Ten books and more than 550 reports of MBP have been published, yet those figures clearly underestimate the actual incidence of MBP due to underdiagnosis and selective reporting of cases. A conservative estimate is that there are 1,200 new cases of MBP reported per year in the United States. Documented cases of MBP have come from more than 20 countries throughout the world and have appeared in at least 10 languages. The continual recognition of MBP proves that MBP is not simply a theory or a behavior confined to Western societies, but a pattern of actions constituting a specific kind of maltreatment of international dimensions.

The last point warrants emphasis because groups have arisen that deny the very existence of Munchausen by proxy maltreatment. Their membership consists of individuals who are understandably bitter about having been falsely accused and have important points to make about situations in which the risk of misdiagnosis is heightened. However, it appears also to include actual perpetrators who grasp the brass ring these groups offer to conceal their crimes. Perpetrators who align themselves with the groups insist upon their innocence and present themselves as victims who are being punished for having the courage to speak out against physician incompetence. The group members often target key professionals who have attempted to build awareness about MBP. In an effort to destroy reputations, they have collected and publicized personal information about these professionals and have sent threatening e-mails. Not surprisingly, an entire industry has arisen in which certain psychologists, attorneys, and even those without any clinical experience have become well-known in the field of MBP for writing and testifying exclusively in support of accused mothers. Innocent parents deserve the most ardent and skilled representation possible, but these experts explain away compelling evidence against their clients, the danger to the children notwithstanding.

Survivors of MBP maltreatment usually feel terribly alone, as Lindsay's comments demonstrate.

Lindsay's Words

When I became aware of your work, I was so surprised that there is actually a name for this problem. I had always been told that I was a very sick child—and believed it. It was only when I went away to boarding school, and noticed that I never needed to go to the doctor when my mother wasn't around, that I began to suspect that she had been fabricating my illnesses. I stopped using the inhaler that one of my many doctors had prescribed for my "breathing problems," and I felt fine. [The resolution of symptoms when an MBP parent is absent is called a *positive separation test*.] I can't tell you how many times I have been in an emergency room. I have been to physical therapists, allergists, neurologists, internists, and the list goes on and on. I began to wonder why my mother's stories about my childhood ailments and injuries seemed to change over the years. I began to intentionally expose myself to foods I was "allergic" to only to find that I had no allergic reaction at all. I have never confronted my mother about this; the thought of doing so is too unpleasant.

A small body of statistics is available for MBP, and the data are staggering: For instance, the estimated mortality rate is 9 to 10 percent, making it perhaps the most lethal form of child abuse. Mothers are the perpetrators in around 75 percent of the cases, with females such as grandmothers, babysitters, foster mothers, and stepmothers comprising most of the remaining 25 percent; fathers and other men account for fewer than 25 cases (less than 3 percent) in the literature. Hypotheses abound about the female predominance, but the main reason may be the greater time spent by women in caretaking roles and the correspondingly greater unsupervised and unwitnessed access to children. Boys and girls are victimized approximately equally.

The original term, *Munchausen syndrome by proxy*, was coined in 1977 by Dr. Roy Meadow, a Professor of Pediatrics at the University of Leeds in England, who was knighted for this work. He created the term as a way of distinguishing these cases from adult factitious disorder and Munchausen syndrome. Most authorities have dropped the word "syndrome" from Meadow's creation because it tends to suggest that MBP is a group of symptoms rather than a scientifically recognized public health tragedy. Dr. Meadow has done so as well.

In 1993, MBP was added to an Appendix of the fourth edition of the *Diagnostic and Statistical Manual of Mental Disorders* as a "research" mental diagnosis called *factitious disorder by proxy* (FDP). It remains in the Appendix to this day, meaning that further study is still necessary before FDP can be established to be a mental disorder. I take the stance that a perpetrator can no more have MBP or FDP than have shaken baby syndrome. In other words, I conceptualize MBP exclusively as a particularly dangerous form of maltreatment and reject use of the term FDP or its inclusion in *DSM-IV* and *DSM-IV-TR*. Alternatives that some authors have promoted, such as "Pediatric Condition Falsification," "Meadow's syndrome," and "Polle's syndrome," only add to the confusion in nomenclature. (Polle, purportedly the child of Baron Münchhausen but one he disavowed, died in childhood for reasons that are unclear.)

In MBP, a child may undergo an extraordinary number of unpleasant and often painful diagnostic tests. He or she may also be exposed to numerous pointless medication trials and/or surgeries with all their attendant risks. Some children have had as many as 300 clinic visits and 14 hospitalizations in their first 18 months of life. The youngest victim stemmed from an assertion of fetal illness: a 25-year-old woman continually made deliberately false claims during the second and third trimesters that her fetus was not moving. These claims led to repeated and unwarranted testing, but all test results were normal, as was the birth of her child.

Collision, Not Collusion

MBP victimization is more common among infants and toddlers who are too young to talk. When the child begins to talk and can describe things, the probability is higher that the perpetrator will be detected. However, MBP doesn't necessarily end with the development of the child's verbal skills. Young children are not always able to see relationships between events or people, so a child who is being victimized through illness may not make the connection that a parent or trusted other is making him or her sick. Besides, parents of legitimately sick children must usually fight to get medicine down a child's throat, so a child who is the target of MBP isn't necessarily going to understand when ipecac or a laxative is being force-fed needlessly. It is also well-established that many abused children internalize the problem and blame themselves rather than their parents, believing perhaps that they deserve the illness due to some wrongdoing on their part.

Older children may not disclose the true sources of their illnesses out of fear of abandonment by their mothers (again, the usual perpetrators) if they stop being sick. Other elements of classic child abuse creep into the MBP picture as victims and abusers enter into an almost symbiotic relationship, much the same as hostage and hostage-taker. This phenomenon, Stockholm syndrome, was introduced in chapter 8. The best-known example in the United States is that of Patty Hearst

who, after being kidnapped and tortured by the Symbionese Libera-
tion Army, joined their cause and helped their members commit
armed robbery. In a parallel way, children often protect their abusers
and resist making revelations to the medical and social service personnel who could rescue them. Dr. Meadow has noted that as children
grow older, they may in fact come to believe that they are disabled and
may actually participate in the medical hoaxes, ultimately developing
factitious disorder themselves. Others grow up with post-traumatic
stress symptoms or difficulties discerning reality from fantasy.

Signs and symptoms created in children include fabricated or
induced apnea (respiratory arrest), seizures, blood and bacteria in the
urine, unremitting diarrhea and bloody stools, vomiting, rashes,
dehydration, fevers of unknown origin, depression, heart arrhyth-
mias, bacterial arthritis, vaginal and rectal bleeding, coma, and cardiac arrest. And one of the most shocking revelations to emerge from
the study of MBP is that, while the precise numbers are unknown,
some Sudden Infant Death Syndrome (SIDS) casualties (or "cot
deaths") are actually due to suffocation as part of MBP that went too
far; bruises or blood on the face are especially suggestive of homicide
rather than SIDS. More subtle indicators of suffocation are being
developed. In addition, in a study at a Boston hospital, Dr. Thomas
Truman found that more than one-third of 155 infants who had suffered repeated apparent life-threatening events (ALTEs) were in fact
MBP victims. The American Academy of Pediatrics has issued a policy
statement that all children whose deaths are unexplained should be
examined specifically for possible fatal child maltreatment, including
MBP.

In the U.S., the most common among the MBP symptoms are
apnea, seizures, vomiting, and diarrhea. Two cases from university
medical centers are presented as illustrations.

Tamika's Experience

One mother began making emergency room visits with her daughter when the girl, Tamika, was six months old. By the time she was
three years old, Tamika had had at least nine hospitalizations for
alleged apnea. Because the mother's account of her child's illness was
so believable, doctors disregarded the normal tests and prescribed a
home apnea monitor, also treating the child with a powerful anti-
convulsant medication. (The shockingly shoddy science behind

home monitors was later exposed in the award-winning true-crime book, *The Death of Innocents.)*

By the time Tamika was five years old, none of her symptoms was consistently better, and some of her medical specialists and subspecialists had become suspicious. A visit to the child's home by the local child protection agency uncovered the fact that Tamika's room had been organized by her mother, a former nurse, to look like a hospital intensive care unit. It even included an in-home laboratory! Doctors who finally obtained most of the child's records learned that her mother had not only reported symptoms of near-miss SIDS, but also blood in her child's urine and feces, seizures, hypoglycemia, abnormal eating habits, and bowel and urination irregularities. They found that the child had been subjected to a host of pulmonary, cardiac, endocrine, gastrointestinal, neurologic, and urologic exploratory operations. Even though the child's tests were consistently normal, the strength of her mother's continued reporting of symptoms led physicians to treat this child with an alarming variety of medications. None of the physicians had known that so many other doctors were involved in her care. They also discovered that Tamika's mother had arranged for her to receive unwarranted physical and occupational therapy and special education for the handicapped!

Eventually, doctors came to believe that this woman had been preoccupied with making other health care professionals believe that Tamika was ill because she felt so unhappy and abandoned in her marriage. In other words, Tamika had become an object to be manipulated to meet the mother's needs.

Even though MBP is not a mental disorder, the behaviors of MBP, like factitious disorder and Munchausen syndrome, are often accompanied by emotional or psychological disorders that can sometimes be successfully treated. The challenge is in getting the perpetrator to acknowledge and admit to her abusiveness. If this step is achieved and if the perpetrator is truly motivated for change, she can sometimes learn through counseling how to parent more appropriately. Stress reduction and relaxation techniques can help reduce anxiety and anger if those emotions are contributing to the MBP. According to doctors' reports, Tamika's mother, in contrast to most, did benefit from long-term therapy and could be safely reunited with her. Oddly enough, however, the treating psychiatrist had difficulty getting naïve doctors to stop prescribing the unnecessary medications.

Katie's Drama

Seven-year-old Katie was victimized by her mother for six years. During five of those years, the child was seen 126 times at different clinics and by a private physician and was treated for several disorders, including a condition that required pressure equalization tubes to be placed in her ears. The fever of unknown origin (FUO) that finally led to the discovery that her disorders were false began when she was only one year old. The FUO supposedly continued as the child grew, but each time she was admitted to a hospital, her temperature would quickly return to normal. Tests that included cultures of blood, urine, stool, and spinal fluid were always negative.

At the age of four, based on the medical history supplied by her mother, Katie was put on medications for asthma and allergies. By the age of six, she was receiving five asthma medications that had been prescribed by her primary care physician, and her diet was limited to ten "safe" foods. Despite the way the child was being forced to exist, she had shown no signs of wheezing, and skin tests for inhalant allergens were normal.

This girl lived with her mother, stepfather, stepbrother, and stepsister. Her stepfather was a blue-collar worker and her mother was an emergency medical technician. The child was supposedly so ill that she couldn't attend school and had at-home tutors. At one point, she developed severe diarrhea and vomiting requiring administration of intravenous fluids. She then displayed the symptoms of an overdose of the asthma medication theophylline. Her mother, who had refused to relinquish an active role in monitoring the child's vital signs and administering her medication, denied playing a role in this latest medical dilemma. However, the baffling constellation of physical problems, which came and went, and the onset of theophylline poisoning finally alerted doctors to the likelihood of MBP.

They admitted Katie to a pediatric intensive care unit and notified her stepfather, Children's Protective Services, legal counsel, and her primary care physician. It was discovered that the mother had a chronic history of abuse as a child, and also as an adult at the hands of her first husband. An investigation concluded that she had indeed induced the child's frightening medical signs and symptoms. By devoting her life to "helping" her "sick" child, she could, in the eyes of the world, be a nurturing, martyr-like mother, unlike her own abusive mother.

After a court arranged alternate care for Katie, the child thrived without medications and was able to attend school regularly.

"We may teach, and I believe should teach, that mothers are always right," Dr. Meadow once wrote, "but at the same time, we must recognize that when mothers are wrong they can be terribly wrong." Dr. Meadow warns that the realization that a child is a victim of MBP evolves slowly. The point at which intervention should occur, he says, depends on the amount of proof a doctor is able to accumulate and the level of danger faced by the child.

Disease Devotees

As we have seen, mistreatment in MBP runs the gamut from sad to horrific. The disease forgery can include any of the manipulations discussed in chapter 2, including exaggerations, false reports, falsifications of signs, simulations of signs and/or symptoms, dissimulations, aggravations, and induced signs or diseases. Exaggerations and false reports are not necessarily less harmful than aggravations or induced ailments because the ultimate consequences to the child may be the same: misdirected investigations, medications, and medical/surgical procedures as well as confinement to the role of patient. Also, perpetrators who engage primarily in one type of manipulation can choose to engage in any other as the circumstances seem to dictate.

Mothers may put their own menstrual blood in their child's urine specimen or inject feces into the child's intravenous line. An extraordinary number of different substances, including both prescription and over-the-counter medications and preparations, have been utilized to cause diverse physical symptoms: diuretics to induce dizziness, ipecac or salt to force vomiting, narcotics to create breathing problems, laxatives to produce intractable diarrhea, barbiturates to cause lethargy, antidepressants to trigger coma, and insulin to manufacture hypoglycemia. One mother pricked her own finger and added the blood to her 5-year-old child's urine, knowing that tests would read positive for bleeding from the urinary system. Another mother produced the illusion of diabetes in one of her children by putting sugar and acetone in her urine. She produced actual illness in another of her children by poisoning him with medication to induce seizures. Other mothers have caused seizures by stopping oxygenation of the brain; they do so by restricting the child's breathing.

In one case, a mother induced seizures through coercive training, rather than drugs. Her little four-year-old told teachers and students that he was epileptic, and on numerous occasions was observed lying on the ground at school, trembling as if having a seizure. However, suspicion grew when he was easily roused by the mention of his favorite food. He later told his teacher that his mother had trained him to simulate epilepsy, and rewarded him with candy when he acted in this manner. The child was placed in foster care and his "epilepsy" resolved.

Children often have to endure far more than that four-year-old before their false illnesses are resolved. They have had unnecessary operations, such as removal of part of the intestines and removal of the pancreas. One child was unsuccessfully treated for five years for strange ulcerations on his back; it was only discovered much later that his mother had been rubbing oven cleaner on his skin. Another mother altered test results and stole sputum from patients with genuine cystic fibrosis (a hereditary disease affecting the mucous and sweat glands) to make her child appear to have that disease. And another woman gave her child ipecac to cause the appearance of bulimia.

In a case in which the father was the culprit, the man reported that his 11-year-old son had a long history of cystic fibrosis. This claim was easily disproved by testing. When confronted, the father readily backed down from his claim, which contrasts with the tenacity generally seen with maternal perpetrators. Another father added cooked meat to his son's urine samples to create the impression of hematuria.

Family Ties

Medical investigators warn that sometimes an initial tip-off that a child is a victim of MBP is a deceased or chronically "sick" sibling; if there are several children in a family, abuse may not be reserved for just one child. In a representative case, MBP was found to have affected four siblings after one child died at the age of two and another at the age of twelve months. A third had suffered for six years before MBP was discovered. Another mother repeatedly brought her infant twins for medical attention, claiming that they were vomiting blood. While one of the babies was hospitalized, she reported that he had vomited blood and displayed blood-stained clothing as proof. The mother and child had different blood types and analysis showed that the blood on the clothing did not belong to the child, but to the mother. She was later caught pricking the lip of one of the infants with a pin to create bleeding, and the children were removed from her by a protective services agency. The mother later falsely complained to doctors that she herself was coughing blood, seeming to be preoccupied with this medical condition. In another family, illicit insulin administration was found in a one-year-old girl. Doctors then looked at the history of her siblings and found that there had been 30 separate episodes of factitious illness in four family members.

Further evidence of multiple MBP victims in the same family comes via a case in Australia in which a woman's son had 18 hospitalizations in his first 18 months of life. Her daughter had 15 hospitalizations in her first nine months of life. Police were able to intervene only when the mother was seen trying to choke her daughter, and she was sentenced to six years in jail.

In 2003, Mary Sheridan, Ph.D., published a review of 451 cases, replete with reported life-threatening episodes. Perhaps her most shocking finding related to the 210 known siblings of the 451 victims described, proving that the identification of one victim raises concerns about other children in the perpetrator's care: 25 percent of these siblings were known to be dead (from all causes), and 61 percent of all siblings either had symptoms similar to those of the victims or symptoms of potentially suspicious origin. There is every reason to believe that many, if not most of the deceased siblings represented MBP that had gone undiscovered. Often, only when one or more children in the same family die under odd or vague circumstances do authorities realize that the lightning that keeps striking this family may have been induced through reprehensible actions.

Characteristics of the Perpetrators

Analyses of the characteristics of the perpetrators in proved cases are surprising. Despite their chilling actions, most MBP mothers appear completely normal on the surface. Even on detailed psychological testing, they do not necessarily appear disturbed in any way, and so psychiatric and psychological examinations are typically futile in establishing or refuting the diagnosis.

One way to help differentiate between appropriate mothers and potentially lethal ones is to be suspicious of a mother (or other caregiver) who is angered by negative test results. It is also telling if a mother shows a peculiar eagerness to have invasive procedures performed on the child. Most caregivers are understandably reluctant to allow painful interventions without a thorough explanation.

Also, a pattern often emerges in MBP in which the child is sick and the mother continuously stays at the hospital for several days. She then becomes exhausted and goes home to rest at the urging of staff. During that time, the child suddenly gets well. The mother returns after a couple of days and the child gets dreadfully sick again. Thus, the occurrence of symptoms very closely parallels the mother's presence.

Callie's Tales

One mother, Callie, took her three sons to doctors so frequently that, though her husband was gainfully employed, she had to get a part-time job just to keep up with the portion of the bills that their insurance company didn't pay. The vague symptoms she reported, and that she insisted were signs of chronic illness in the boys, ranged from pallor and headaches to tiredness and sprains.

As the children grew older, the complaints Callie issued worsened to include asthma, chronic allergies, sinusitis, and arthritis. Apart from some valid sports-related injuries and the occasional cold, however, doctors never found anything wrong with the children. Nonetheless, they missed blocks of time from school and their activities were curtailed because Callie insisted that they were ill and that doctors had misdiagnosed them. She also managed to talk doctors into prescribing antibiotics and other medications for her children on the strength of her descriptions of their symptoms. She kept a medical reference book in her home and frequently checked it to match symptoms with illnesses.

Callie, who appeared to be a genuinely concerned and loving parent, admitted that she had always wanted to be a nurse, but said she couldn't go to school to fulfill her dream because her children were always sick. She had a keen interest in medicine and often accompanied relatives on doctor visits. Her abusive behaviors tapered off when her boys were in their teens and old enough to resist going to doctors for what they described as nothing, but by that time one of them showed signs of factitious disorder himself, complaining about vague symptoms without prodding from his mother.

Motivations

MBP perpetrators are motivated by an intense desire for emotional gratification. Examples follow:

They may simply adore the attention MBP produces for them. Having an ill child brings them a certain kind of misguided status. Their child's illness is their claim to fame, and they bask in accolades from medical caregivers or the community about their devoted parenting.

The father may be emotionally distant from both mother and child and unconcerned about or literally unaware of the child's illness. He may be a traditionalist who believes that anything involving the children is his wife's responsibility, and that he is a great father by virtue of being a single-minded, dependable breadwinner. The mother then aims to prove her worth by caring unwaveringly for their offspring despite the adversity of illness.

The child's illness may bring about a closer relationship between the parents. Arguments cease and the parents unite when faced with the common adversity of a sickly child. This closeness may suit the mother, who sustains it by keeping the child ill.

Some MBP mothers find that the child interferes with a satisfying social life. Repeated hospitalizations of the child allow the mothers to escape the responsibilities of parenthood.

MBP maltreatment allows the perpetrators to express rage not only toward their children but also toward those whom they see as responsible for their dissatisfying lot in life. For instance, they may blame their own parents, who will be predictably distraught that their grandchildren have perplexing ailments and who can therefore be "punished" by ensuring that the child is never cured.

Others need to feel that the child is totally dependent on them and force this dependency through induction of illness.

Many find gratification in manipulating high-status professionals, such as doctors, and prestigious institutions such as the Mayo and Cleveland Clinics. They may also be emotionally satisfied by gaining the attention of lawyers, judges, and others within legal circles, as well as television and print reporters.

Not surprisingly, an element of sadism is involved in most cases, particularly those leading to painful, repeated interventions. I believe that a person's being repeatedly brought to the brink of death, as in many MBP cases, is properly termed torture, and in such cases I advocate that criminal courts put aside the term Munchausen by proxy and address unflinchingly the torture that has befallen the victim.

Interestingly, contact with the medical establishment is not inevitable. If the mother can gain enough gratification simply by misinforming others that her child is sick, she can sidestep taking the child for actual examinations and tests. One mother falsely claimed for almost two years that her child was dying of cancer. She shaved the child's head to mimic the hair loss from chemotherapy, gave the child sedatives to cause her to appear "spacey" (claiming it stemmed from brain damage from radiation treatments), and received the prayers of everyone with whom she shared the story—which was the entire town and beyond. Finally, the mother's crudely forged doctor's note to the child's school proved to be her undoing. It was full of misspellings and factual errors about health care. The mother soon acknowledged hundreds of lies, big and small, that she had told to keep everyone riveted with the invented tales of her child's battle with cancer.

Spin-offs

Several variants of MBP have emerged over the years, causing doctors to urge vigilance among all professional caregivers. As mentioned before, the victims can include pets. An equivalent of MBP is seen by veterinarians in which a woman, usually middle-aged, fabricates medical signs and symptoms in her pet—typically a dog or cat, but sometimes a horse, goat, or other animal. For many people, a pet is a substitute for a child, and the animal's illness is also a way of maintaining a relationship with the pet's doctor. Pet owners have precious few legal responsibilities, and cases have been reported to me in which an abusive owner maimed or killed more than a dozen animals in the unmistakable pattern of MBP. One such owner bragged on the Internet about the resulting amount of contact she had with the veterinarian, and was thrilled when he gave her his home address and phone number in case the next tragedy occurred after business hours. It promptly did.

A peculiar variant of human MBP surfaced in 1980 in Israel, resulting in the first known incident of what doctors termed *Munchausen by adult proxy*. The central figure in this case, a 34-year-old man, began inducing illness in his wife by putting sleeping pills in her coffee. While she was sedated, he injected gasoline into sections of her body to create abscesses. The perpetrator kept an almost 'round-the-clock vigil at his wife's bedside under the guise of assisting in her care. She died from the ailments he had induced and his role in the death went unrecognized.

Three years later, the same man hired a nanny to help him care for his daughters. Eventually he proposed marriage to her. When she expressed a lack of enthusiasm about his offer, he drugged her coffee and injected gasoline into her breasts, neck, and buttocks. Extensive lab tests ultimately led to his being discovered and he was sentenced to 46 years in prison for the murder of his wife and the assault of the nanny. This man became publicly known as the "Gasoline Injector."

The Value of Surveillance

Proof is what doctors at Yale University School of Medicine in New Haven, Connecticut were after when they set out to catch a mother whom they believed was creating chronic diarrhea in her son. The 18-month-old child developed severe diarrhea when he was only two days old, and was first admitted to a local hospital at 3 months of age. He was then transferred to Yale-New Haven Hospital, where he underwent costly and comprehensive bacteriologic, radiologic, endocrinologic, and metabolic studies, all of which had normal results. After two months, the diarrhea suddenly stopped and he was sent home, where he thrived for six months. Then, once again, he was readmitted for diarrhea after having been treated with several antibiotics for an unresponsive inflammation of the middle ear.

Agitated and underweight, the child had to be fed through a catheter instead of his mouth and he was given a multitude of antidiarrheal medications. Still, the diarrhea could not be controlled. As part of their investigation into the cause of the depleting illness, doctors examined every aspect of the child's hospitalization, and noticed that his diarrhea subsided when he was sleeping or away from his room for tests. A common denominator during all of his episodes of diarrhea was his mother, a vigilant guardian who stayed by her son day and night to assist in his care. She spent so much time at the hospital that she cultivated friendships with some of the nurses, who offered her food and money because she complained that her husband was stingy and uncaring.

Doctors convinced the mother that she needed a rest from the hospital. She boldly predicted that her son would improve while she was away. He did, but, as soon as she returned, so did the diarrhea.

This case presented an unusual set of circumstances to the child's physicians, who wanted desperately to help him. They took equally desperate measures to root out the cause of his chronic illness, which they feared could lead to his death. They were reluctant to approach the boy's father because they were uncertain about whether he might have a role in the child's illness or warn his wife. Doctors, nurses, members of the hospital's house staff, and a social worker banded together to gather the proof they needed, which was essential to enable a protective service agency to step in successfully. With guidance from hospital attorneys and administrators, the hospital security team arranged for video camera surveillance of the child; this approach had been effectively used at another hospital in a case of MBP involving twins who repeatedly suffered cardiopulmonary arrest.

A closed-circuit camera was installed above the bed in the private room and staff members were instructed to view the monitor continuously. If they saw the mother doing anything dangerous, they were to contact a security officer and confront her. Within 24 hours, the video camera showed the boy's mother giving him three doses of a substance that she administered orally with a syringe. She was taken into custody, and a search of the child's room turned up syringes and a number of different substances that would cause diarrhea.

Doctors had been concerned about what this woman might do to herself or her child when confronted, so they had alerted the psychiatric emergency room staff beforehand and asked them to be ready for any eventuality. As predicted, the woman became extremely upset when she was confronted with the evidence and could only be controlled through admission to a psychiatric hospital. The child, whose diarrhea once again stopped in his mother's absence, was released into the custody of his father.

After the mother was hospitalized, her complicated personal medical history surfaced. It included numerous hospitalizations and surgical procedures for reasons that were not well-established. She had worked as a nurse's aide but was terminated for stealing patients' medication, and also alleged fainting spells and chronic insomnia. During her two pregnancies, she was hospitalized for severe vomiting and diarrhea, the causes of which were never determined. Her records had all the indications of someone with a history of factitious disorder, if not Munchausen syndrome. With the birth of her son, she decided to use his body rather than her own as the instrument for her deceptions. In doing so, she willfully became a child abuser.

Inpatient *covert video surveillance* (CVS) is the medical staff's most definitive way of proving MBP. CVS has been used with great success in the identification of MBP abuse both in the United States and United Kingdom, and is accepted as legal and ethical when applied according to written protocols. In the U.K., pediatrician David Southall and his team used CVS at two hospitals to uncover life-threatening child abuse in 33 of 39 cases in which induced illness was suspected. In the U.S., Dr. David Hall and colleagues, who reviewed 5 years of CVS data at an Atlanta children's hospital, concluded that CVS is *required* to make a definitive and timely diagnosis in most cases of MBP. They added the following concern and imperative: "Without this medical diagnostic tool, many cases will go undetected, placing children at risk. All tertiary care children's hospitals should develop facilities to perform CVS in suspected cases."

When confirmed perpetrators are confronted with video evidence, they may claim that "this is the first time" they've ever engaged in this behavior; alternatively, they may try to explain away suffocation as "cuddling" or tampering with IV lines as "just straightening out the tubing." Videotaping may therefore represent only the beginning of the medical investigation that must follow. Checking on the real histories of the child patient and his or her siblings (with the help of other family members and caregivers) often leads to unearthing the full story. Also, the "first time," "cuddling," and "straightening the line" claims have been offered so often as desperate lies that they have largely lost their capacity to influence.

Advocacy...For Whom?

Although the mother just discussed was not criminally charged, others who have subjected their children to MBP have indeed had criminal charges leveled against them. It seems obvious that maltreatment, up to and including murder, should be criminally prosecuted. Yet, because the victims in MBP cases usually cannot speak for themselves, such prosecutions are infrequent. In case after case, the mother is able to mobilize lawyers, court the media, write to politicians, and, shockingly, portray herself as the victim. It takes exceptional circumstances for district attorneys not to turn a blind eye. For instance, in one celebrated case, Floridian Kathy Bush was convicted of child endangerment for spending years sickening her daughter Jennifer. She also misappropriated state health care funds to buy a motorcycle and a swimming pool while pleading poverty. An earlier investigation by law enforcement had been stopped and so, by the time of the conviction, Jennifer had gone on to have dozens of surgeries and 200 hospitalizations. In response to Mrs. Bush's spirited letter-writing campaign, Jennifer became a poster child for national health care reform who was feted by then-first lady Hillary Rodham Clinton. A well-known baseball player was so touched by her plight that he became a kind of "second father," leading to even more media attention. When protective services and law enforcement finally stepped in definitively, they found that Jennifer's extreme medical problems entirely resolved upon separation from her mother. Mrs. Bush was proved to have been recurrently poisoning her. As the awareness of MBP grows among health care professionals, law enforcement agencies, and the judicial system, offending parents are gradually being prosecuted and jailed more frequently for doing harm to their children. Kathy Bush is now serving a five-year sentence. Jennifer, who was placed in foster care, sent a bitter, castigating letter about her to the judge in the case shortly before her mother's incarceration began.

Some health care professionals have accused the medical, legal, and social service worlds of collusion with MBP perpetrators through their ignorance of this form of maltreatment and their failure to intervene swiftly. In one paper, Dr. Basil J. Zitelli and others stressed early recognition of MBP to help professionals from becoming "unwitting collaborators" with the abuser and "professional participants" in the abuse. They also emphasized that participation from all involved health care professionals is generally necessary to identify the factors which contribute to this type of abuse in a given case.

Detection depends upon an awareness that MBP exists. In a 1988 study of a pediatric nursing staff, 55 percent had never even heard of Munchausen by proxy, and more than 70 percent felt professionally and personally unprepared to deal with such a case if it arose. The results were scarcely better in a 1996 study of social workers and family physicians, though the term itself is becoming more familiar to professionals and the public at large. Education is the key to early detection and treatment, and education is the primary reason for this book.

As with factitious disorder, MBP can involve the feigning or production of *psychological and/or behavioral signs and symptoms*, not just physical maladies. For instance, one father surreptitiously gave his child sedating medications, then presented the boy as inexplicably lethargic and inattentive, and in need of services for the developmentally disabled.

Bethany's Exploits

Two even more disturbing cases were described by a woman writing about her sister-in-law, Bethany:

Bethany has been "by proxying" on the children since they were born. Right now, she has both of her children mentally hospitalized and is trying to convince their doctors that they are mentally ill. She claims that her adolescent daughter suffers from bipolar disorder with manic episodes. She claims that her daughter is violent, which we have never witnessed. She says both children suffer from ADHD [attention deficit hyperactivity disorder] and has insisted that they be medicated. More recently, she claims that her daughter was hearing voices and that the voices told her to kill her brother and that she was beating up her brother a lot and trying to kill him. A few months ago she had her son committed to a psychiatric facility because she claims that he told her that he was hearing voices. I spoke to the boy on the day before the commitment, and he was cheery and fine. He was being seen regularly by his grandparents and aunts and uncles who said he seemed relieved to be at their house. She will not let anyone visit the children unless she is present so they won't tell us about what is really going on.

Regarding the first facility at which she had her son admitted, she said that she had him removed and sent to another because she saw an attendant kick a child. In reality, she had him removed because she wanted all kinds of testing done and he was starting to talk about what mom was doing to him.

Bethany owes her father thousands of dollars from a loan she took to keep her out of jail for embezzlement and he is in desperate need of the money. She just started (after nine years) paying back the money and he will not confront her for fear that she will stop paying the money. She told her mother that if she ever insinuated that she had done something to the children she would never see or hear from her grandchildren again.

About 3 weeks ago, she had her son put in another residential home. We tried to alert the staff, but they seem not to know anything about MBP and didn't want to receive this information. It seems we are at a dead-end.

Bethany is an example of a perpetrator who uses intimidation to prevent the children, relatives, and professionals from stopping or reporting her behavior. As teenagers, Bethany's children are older than most victims. Still, she has effectively controlled their ability to speak out by restricting the people to whom they can talk and the topics they are allowed to discuss. She defines for health care professionals what the children's presenting problems are and uses her version of those problems to undermine the children's own credibility. By claiming that her daughter was thinking of killing her younger brother, Bethany would easily have influenced professionals to keep the siblings apart. This claim could also have undermined the boy's ability to trust his sister, sadly reducing the likelihood that he would turn to his own sibling for support.

Whether the MBP is manifested physically or psychologically/ behaviorally, initial suggestions that MBP is at work may be viewed angrily by many staff. No one wants to believe that he or she could be duped so completely. Also, in our litigious society, doctors may worry about the consequences if they make an accusation of MBP and are proved to be wrong. But even when confronted with iron-clad proof, staff *still* may be reluctant to believe that the parent is the cause of the child's illness. Gross evidence of child abuse, such as burns or bruises, is uncommon. These cases are further muddied by the falsification of the child's medical history and background. The child's birth date may be the only accurate information the parent provides.

Warning Signs and Detection Techniques

These are the most significant warning signs of MBP. They assume that the mother is the perpetrator and her child is the victim:

- Signs and symptoms begin only when the mother is, or has recently been, alone with the child. (Suspected MBP perpetrators and others often declare that someone else can verify that they "saw the problem," such as respiratory arrest. This claim may or may not be true. One must attempt to determine whether the observer actually saw and heard what happened at the original moment when the child changed from "normal" to having symptoms.)

- The problems resolve when the mother is separated from the child (i.e., there is a positive separation test).

- Other children in the family have had unexplained illnesses or died for unknown reasons.

- Data from tests and procedures are consistent with feigned or produced problems. For example, particular blood studies can help indicate whether insulin or other drugs have been administered unnecessarily.

- The problems consistently fail to respond to appropriate treatment. (One MBP mother boasted that her child's infections persisted despite 52 antibiotic trials.)

- The mother is proved to have provided false information or fabricated a problem.

- The mother has a history of feigning or inducing illness in herself (and may even have Munchausen syndrome).

- The only diseases that remain as possible diagnoses are exceptionally rare.

Accurate detection can be enhanced by

- Separating the child from the mother and seeing if illness persists (but the children themselves may resist separation or develop apathy and passivity until reunited with the abusive parent).

- Analyzing the previous medical course for a temporal relationship between illness and the presence of the mother.

- Retaining selected specimens and supplies for detailed investigation (e.g., for the presence of poisons in infant formula mixed by the mother).

- Obtaining psychiatric consultation—if only to support the befuddled staff—if the question of MBP arises.

- Stationing a nurse near the child's hospital room to observe the mother's interactions with the child.

- Asking the child himself or herself whenever possible.

- Performing specialized testing. Examples include testing for laxatives in the child's stools; seeing if blood in urine samples matches the mother's (but not the child's) blood type; and performing an EEG (electroencephalogram), which may reveal brain effects from surreptitiously administered drugs.

- Finding time to spend with the child's mother during regular visits. During that time, gentle questions asked about the mother herself and the child's home life may be enlightening and give the doctors and staff insight into possible motives for maltreatment.

- Considering alternate possibilities, such as the mother's being overanxious but not deceptive or the child's having troubling side effects from medications that had been misperceived as entirely benign. Another option is *malingering by proxy*, abuse in which the mother invents illness in the child to accrue *tangible* benefits, such as cash gifts. For example, Ohio's Teresa Milbrandt faked her daughter's leukemia to gain thousands of dollars in donations, even putting the child in counseling to prepare for death though Mrs. Milbrandt knew all along that the child was well. She was sentenced to more than 6 years in jail.

- Utilizing covert video surveillance, as discussed.

MBP in Schools

Throughout this chapter, I have pointed out that MBP can play out in settings that extend beyond hospitals and doctors' offices. Just as church congregants and other community members have provided the desired sympathy in many cases, MBP may primarily involve personnel from schools and other educational programs.

There has been increased recognition within the field, mirrored in my own practice, that schools can provide nearly the ideal environment for MBP perpetrators. Typically, mothers claim to school personnel that their children suffer from serious medical or emotional problems that often include intellectual, learning, or physical disabilities. The perpetrators simultaneously demand specialized classes and teachers; personal tutors; continual nursing availability; transportation to and from school even when they live outside the service areas;

administration of complex daytime dosing regimens of numerous medications; and/or intensive counseling, and then only when performed by hand-picked professionals. These services emerge as flatly unnecessary even as they strain the limited funds of school districts. In one case, for instance, a mother demanded that a registered nurse sit next to her child at all times throughout the school day; when the superintendent pointed out that the child appeared perfectly well at school, the mother complained to innumerable local and state officials, including the governor, about the discrimination against her handicapped daughter. Her request was granted—though, after consultation with me, the superintendent intended to revisit the matter, now armed with knowledge about MBP. Thus, much as some MBP perpetrators raise the stakes when their requests for invasive procedures and ever-stronger prescriptions are not met by doctors, others create untenable situations for educators and other school personnel who dare to raise questions about what *really* is in the child's best interests. In the following account, a teacher, Dianne, writes about her feeling of sinking in the quicksand of MBP.

Dianne's Encounter

I am a teacher of a student whose mother's behavior fits all the warning signs of MBP. The child, Molly, is six years old. Her mother claims that Molly has extreme symptoms of emotional illness where the treatment does not work well. I have observed Molly for countless hours and never seen evidence of mental illness. The mother has said that she gives the child medications that are banned in the United States and is obviously proud of that fact. She has taken Molly to a large number of psychologists and psychiatrists—she really goes through them. She loves to talk about Molly's "problems" down to the microdoses of medications she gives her child.

The mother is very acquainted in the community with other parents whose children have real mental illnesses and is supposedly writing a book on the topic. She was spending hours in my classroom every day to monitor Molly until I got a district supervisor to mandate her removal. She had extreme difficulty in not coming into our class every morning and creating a disturbance in which we would all focus on her and her daughter.

The mother has been so loud and demanding about the specific ways in which Molly should be handled that I had to again seek district intervention because I feared for my own and other children's physical safety. The father is very rarely a part of the picture. I met him once, and his wife did all the talking. She is obsessed with people thinking that she is a great parent and going over details of how devoted she is to her daughter's "illness" and the sacrifices she has made.

She claimed one day to be a lawyer, something she had never mentioned before, and said she knows what she is entitled to as far as education for her child. She has invented scenarios where I have done things that have been harmful to Molly, and the principal believes her before even asking me my side of the story. I am ready to leave my job because of this situation.

In this case, I advised Dianne to request that school officials promptly contact a MBP consultant in her area. I also pointed out that, in some states, teachers are required by law to report suspected abuse to child protection. However, because loss of life or limb was not in the balance, I believed that that step should first be discussed with supervisors and, optimally, the consultant. I suggested that, as part of an abuse report, she or her designee be aware of likely knowledge deficits among the local child protection intake and investigative workers and be prepared to "teach" them what she had learned.

MBP or Not? A Warning About Misdiagnoses

The possibility of a misdiagnosis of MBP was mentioned earlier in this chapter. A 1999 review of published reports suggested that, in around 3.5 percent of cases, MBP is diagnosed when it has not occurred. For example, even health professionals who are well-informed about MBP may have difficulty distinguishing MBP mothers from mothers who are genuinely loving but who, out of misguided concern and not an effort to deceive, exaggerate minor problems their children develop. In such cases, MBP can be erroneously diagnosed. The key difference: such mothers hope merely to get the child's care prioritized and, unlike MBP perpetrators, they are delighted when the doctor finds nothing wrong. Other mothers may not give the child badly needed medications, such as antibiotics, not because they want the underlying illness to worsen, but because they fear the side effects of the medication or do not understand the consequences of noncompliance. Education will usually assist with such non-MBP behavior. Some children (e.g., with asthma) have signs and symptoms that come and go. They may wheeze at home but breathe normally in the doctor's office; this phenomenon represents the variability of the underlying disease and should not be assumed automatically to represent MBP. Also, older children may unilaterally feign illness to gain attention or miss school; their doing so does not mean that a parent has been involved. Prescribed medications such as metoclopramide and cisapride can cause respiratory distress, heart rhythm disturbances, muscle and movement abnormalities, and even sudden death; these potential side effects can be misattributed to MBP. (The latter drug has been removed from the U.S. market; the former is still used regularly—if not overzealously—in children with digestive problems.) And inevitably, there are children with rare genetic ailments who are diagnosed with MBP because the basis of their maladies is so very difficult to uncover.

Obviously, the consequences for a falsely accused parent are devastating, and a beautiful and loving family can be torn asunder. The mother of a child whose brain disorder was initially thought to be a sham wrote,

> I was basically a soccer mom. Suddenly a social worker took all of our children away and I had to defend my parenting. How do you prove you're NOT a bad parent? The children were returned after the court hearing but our lives never returned to normal. Our daughter was entitled to special services through the state, but we were afraid to be strong advocates for her. We were afraid for all of our children. Every normal bump and scrape made me panic about whether I would again be reported as an abuser. We all could have used counseling, but we couldn't trust anyone enough to get it. We hid from the world. Looking back, dealing with the MBP accusation was worse than handling our daughter's medical problem.

Becoming Aware, Responsive, and Responsible

Despite the caveats in the last section, MBP remains all too real in all too many situations. Mary Sheridan, Ph.D., whose extensive review of the MBP literature was cited earlier, knows first-hand the devastating effects MBP can have on children and professional caregivers alike. She finds it hard to accept that there are health care providers, including pediatricians, who still don't believe MBP occurs, and she provided this perspective:

"I think that health care professionals actually have to be exposed to MBP before they understand that it's a reality and want to know more about it. The experience of dealing with a MBP situation is extremely painful and difficult, especially if you don't know anything about it when you're starting. Most people don't, even within the mental health and medical professions. They don't know that this form of abuse exists. It's not been adequately and accurately publicized.

"My first case was a very difficult situation of a mom who, we believed, was creating the appearance of apnea in her child through smothering, although we never proved it. A typical baby with apnea usually doesn't have severe episodes. If he or she does, there should be one or two at the most. With proper treatment, the child should get better over the course of time. This child, according to her mother, was constantly having very severe episodes and we couldn't keep her out of the hospital. Every time she went home, her mother reported, she would have another severe episode.

"When apnea episodes recur with great frequency, caregivers have a little checklist in their minds that they run through to determine what's causing them. We work our way down from the most likely to the least likely, and children whose symptoms are being induced don't fit the pattern. The tests come back normal. They don't respond to medication the way they should. So, it becomes a very difficult intellectual challenge because we're working our way farther and farther down the list into more and more esoteric diagnoses. We consult colleagues who come up with more and more exotic possibilities. It's very easy to get emotionally sucked into one of these cases if you don't know what's going on. Later you stand back and look at the process that you've been through, and you look at the number of hospitalizations, and the number of ambulance calls, the diagnoses that you were considering and the timing sequences. After the dust has settled, you say to yourself, "I should have recognized this a lot sooner."

"I didn't know about MBP before I first encountered it many years ago. I came to believe it was occurring because nothing else made sense anymore. I was grappling with these concerns when one of the residents at the hospital saw an article in a medical journal about MBP and gave it to me, saying, "This sounds just like the family you're dealing with. Do you think it's remotely possible?" A mother had been caught smothering one of her children at a hospital in Texas and they recorded it on video. The similarities to our patient were striking. The case history was the same and the profile of the mom was the same.

"Then I discovered that there's a body of literature on MBP, and I read as much as I could and I found that so many of the cases had the same pattern. That's when my faith in the mother started cracking. Our apnea director was also heavily involved in this process. He suspected the mother before I did. Ultimately, we reported the case to child protective services. They confronted the mother, the child was placed in foster care, and the apnea episodes ended. I found out that the mother was known to have actually created illness in herself as a teenager.

"Painful is the word that comes to my mind when describing the whole process of being involved in such a case. It was very, very difficult for me to believe that a mother had done this. Just before the child was placed in foster care, I believe the mother unconsciously told me what was going on. She did it in a very subtle way. She knew at that point that anything that she said to us would be checked. She happened to mention that a relative of hers had just had a child die of SIDS. It was a fabrication. I believe that at some level she knew that I'd go straight to the SIDS coordinator and ask if that was true. One of the things that one does after one begins to suspect a parent is to take any piece of information that's checkable and use it to establish a pattern of truth-telling or falsification. When the child was placed in foster care, the problems resolved immediately. Eventually the apnea monitor was taken back and so my involvement with the patient was over. Later, the child was returned to her mother. A couple of years after that, there was a segment on the television news one morning in which this same mother was claiming that some chemical that was being used near her home was making her child sick! That was the last I heard of them."

Infrequently, the perpetrators do admit to the maltreatment, but usually only after there is an adverse judgment against them in court. One mother who fought unsuccessfully to retain custody of her child eventually thanked the child protection agency social worker. She admitted she probably would have seriously injured the child if he had remained with her. Another MBP mother chose to share the following words with me while she was in prison.[1]

Jolene's Realization

Factitious behavior was a learned behavior in my case. My mother had Munchausen syndrome. I can remember having factitious behavior in childhood and early adulthood. It was a way to escape and hide from my real problems. The person is getting the attention of a parent figure but also the pain. The pain of medical tests is punishment for past sins. For me, the full-blown Munchausen and MBP did not start until after my twin sons were born. One was stillborn and I lived with the fear that my daughter and remaining son were going to die. I began emotionally detaching myself from them. This allowed me to treat them as things and not human beings. I felt that if I were able to keep them sick in the hospital they would be safe.

I would like to see more done on stopping women with MBP before serious injury or death to a child occurs. My son died when he was almost 3 years old, when I gave him an overdose of a blood pressure medicine that was for me. I believe that my daughter would also have died had I not been stopped. I am now serving 12 years for manslaughter and assault. I would like to think that I could help professionals be able to see MBP better in people so that children can be saved. Knowing that maybe I can help allows me to deal with the shame and guilt I feel for what I have done.

I'm delighted that Jolene has gained perspective on her past behavior and taken responsibility for it. I'm encouraged that she seems so intent upon raising awareness about MBP maltreatment (and inclusion of her comments in this book will help). But I am also profoundly saddened that her insight developed too late to preserve a human life.

11

Munchausen by Proxy 2: After Detection

Due to cultural beliefs about the sanctity of motherhood and the devotion that MBP mothers publicly display toward their children, it is extremely difficult to intervene in these situations, let alone proceed with formal prosecutions. However, there are actions that concerned individuals can take to assist the victim, and ultimately the family. Steps in post-detection management include assisting the work of an array of professionals in formulating a team-driven plan; being prepared for the likely reactions of the child, mother, and wider community; working with police, attorneys, and others in cases in which court possibly including criminal one—must be engaged; remaining realistic about the potential for a new standard of safety in each affected family; and being sensitive to the likely mental health needs of those involved.

Post Detection

Once MBP has been suspected, the child's safety must be the first priority. Legally, reasonable suspicions need to be reported promptly to child protection agencies. If MBP is actually detected, the child usually needs to be removed from the home, if only temporarily. Health care professionals must also recognize the need to protect other children in the family, including those not yet born. The maltreated child's health status must be monitored on an ongoing basis to ensure that any subsequent medical treatment is appropriate, and care should be consolidated at a single medical center where physicians are familiar with the history.

Victims of MBP may be permanently damaged physiologically and/or psychologically, either directly by the perpetrator's manipulations or by the treatments and tests administered. For example, children may develop brain damage or cerebral palsy from induced anoxia (inadequate oxygen to the tissues in the body), or severe damage to internal organs from recurrent infections. Children may miss a lot of school and suffer educationally and socially. They may go on to display intense anxiety or hyperactivity, fearfulness, or passivity and helplessness. Later in life, some of the children develop factitious disorder themselves or become convinced of their own "invalid" status. One healthy 26-year-old was confined to a wheelchair because his mother had persuaded him that he had spina bifida.

The effects on adults victimized as children or adolescents were evaluated by MBP expert Dr. Judith Libow. She assessed ten volunteers who believed they had been subjected to MBP abuse while growing up. Her subjects reported receiving bizarre medical and surgical treatments in childhood, though five did not suspect their parents of subjecting them to medical child abuse until, as adults, they learned about MBP through the news media. Two reported that, in adult life, they staunchly avoided seeing doctors. Although the others did describe an ongoing struggle to avoid playing the sick role, they felt confusion about their illnesses even when they were legitimately sick. Similarly, they had difficulty making decisions about medical treatment. Lindsay, whose story appeared toward the opening of the last chapter, poignantly describes the confusion:

> Over the years I have found that, even as an adult, I have a hard time knowing when I am sick and when I am not. I find that when I have real illnesses with real symptoms I try to ignore them and convince myself that nothing is wrong with me, and sometimes I overreact to normal, minor sicknesses. The worst part is that I feel so stupid for being duped into believing, well into my teens, that I was sick when there was nothing wrong with me at all.

A good deal of Lindsay's ongoing therapy will be to reassure her that she was hardly stupid for believing what her mother told her and doctors about her health, and that puzzlement about health and illness is a predictable residual effect of MBP abuse for which she is not responsible.

Stephanie's Perspective

The wife of a man victimized by maternal MBP in childhood, adolescence, and early adulthood wrote to me about a situation that illustrates the same point—as well as the effects on the spouses and partners of past MBP victims:

My husband and I need to think carefully about how to manage my mother-in-law's behavior now that we recognize she perpetrated MBP on him. Fortunately, as we now live in our own house, we have removed ourselves from any potential danger. But I have noticed that if my husband and I argue—which is not very often—he will suddenly develop a severe headache or stomachache and complain of feeling sick. It seems to me he may have learned this response as a way in which to protect himself from his mother's violence—and consequently from the potential threat that I may become violent if we argue. Sometimes I almost feel angry if my husband becomes "ill." Not so much angry at him, but angry at his mother: anger and resentment, not only because of things she has done, but also, in some small way, because she still has control over him. Also, more often than not I will assume the role of caretaker and look after him as his own mother would have done. Perhaps it has become his subconscious desire to reassume this role in our own relationship.

Separation as Key to Protection

Although it is virtually always an essential course of action, separating children from their parents becomes a major issue in MBP cases. When you take children away from their parents, the focus shifts to the separation, not the maltreatment. Because abused children may assume they're to blame, they often have difficulty separating from their parents and will need counseling and a supportive, informed environment.

If these children are returned to their parents prematurely, disastrous results can ensue. To achieve a situation where a child can be reunited with his parents, I usually recommend continuous surveillance of the situation for an indefinite period of time. There must be universal acknowledgement: everyone involved—the perpetrator, her spouse or partner, the child's grandparents and other relatives, the physicians and health workers—must accept and understand the reality of what has happened to this child

Although attempting to preserve the family unit is admirable and important, protection of the abused child must be the primary concern. While it's helpful to be optimistic, the involved parties still have to keep in mind that the bottom line is the safety of the child. One must bear in mind that the hallmark of MBP maltreatment is deception. MBP perpetrators are usually accomplished deceivers. They are typically extremely convincing and are able to give seemingly plausible reasons for any inconsistent or odd findings or personal behaviors. They do not necessarily have to have extensive health care knowledge or be particularly intelligent; it does not take special knowledge to engage in many kinds of MBP maltreatment. MBP perpetrators usually deny that they have engaged in maltreatment, even when there is incontrovertible evidence, and may not stop their MBP behavior when they are suspected or even caught. However, the type of MBP behavior may change or seem to subside temporarily. Even if they have no contact with the victim, they may continue to use the child as an object and gain attention by asserting that the child does or did have problems. They routinely blame the involved physicians or medications they insisted the doctors prescribe. (As noted, some of these medications can indeed have untenable side effects.) If perpetrators do have contact with the child, they may escalate the MBP in an attempt to prove that the child has problems that have developed and occurred naturally.

Even in the rare cases in which the mother admits to the abuse and requests therapy to try to change her pathological responses, there will be setbacks. In MBP, the consequences are high if the work of therapy is going badly. The therapist has to be realistic about what can be accomplished. If the child has been reintroduced into the family, he or she may have to be pulled out again and the therapist has to be fully prepared to make that recommendation. There is no doubt that these children also require intensive individual therapeutic work if they are old enough. These can be heavily conflicted, compromised children.

Being able to follow through on treatment recommendations made to MBP perpetrators is just as difficult as winning the cooperation of Munchausen patients, primarily because of their denial. These mothers are usually emotionally fragile and, as indicated, vehemently deny the allegations of abuse. The offending mother should be approached when she is alone; otherwise, the father tends automatically to defend her, sometimes very angrily if not violently. Fathers in these cases tend to add to the mothers' denial out of their own ignorance of her behavior. In one notorious case involving multiple dead children, the father refused to believe the mother was the perpetrator even after her confession. His dismissive response? "The Lord needed angels, so we got a ton of them up there."

The denials from these child abusers may be so convincing that the doctors involved may start to doubt the evidence themselves. Mothers usually turn to others, such as the family pediatrician, to marshal support. Perpetrators are usually absolutely believable: Despite her guilt, one perpetrator got five physicians and 17 community members to testify to her integrity as a parent. Unless protective provisions are in place, mothers sometimes respond to detection by running away, even to other parts of the country, only to seek medical services elsewhere for the child.

The impact that MBP has on hospital staffs is intense and lasting. Twenty nurses at a Midwestern children's hospital who were questioned after dealing with a MBP perpetrator were mostly reluctant to admit that they had been duped. They were equally unwilling to accept that the seemingly doting mother was the perpetrator. The case with which they had been involved concerned a 17-month-old girl who was hospitalized for recurrent urinary tract infections with hematuria, fevers, weight loss, vomiting, hypoglycemia, and developmental delays. Her three-year-old sister, who had recurrent hematuria as well, had had approximately 13 hospitalizations. The mother had been trained as a licensed practical nurse but didn't have a degree, and she enjoyed strong camaraderie with some of the nurses. Once the MBP was confirmed, the child was released into the custody of the paternal grandparents and the father. The mother, who was charged with attempted murder and neglect of a dependent, pleaded guilty to battery causing serious bodily injury. As in other MBP cases that are criminally prosecuted, her sentence was notably light: she received a five-year suspended sentence and probation.

Cases such as this lead nursing and other staff members to be less trusting of parents in general. They may feel shame and sadness when they realize that they helped administer extensive and painful procedures that were unnecessary. Training programs need to do a better job of teaching physicians, nurses, and other professionals to recognize MBP.

MBP in the Legal System. Child protective programs need to alert attorneys and court officials proactively to facilitate appropriate prosecution of these cases when they come up. One judge dismissed a MBP case by stating that the charges were inherently defamatory; he didn't believe such a phenomenon could occur. In another case, the lawyer representing the state *on behalf of the child* commented that no mother would ever behave in this manner. Defense lawyers and their expert witnesses may attempt to dismiss the whole phenomenon of MBP as overblown, exotic and fashionable, or unproved. Sometimes abusers have tried to turn the tables on the medical staff as suspicions arise: They divert attention by inducing naïve or conspiratorial attorneys to sue the innocent doctors for negligence in failing to end the child's ailments. They may introduce an array of other distortions and falsehoods, and attempt to impugn MBP experts through scurrilous personal attacks.

When legal arrangements are made, they often do not adequately protect the child. For example, one judge ordered a psychiatric evaluation of the parents, but it was performed by one of their closest friends. Based on the sympathetic report, the child was returned to the parents—and later died of "unknown" causes.

In an article for *Juvenile & Family Court Journal,* Beatrice Yorker and Bernard Kahan examined a sampling of MBP cases that made it into the courts in order to highlight the different actions taken against accused parents. One of these cases, *People of California v. Phillips* (1981), has been credited with helping the legal community to recognize MBP as a form of child abuse. In this early case, the California Court of Appeals upheld the use of psychiatric expert testimony to describe MBP and to render an opinion on whether the mother in question could be such an offender. The mother, a child abuse agency volunteer who claimed she had never harmed her children, was accused of adding massive amounts of sodium to the formula of her adopted infants. She was found guilty of having murdered one of the children in 1977 and willfully endangering the life of the other at a later time. She served several years in jail and has since been released. Now she seems to have turned to false or exaggerated claims and enactments of illness involving herself.

Yorker and Kahan contrasted that outcome with one in which a mother was accused of giving her son diuretics. Syringes and vials of a diuretic were uncovered in a search of her home. The judge in that case found that the child was in jeopardy, but on appeal the boy was returned to his parents under supervised custody despite the dangers. The way in which judges "understand" MBP—even when they're flatly wrong—shape the rulings and the possibility for reunification, even when the danger is palpable. In a third case, one involving laxative administration to an infant by her mother, the court found evidence of a number of warning signs of MBP, including the child's marked improvement in her absence. Significantly, the court noted the reluctance on the part of legal authorities to believe that a parent who seemed to be extremely caring could actually cause her child's illness. Two nurses provided evidence in this case linking the mother to laxatives in the bottled formula. The court found the mother guilty of child abuse, placed the little girl with her father under the supervision of the Department of Social Services, and ordered monthly visits to a pediatrician and a psychiatrist. A six-month court review was also required. This outcome was far safer for the child.

A subsequent judgment in Ohio is worth noting as well. In this case, the Court of Appeals expressed concern about the evidence attributing MBP to the mother. Indeed, while the psychiatric expert had pointed out that the parent's infant daughter had been repeatedly hospitalized for minor medical problems, there was no evidence that the mother had ever induced any medical problems. Instead, the Court viewed her as unreasonably worried about medical issues but not overtly hurtful. The Court did go on to acknowledge that the legal community has at times been an obstacle to the diagnosis of MBP cases because of its doubts about the entire phenomenon. The Court also discerned two trends in its review of earlier cases. On the one hand, the judicial system has been likely to find that a child was abused whenever a parent has introduced a foreign substance into the child's body to induce symptoms. On the other hand, even in the absence of indications of such overt behavior, courts have frequently terminated parental rights based upon a finding of MBP combined with other factors, such as a patently unstable home environment. However, courts, like professionals, may not understand that a perpetrator who begins by giving doctors false reports can escalate into the direct induction of illness through means such as suffocation and poisoning.

Effectiveness in MBP Case Assessment and Management

The following overview is based in large part on the work of international MBP expert and author Louisa Lasher, M.A. It presents the general guidelines for successful intervention in cases thought to represent MBP.

Successfully resolving suspected or confirmed MBP cases—whether it means removing the child from the home or exonerating the accused individual—means that someone must take the initiative. A health care professional may be the first to recognize the indicators of MBP and pursue the actions outlined below. However, family members and friends might be in the best position to understand the acuity of the risks to the child's safety. They can attempt to contact the child's primary physician to alert him or her to the dilemma. In doing so, relatives and others can explain to the professional that the confidentiality of the doctor-patient relationship is not compromised if the caller or letter writer merely provides details about the possible MBP but does not receive any information in turn. Professional caregivers may or may not be receptive or responsive to the worries, but the chance of acceptance and action are increased if the presentation is clear, cogent, and fact-based. An interested party's doing something as simple as sending reprints of published case reports may be very helpful as well. In cases in which there is acceptance, the caregiver or his or her designee should contact child protective services (which goes by various names in different jurisdictions, such as "Child Protective Services" [CPS], "Department of Social Services," "Department of Public Welfare," "Department of Human Resources," or "Department of Human Services").

If the health care professional is unavailable or not persuaded, an alternative is to telephone a report directly to the local child protection agency hot line. Predictably, those family members or friends who make the report of suspected maltreatment fear that their role will be discovered and, as a result, they will be scorned or threatened by the parents and extended family. However, the alternative—allowing likely abuse or neglect to proceed unfettered—is to acquiesce to it, if not to endorse it tacitly. Such agencies prefer that callers identify themselves but may not force the issue.

Once the initial report is made, CPS (or its correlate) will contact the police and an objective and thorough investigation by professionals must follow. If MBP is confirmed, specialized intervention, case planning, and case management are required in the short and long terms to protect the child. The following six ingredients are crucial.

First, basic MBP maltreatment education for all involved professionals is the foundation of work with suspected or confirmed MBP cases. It is counterproductive, even dangerous, for professionals to discuss, make decisions, or formulate strategies if they do not know about MBP basics, investigative and confirmation-disconfirmation techniques, and case planning and management elements. Reading an article on the subject does not equip one to make important decisions about the fate of a child and the family; one must seek out education. A teaching program conducted by an expert (if only by telephone) is always of benefit. Of course, it would be better if all health care professionals were educated about MBP as part of their early training.

Second, a thorough and appropriate MBP maltreatment investigation should be performed by or with the assistance of a professional who has credible MBP knowledge and experience. Child abuse teams at hospitals, departments of psychiatry or pediatrics at university medical centers, newspaper and academic articles on the subject, and material on the Internet can help individuals in smaller communities locate suitable professionals, even if they are geographically located elsewhere.

Third, a multiagency-multidisciplinary team (MMT) should be developed that is composed of CPS workers, law enforcement, physicians, mental health professionals, nurses, social workers, school staff, and/or others who are, have been, or will be involved with the family and case. The precise membership of the MMT is dictated by the unique facts of the case. A MMT should be convened—if only by conference call—even if there is a permanent hospital, county, or state team that regularly reviews all apparent child maltreatment cases. The MMT can join together disparate information and make decisions about future steps. At this point or any subsequent one, if MBP maltreatment is disproved, the team can disband and other avenues pursued that address the victim's and/or family's problems. Further CPS involvement will be necessary only if facts emerging over time point to MBP or another form of maltreatment.

Fourth, an MBP expert consultant is commonly needed to provide ongoing education, review information, offer comments and recommendations, guide or conduct the investigation, provide on-site technical assistance, present a final opinion and recommendations, and work with the assigned attorney(s) in preparing the court case. Again, many communities will need to engage in considerable legwork to locate an available expert consultant. An Internet search can expedite the process, and aid can be accessed through some of the pages listed under "Selected Websites" near the end of this book. As more and more professionals gain an understanding of MBP and assist in case work, the legwork should be lessened.

Fifth, a MBP expert witness (usually the same individual as the MBP expert consultant) is invaluable in educating the court (family, civil, and/or criminal), relating that education to the case at hand, providing an opinion and recommendations to the court, and responding to rebuttal. MBP expert testimony may also be necessary in motions and other kinds of hearings.

Sixth, an attorney who is properly educated about MBP, is willing to work as a team player with the MBP expert, and is fully prepared for court and related activities is essential. No matter how strong the evidence for MBP, the hearing or trial is likely to be for naught unless the attorney and expert work closely together throughout the process.

Following the Court Judgment

If the judge does find clear and convincing evidence of child endangerment in family court proceedings, the victim is generally taken into protective custody and placed in alternate care. Relatives and friends of the family should rarely serve as foster parents in MBP cases because of the danger that the perpetrator will still be given unsupervised access to the child. The situation of any siblings should be considered carefully and thoroughly because of the high frequency with which brothers or sisters are past, present, or future victims.

A service plan will generally be developed for MBP perpetrators and victims. This plan should include elements specifically addressing the problems associated with MBP; for example, the plan should require coordination of the victim's ongoing health care by a single provider with full disclosure to CPS. It should also include involvement by one or more of the health care providers who initially suspected the MBP maltreatment to help counter the skepticism ("No mother would *really* have done all that, right?") that commonly creeps into these cases with time. Though MBP itself is not a psychiatric affliction, psychotherapy can still be offered to the perpetrator (particularly those with concurrent mental disorders). However, as mentioned, it is often refused or rendered of limited value due to the perpetrator's continued denial. The therapist should have experience in working with cases of MBP or at least in working with clients who have deep-seated problems such as personality disorders; should receive education about MBP if necessary; and should communicate fully with the relevant CPS staff. Issues of confidentiality and federal regulations governing access to health care records must be considered by the judge, who can mandate that the perpetrator sign the necessary releases of information. The victim should stop undergoing unnecessary treatments, though medical help may be needed to repair or treat objective physical damage (e.g., bowel adhesions from exploratory gastrointestinal surgery prompted by fallacious maternal complaints). If the child is of appropriate age, mental health evaluation and treatment become essential. Central tasks will be to correct the child's self-image as sick, his or her likely feelings of guilt about the separation from the mother, and his or her confusion between illness and love. More detailed recommendations regarding victims and perpetrators can be found in the book by Lasher and Sheridan under "Selected Readings."

Reunification?

Long-term decisions about placement, visitation, and similar matters will be made by a judge at a dispositional hearing. While every effort should be made towards reunification, this goal is often not achievable and planning for legal termination of parental rights and permanent placement outside the family must be undertaken. Exceptions do exist, however, and the following criteria can be used to determine when reunification may be safe:

- The child is old enough to report any recurrent maltreatment.
- No siblings have died under circumstances suspicious for MBP.
- The mother, her partner, and others accept that a pattern of MBP behavior occurred.
- The mother and partner have achieved insight about why the MBP took place, the personal needs prompting it, the situations that triggered it, and the reasons the partner remained unaware or silent.

- The mother, partner, and others do not claim any ongoing unexplained problems in the child.
- The family accepts the case management plans, and the court and CPS can provide long-term monitoring, with readiness to remove the child again if necessary.
- The mother, partner, family, and friends are committed to the child's safety.

A Daunting Challenge

Those working with even a single MBP case will find it labor-intensive and emotionally challenging. As with other areas of child protection, however, this is important work that must be carried out regardless of any impediments and disincentives. The desperation of victims for answers and help is so keen that any gift of understanding is powerful, as the following e-mail proves.

Georgie's Chronicle

I cannot tell you how many times I was rushed to the hospital by my mother, or how many times the spoon with the purple or pink medicine clanked across my little teeth. There were also many pills, usually the little red ones for my many bladder infections that didn't really exist. Not to mention the day I found out I had two normal kidneys and not just one non-functioning and one fine. My mother also did this to my daughter. My daughter was injected with 50 needles to test her for allergies that my mother had made up—and I believed. My mother even tried to get tubes put in my daughter's ears. I didn't realize what my mother was doing until about a year ago. I thought it odd to find out from a specialist that my daughter had always had perfect ears. I am also finding out things about my siblings. I don't know if any of my information is useful to you, but if it is I would be happy to help. I am very happy to know that you are out there. One person really can make a difference.

12

Cyber-Deception: Virtual Factitious Disorder and Munchausen by Internet

Thousands of virtual support groups have sprung up over the past few years, offering patients and their families the chance to share their hopes, fears, and knowledge with others experiencing personal crises. At the same time, the Internet has opened the door to the possibility for far-reaching deception. Anyone can log on and pretend to have an illness, compromising the integrity of the group. This chapter looks at several cases of cyber-deception, revealing how some posers even stage their own "deaths" and adopt the voices of family members and friends via e-mail when their extreme stories are challenged by group members.

The Internet is a medium of choice for millions of people who need health-related information. Medical websites have multiplied exponentially over the past several years. Thousands of virtual support groups have sprung up for those suffering from particular illnesses. They offer patients and families the chance to share their hopes, fears, and knowledge with others experiencing similar crises. These online groups can reverse isolation and serve as bastions of understanding, deep concern, and even affection.

Unfortunately, cyberspace resources are sometimes deliberately misused by people intent on deceiving others. Spam, with its outlandish product claims, is the best-known example. Less attention has been accorded health-related claims and suggestions transmitted person-to-person over the Internet. Formats for such direct communication among patients, family members, and others include newsgroups and mailing lists (listservs); chat rooms, clubs, and communities; independent bulletin boards; Internet Relay Chat (IRC); private electronic mail (e-mail); and discussions sponsored by Web sites. These interactions typically take place via the World Wide Web (WWW) or Usenet, a bulletin board system in which messages are arranged into categories. Not uncommonly, individuals mislead others by pretending to have illnesses—or to be experiencing crises—that are fake. They divert the attention of the group toward their feigned battles with cancer, multiple sclerosis, anorexia nervosa, or other ailments. The eventual discovery of the deceptions can be devastating.

One of the paradoxes of Internet discussion groups is the level of intimacy that can be established while maintaining near-perfect anonymity. This unusual circumstance affords a risk-free opportunity for deceptions that may serve as a practice arena for individuals not yet bold enough to try their deceptions openly. Such online behavior can be easily viewed as a manifestation of factitious disorder or, as we will see in two cases that follow, MBP. Instead of seeking care at numerous hospitals, these individuals can now gain new audiences merely by clicking from one support group to another. Under the pretense of illness, they can also join multiple groups simultaneously or establish different personae in a single group or one-on-one interactions. In a startling development, factitious disorder and Munchausen patients have recently banded together in their own online group, one focused on how to be more convincing as they ply their deceptions!

The following cases illustrate the misappropriation of the online community of support through the use of spurious illness or victimization. I was alerted to them by one or more of the deceived participants through my Web site on factitious disorder and Munchausen by proxy, and the material was confirmed. Names have been changed to preserve anonymity though, having been sent and/or posted unsecured via the Internet, the information is a matter of public record. I originally presented some of the cases that appear below elsewhere.

Barbara's Guise

An individual claiming to be a young woman posted messages to an Internet support group for those suffering from cystic fibrosis (CF). She said that she was in the terminal stages of CF and was at home waiting to die. She added that she was being cared for by her older sister, Amy, and that her dream was to die on the beach. Many CF patients and their families sent emotional messages back to her, sharing their own experiences and offering prayers. A few days later, Amy posted tragically that the girl, Barbara, had died, but that she had been able to transport her to the beach just in time. Group members were distressed by the news, but some did question the report that Barbara had been taken to a beach without having access to oxygen. They also noted that Barbara's constant spelling errors, which they had attributed to her being hypoxic (lacking oxygen), were made by Amy as well. In response to questioning about these issues, the individual admitted that she had made up the entire story and taunted the group members for their gullibility. The lay moderator of the group alerted Barbara/Amy's Internet service provider and requested a suspension of Internet access to the person using the screen names attached to the posts. He noted that the explicit intent of the group was to provide emotional support and information to CF patients, and that they had been completely diverted from this goal by the anger and betrayal caused by the hoax.

Chris' Dishonest Chat

A person describing himself as a 15-year-old boy began to post to a Usenet group for people with migraine headaches. His reports about his struggle with intractable migraines were moving, particularly in view of his youth and the unique personal qualities he described. Over time, Chris disclosed that he also suffered with hemophilia as well as a seizure disorder due to abusive head trauma his estranged father had inflicted. Despite these ailments and his brother's recent death from AIDS, he was performing superbly as a fourth-year medical student. His mother was described as deaf and his stepfather as alcoholic. Their lack of interest in his education resulted in his having to skateboard three miles daily to a bus stop to get to his medical school classes. His nighttime employment as a drummer at a nightclub was a useful distraction, however, and helped pay for his pain medication.

Although this information was provided only very gradually, some group members could not escape the impression of escalating implausibility. For example, it strained credulity that Chris played the drums even in the throes of a migraine. One group member privately e-mailed others, and Chris was gently questioned about some of the dubious information. In response, Chris's "mother" signed on and chastised the group for doubting him and subverting his faith in the group's caring nature. She warned that the questioning might precipitate a recurrence of the profound depression Chris had suffered in the past. As some continued to ask him questions (e.g., the name of his medical school or even the state it was in), Chris complained that they had violated the "spirit" of the Internet and stopped posting to the group.

Darlene's Fraudulent Posts

In another case involving a false report of CF, Darlene, claiming to be the mother of a baby girl battling the disease, posted to a bulletin board for parents of children with special needs. Erica, another mother of a CF child, responded warmly. However, she acknowledged feeling persistently guilty for not being able to extend herself more because her own child was seriously ill with respiratory syncytial virus (RSV), responsible for many lung infections in childhood. Once the child recovered, Darlene questioned her about RSV, and Erica provided general information with the intent of assuaging Darlene's apparent concern. Weeks later, Darlene suddenly reported to the devastation of the group that her baby had just died of RSV superimposed on her CF. Erica recognized that the details in Darlene's reports about RSV and its treatment were full of inaccuracies; in retrospect, she also realized that Darlene's comments about CF had simply duplicated material already posted. Many group members whom Erica alerted were not persuaded, however, and several went on to contact the hospital and funeral home to send flowers and offer assistance. When they learned that no information existed about such a child, they were satisfied that Darlene's fakery was proved. Her posts abruptly ended.

Glenda's Personae

Frank and Glenda met in an Internet chat room and became friends, switching to communication via ICQ, a popular direct messaging program. The tenor of Glenda's posts changed as she talked about a bitter break-up with a boyfriend years earlier. Shortly thereafter, Frank received a message through her ICQ account that was ostensibly not from Glenda but from her father. He reported that Glenda had been assaulted at home earlier in the day, and that she had been screaming for Frank ever since. Frank offered to call the father in lieu of their typing back and forth, but he declined, claiming that he had promised Glenda that no such call would occur. Frank found his resistance unusual since he also stated that he was a police detective. As the communication continued, Frank noted remarkable parallels between his writing style and Glenda's (e.g., the overuse of exclamation points and the absence of capitals). The father then said that Glenda wanted to talk to Frank alone and that he was going to leave the room. After a pause, Glenda appeared and declared that the ex-boyfriend was the perpetrator. As Frank asked additional questions, Glenda interrupted to insist that she had suddenly remembered her repressed past. She demanded that he not interrupt as she recounted a story of molestation, forced prostitution, homelessness, financial exploitation by her parents, and serial rape, culminating in her somehow being permitted to adopt two troubled teenagers. Frank noted profound inconsistencies in her tale but she warned him that it would undermine her recall if he were to try to clarify details. Indeed, after providing her report, she claimed to have totally forgotten it and asked Frank to tell her what she had just said.

Weeks later, Glenda came online to report a sadistic physical assault and rape, this time by a family friend. Following her report, a different friend named Hal took over the computer. Frank noted that Hal's word choices and punctuation duplicated those of Glenda. Without explanation, Hal declined telephone contact at the time but, pressed by Frank, scheduled it for the next day. When Frank called, Glenda told him that Hal had suddenly left town. He was never mentioned again.

Subsequent posts included two other assaults. They also included Glenda's claims that she had become severely underweight because one of the teens she adopted had misused her bank card, stealing $70,000 and leaving her with no money for food. Later, Frank was confronted online by a different ex-boyfriend, this one jealous of his relationship with Glenda, but his writing style also mirrored that of Glenda herself. Glenda claimed that he went on to rape her.

Faced with the continual dubious crises, Glenda's refusal to provide any evidence of her claims, the unwillingness of rescuers to speak by phone, the uncanny similarity among the writing styles of different people, Glenda's inaction in response to professed attacks, and an episode in which she admitted to impersonating her sister, Frank reluctantly recognized that he had been manipulated into expending vast amounts of time and emotional energy. Still, he has elected to continue to talk online with her from time to time. The reason isn't clear. He may believe he can change Glenda, or he may simply be fascinated with the perverse.

Herman's Masquerade

Herman, a participant in an e-mail support group for persons with cancer and their loved ones, posed as an ordained brother in the Catholic Church who was living a monastic life. He claimed to have a rare, quickly-progressing form of cancer and further asserted that, because of his vow of poverty and the constraints of monastic life, he was unable to seek treatment for his disease. He requested the assistance of the support group in dealing with his loneliness and his fears about dying. At one point, he discussed a visiting nurse who had begun to assist him in his daily activities. Over time, however, the energy level suggested by Herman's lengthy and frequent communications to the participants, combined with his remarkable longevity without treatment, created suspicion among several members. One of them confronted him and, in a private response to that member, Herman confessed that he had fabricated the information about his illness and his vocation. He withdrew from the list.

Ida's Account

Ida contacted me to request more information about the psychological underpinnings to MBP. She indicated that, as the parent of two children with an uncommon genetic disorder, she had found support by communicating via the Internet with other parents of similarly-afflicted offspring. As her virtual encounters developed, she became especially close to one woman, whose children apparently suffered from the same ailment. Their friendship blossomed, and she had offered more and more personal information. She was writing now, however, because she had just learned from a reliable third party that, in reality, her new-found friend had lost custody of her children because of MBP: she had repeatedly misrepresented them to health care professionals as ill, both with the genetic disorder and other medical problems. Unwilling to continue to communicate with the woman, but wishing to avoid a direct confrontation, Ida quietly reduced the frequency of her own postings. She finally withdrew entirely from the online support group. The experience left her deeply shaken.

There can be enormous benefits from the personal narratives of illness or crisis that are shared via the Internet. The Internet offers unlimited opportunities for patients—even those with rare diseases—to find like-minded and caring communities 24 hours a day. In particular, members of virtual support groups offer an instantly accessible conduit for information to be provided and isolation to be countered.

However, these case reports illustrate that individuals sometimes go online deliberately to provide misinformation about their own medical and personal histories, and that they may do so because it is inherently gratifying. Like the factitious disorder patients and MBP perpetrators who make false reports to health care professionals, the only recognizable purpose to this behavior is to garner attention, mobilize sympathy, act out anger, or control others.

Detection

Clues to the detection of false Internet reports include the following:

- The length, frequency, and duration of the posts do not match the claimed severity of the illness (e.g., a detailed post from someone claiming to be in septic shock).

- The posts consistently duplicate material in other posts, in textbooks, or on health-related Web sites.

- The characteristics of the supposed illness and its treatment emerge as caricatures based upon the individual's misconceptions.

- Near-fatal exacerbations of illness alternate with miraculous recoveries.

- Personal claims are fantastic, contradicted by later posts, or disproved (e.g., a call to the hospital reveals that there is no such patient).

- There are continual dramatic events in the person's life, especially when other group members have become the focus of attention (e.g., as interest in one person started to wane in her group, she announced that her mother had just been diagnosed as terminally ill as well).

- The individual complains that other group members are not sufficiently supportive and warns that this insensitivity is undermining his or her health.

- The individual resists telephone contact, sometimes offering odd justifications (e.g., it would be so upsetting as to cause a medical catastrophe, or the telephone lines in the building do not permit incoming calls) or making threats (e.g., he or she will run away if called).

- There is feigned blitheness about crises (e.g., a cardiac arrest or assault) that will predictably attract immediate attention.

- Others ostensibly posting on behalf of the individual (e.g., family members) have identical patterns of writing, such as grammatical errors, misspellings, and stylistic idiosyncrasies.

As with factitious behaviors as a whole, detection is particularly difficult when the content appears to mix fact and fiction.

Arline's Perspective

Arline, who did have some mild physical problems, exaggerated them into a condition requiring repeated intensive care when, in reality, she was not hospitalized at all. She also invented detailed conversations with her parents and a death in the family that never really occurred. A sample follows. It also illustrates how Arline kept her Internet friends from contacting others who would obviously dispute her claims.

Well, I had the meeting with my parents. Let's just say it didn't go too well. This is going to be pretty matter-of-fact cuz I honestly am not feeling anything (well, I'm not letting myself feel anything). First my parents walk in and tell me that my aunt, whom I was close to, was killed Thursday night. I can't even physically get to her funeral or wake for closure because I'm too sick.

Then we moved on. They weren't upset at all about me not telling them I was in the hospital. My dad just sat there like a lump the whole time because he has always felt that he has no right intruding upon my mom and I. True, he's only been my dad since I was nine, but he IS my dad, and no matter how many times I tell him that, he will never speak up against my mom. My mom did admit why she can't accept this, which is good in a way, I suppose. If she admits I'm going to die, then she will have no reason for living. Ooh, I'm sure my dad felt great when she said that. They did agree to see the social worker on one condition: that neither I, my friends, any other relatives, nor even my doctors contact them about my medical situation until they are able to work through some things. So, the deal is that if they get contacted by ANYONE (umm, how am I supposed to tell everyone I know not to call my parents?), even me, about anything medical until they work it out, then they will stop seeing the social worker.

Reactions to Exposure

The common reactions following detection, both among the deceivers and those who have been misled, are listed below.

Among individuals who have misled others:

- Protesting their innocence via e-mail or telephone calls
- Scapegoating group members (e.g., "If you had been more supportive, I wouldn't have had to make up stories")
- Abruptly disappearing from the group, sometimes only to engage in the same behavior elsewhere on the Internet
- Admitting to the behavior, but either refusing to apologize or claiming that they cannot explain the reasons for it
- Admitting to the behavior but castigating others for their naïveté
- Rarely, making ongoing threats toward and "virtually stalking" those responsible for the disclosure or banning. Totally ignoring the provocations seems eventually to work (though the posts and e-mails may temporarily increase as the deceivers try to reengage the deceived). I am not aware of any cases in which real-life stalking or violence occurred.

Among individuals who were misled:

- Splitting into camps of those believing and disbelieving the claims
- Remaining in the group to process feelings of anger, sadness, or shame
- Leaving the group in disgust
- Sending e-mails to the deceiver that express anger or sadness
- Seeking retribution (e.g., by contacting the deceiver's apparent employer or college)
- Fantasizing about or attempting to arrange a face-to-face confrontation
- Fearing that the deceiver will misuse personal information that had been divulged in the past
- Feeling amused by the sophistication and audacity of the ruses

In most cases, group members' discovery of the ruse leads initially to gentle questioning. The typical response is a protest of innocence and an allegation of cruel mistreatment by the group, followed by disappearance. Exceptions do exist, however, and one is exemplified by the case—admittedly a bumpy one—that follows. Members of a non-medical message board came to a consensus that the posts of one of their fellows, Daniela, contained escalating, constant, and graphic descriptions of personal catastrophes that virtually no one could believe any longer. Indeed, many statements had been flatly disproved. The group was fortunate to have a moderator, Eileen, who explored the options with me and then selected a magnanimous approach for this particular situation:

> I wanted to take the time to follow-up with you and hope-fully add to your research. Last night, we decided to ban Daniela. She did understand that we did this because she is our friend and we wanted to show tough love. I gave her my e-mail address so she can keep me informed about her progress. I agreed to lift the ban when we mutually agreed she was ready to come back. We had already known where she lives, and I was able to track down a psychologist near her. I gave her this number privately. She asked me to call the psychologist for her and ask questions about the process and

cost of the service. I did this. Daniela has lied in the past, but I have the feeling that she is finally serious about her mental health and is ready to take action. She gave me permission to follow-up with the therapist to be sure she made contact. We all care about Daniela and want the best for her.

Six months later, I learned that Daniela's progress had been interrupted when she began contacting members individually to ask if she could tell them about her problems. Eileen posted a letter asking members to continue to be friendly to her, but to emphasize that she needed to discuss her issues with a caring health professional. Though Daniela sent Eileen some nasty notes, Eileen responded with a consistent message about the need for treatment. Slowly, Daniela again accepted that Eileen was on her side and she has chosen again to focus on improving through therapy.

Lessons Learned

In cases involving medical matters, the false information can include personal histories, recreations of conversations with physicians, reports of laboratory data and radiographic studies, and even citations from medical publications. In addition to their providing time and emotional support, users who trust the information may let it shape their own health care decisions. The betrayal is evident in the comments of two women who regard their online groups as sacred as family. In Charlene's case, the deceptions unraveled when several of the group members were about to fly to Arizona to visit their "sick" Internet friend.

Stacy's Response

The support group on the Internet is the only place I can go where others are experiencing life much as I am. I read the mail from those who can help with the illness and write to those whom I might be able to help. I rejoice in small triumphs, births, marriages. I grieve when we lose someone. My reaction to having been deceived is to be suspicious of new people to the list. I am not as confident about responding. An interloper arrived on our doorstep and my family welcomed her into the security of our "home," nurtured her, and offered all kinds of help. She lied to us and took advantage of kind people already overwhelmed by their own problems. I hope that I and others can put this behind us and still extend support to others who join the list.

Charlene's Reaction

I am hurt and betrayed. I have never in my life put so much effort into praying for something, so much emotion into someone I thought I knew. This does not mean I won't be there for Jane to help her heal, but I cannot forget this any time soon. I e-mailed her and told her all my feelings; it was very cathartic and a great help. I have not received a response. When I told my Spanish professor that I would have to miss her class on Monday if the flight from Tucson got back late and explained that my friend desperately needed a liver transplant, she started crying and told me not to do homework for a week. She said she is thinking about me constantly. How the hell do I deal with that now? I've fought with my parents, spent about three hours a night in the chapel when I should've been studying, almost had an emotional breakdown, just to find out that Jane wasn't sick. The news hit me like a hammer blow to the head. The worst part is that my mother has been working to find her a liver.

Like so many others, Stacy and Charlene have recognized the need to question the veracity of online assertions and balance empathy with circumspection.

In every area, the Internet brings with it new opportunities and new problems. It has brought crucial information and bred lies. It has expanded horizons and facilitated distrust and even crime. This mixture of good and bad is no less true for factitious disorder and MBP than for any other human phenomenon, and those who use this new medium must be on their toes—and fingertips—as they approach the keyboard.

13

People Who Care:
The Casualties of Deception

This chapter examines the human casualties of factitious disorder—especially people who befriend or even love the deceiver. These cases become especially poignant when pseudologia fantastica has been layered upon the medical deceptions, and they may include sadism toward family, friends, and others. Paula's personal account is a bone-chilling story of masterful manipulation by her fiancé, Derek. As a physician, Derek knew how to portray his illness convincingly and spared no detail in providing the physical evidence of his disease. By the time Paula discovered that Derek was neither ill nor single, she had devoted two years of her life to a man she thought would one day be her husband. Those who have been emotionally violated need information and understanding, and this chapter offers steps toward recovery.

As with MBP, factitious disorder almost always leaves casualties in its wake. The longer and more intense the relationship, the more profound and devastating the experience can be. This chapter discusses those who know and perhaps love the patient feigning or self-inducing illness. Many have felt victimized as a person has entered their lives, appropriated their attention and sympathy, and then moved on—or been mocking— when the house of cards has tumbled. In the most severe cases, factitious disorder patients have employed "terrorist tactics" in their desperation to retain the mantle of patienthood. They have threatened and launched lawsuits against former partners, libeled individuals on the Internet and in letters to doctors and other health care providers, or retaliated in other ways that can be abhorrent. Even in less extreme cases, the personal costs can be profound.

One victim from a Scandinavian country shared her feelings in the following way. She expresses the powerful feelings that accompanied her betrayal by a female lover who proved to be a factitious disorder patient:

> When the ruse is exposed, you grieve over lost love. But you also feel angry. Marissa put her tiny nails under my kindness, empathy, and love by telling those horrible stories. I wanted to protect her, carry her grief for her. And I did, but her grief was faked. It was like throwing pearls to a pig. The pearls you threw are still pearls. You have to learn to take them back and wash the mud away.

Francois duc de La Rochefoucauld wrote: "It is more ignominious to mistrust our friends than to be deceived by them (*Moral Maxims*, 1678)." So, we give our friends the benefit of the doubt rather than risk ruining the relationship over our own shameful suspicions about their illnesses. As a result, we—meaning everyone who feels sympathy for others—can become unwitting players in the falsehoods.

Because they are directly victimized, the children who are preyed upon by mothers through Munchausen by proxy (MBP) are the most obvious casualties (see chapters 10 and 11). But there are also many indirect victims in MBP: for example, the emotionally drained, guilt-ridden caregivers who unknowingly put children through the torture of unnecessary tests and procedures, and the horrified family members and friends who had unintentionally lent their support to an abusive situation.

The behaviors of factitious disorder are often so contrary to our understanding of human nature that exposure of the ruse often leads to social branding and abandonment of the deceiver, the very circumstance that drove such extreme behaviors in the first place. Caring friends who have felt shattered by the experience may be unable to forgive the deceiver, even though they accept the cause of the deception as a mental illness deserving of empathy. The feeling of betrayal typically overwhelms victims and displaces any feelings of kinship with the individual responsible.

In most cases of factitious disorder, the patient is not seeking to harm others, but only to fill a deep emotional void with nurturance. But in other cases, the deception is so intentionally cruel and egregious that there is no room for compassion, even by objective professionals. When factitious disorder is accompanied by sadism, criminal behavior, and/or antisocial personality disorder (also called sociopathy or psychopathy), the offender may be untreatable. In such cases, criminal prosecution may be entirely warranted.

The following account, from a woman I shall call Paula, is one of the most heart wrenching stories I have encountered. She was generous enough to provide her account.

The History of Paula and Derek

Paula is an articulate, highly educated, and extremely insightful young woman. I first shared her story in the academic book, *The Spectrum of Factitious Disorders*, which I edited with Dr. Stuart J. Eisendrath. Paula's story provides a remarkably dramatic example of the effect of factitious disorder on caregivers. It is a rare case in which the ruse was carried out by a physician. A master manipulator with the expertise to support his deception, this doctor, whom I will call Derek, subjected Paula, his former fiancée, to what amounted to more than two years of psychological torture. As Paula writes:

In the early 1990s, Derek began to complain of excruciating abdominal pain. He underwent a biopsy, and it came back positive for multiple cancerous tumors of his large bowel, the colon. He was given radiation every morning and afternoon. I don't remember the exact schedule, but he had black magic marker X's on his abdomen surrounding bright red marks from the radiation. Over the next six months, the largest tumors shrunk and grew. They were monitored with regular MRIs. Because Derek was a physician, his results were given to him at work over the phone, so I never had the chance to go to the doctor with him. Many times, Derek told me how difficult it was to read the MRI because of all the scar tissue.

After about a year, the tumor metastasized again to his small intestines. He started on an experimental drug that he was able to get through his connections as a doctor. He also began having his stem cells stored so that they could be given back to him if needed at a later date. A year after his first complaints, Derek's cancer again metastasized, this time to his lung and his liver. I was furious with the doctors for not being more aggressive with the treatments. After the first metastasis, Derek said he was told that surgery was not an option.

I cannot begin to describe the pain and anguish my family and I suffered during these times. Tears were shed like rivers and prayers were said until we were hoarse. Derek kept my family informed as to his cancer and, being a physician, he was trusted and believed by all. He would often draw pictures of his tumors to help us understand the situation.

The drug regimen increased and he became very sick with little appetite. With my urging, he went to a nationally-known medical center for a second opinion. After the consultations were completed, he was told there that he would get the best treatment available. I was relieved and started to become hopeful about his future—and our future together. We became engaged and planned a lush wedding. The treatments continued, but the MRIs showed little change in his tumors and this lack of progress was extremely upsetting to all of us. Because of the urgency of his situation, his doctors believed that stem cell recovery was his best option. The plans to proceed with surgery were set and the wedding had to be cancelled. Since my parents and their friends had purchased non-refundable airline tickets, I asked Derek for a letter from his doctor so that they could get a refund. He provided me with the letter, since proved to be a forgery, which I forwarded to my parents. However, a week before the stem cell procedure was to be performed, Derek had another MRI which showed that the tumors had decreased in size by fifty percent. In view of this thrilling and unexpected improvement, the stem cell recovery was cancelled.

Months later, while I was out of town, Derek went into cardiac arrest during a treatment and had to be shocked back to life with electric paddles. When I returned, he had two burn marks on either side of his heart from the paddles. Around this time, he also began bleeding from his colon because one of the tumors was eating into an artery. I gave him sanitary napkins to wear. He spent many weekend days in bed, and I saw the bloody napkins in the trash. I was totally committed to him during this time and was prepared to stay with him until the end, whether that be his recovery or his death. As a young woman, I cannot tell you how devastating it was for me to watch my future husband die.

Derek became extremely depressed and we frequently discussed his stopping the treatments because they were destroying his quality of life. We cried together numerous times, and I told him he had to be strong and continue. Nevertheless, he confided in me that he was considering suicide. One night, in a state of severe depression, he called his brother, whom I had never met. His brother, also a physician, came for him and took him immediately to a psychiatric center. Derek called sobbing from the center and told me they were going to admit him. I asked to speak with his brother for an update. A few seconds later, this cold voice came on the line. His brother made me feel as if I had failed to take care of Derek and was somehow responsible for his physical and emotional decline. He said that he and the doctors decided that Derek could call me only once a day. He would not tell me where they were. For the next five days, I continued to speak with both Derek and his brother by phone.

I had a growing suspicion that something was wrong. I went to the library and looked up his brother in a directory of physicians. Then I looked up Derek's entry. Piecing the facts together, I learned then that Derek had lied about his age, claiming to be nine years younger than he actually was. More importantly, when I used the number in the directory to place a phone call to his brother, I learned that he had been out of the country for some time and had not yet returned. I suddenly realized that the person I had been speaking with for the past five days, and whom I believed to be Derek's brother, was in fact Derek himself. I shudder at the thought of how he could be sobbing one minute and speaking to me in a cold dispassionate voice the next. I became frightened that Derek would come after me and hurt me, knowing now how cruel he could be.

Though I was dumbstruck, I complied with Derek's request that I retrieve his messages from work. I called one of Derek's coworkers to see when I could pick up the messages and discovered that she was at a scientific meeting in Vancouver. The next day, I called the convention center in Vancouver to try and locate his coworker. Something also made me ask if Derek Collier was registered. When the operator said, "Yes, one minute, I'll connect you," I was flabbergasted. Derek was in Vancouver, not a local psychiatric hospital. I tried to call him all night, but he was not in his hotel room. Early the next morning, he called and continued to tell me how he was opening up to the mental health counselors and other patients. I played along, and then called him back at the hotel an hour later. He hung up on me.

I finally reached his coworker, who answered my many questions about Derek's previous behavior. I learned that Derek had not missed work, was always in his office, and had not shown any signs of illness. She said that, quite to the contrary, he had just been playing golf in Vancouver and seemed to be having a great time.

That night, Derek had the audacity to call me and try to continue the charade even though I had discovered his lies. After several minutes, he made a number of startling confessions: He had faked the cancer, was indeed nine years older than he had claimed, and was still married. Then he begged my forgiveness as if I should be able simply to move on. For two years, my family and I had been manipulated for Derek's own amusement into believing he was dying. He has a mental sickness beyond comprehension, and I've had no contact with him since. But, believe it or not, I learned that the day after his confessions to me, he showed up at work wearing an eye patch. Why? For the last year, he's been telling coworkers that he has carcinoma of the retina. He's moved on to a new audience.

Derek's symptoms, cruelly and cleverly executed, devastated his devoted fiancée. So convincing were his disease forgeries that for two years Paula's perceptions and emotions were shaped by falsehoods. Unlike most factitious disorder patients, Derek's motives seem to have stemmed not only from a desire for sympathy; he also engaged in an astounding degree of sadistic lying and manipulation.

Not all patients build their deceptions on apparent physical evidence, such as Derek did when he created marks and burns on his skin and soaked gauze pads with blood. Some rely solely on the power of the story. Even when evidence is absent or contradictory, the deceptions often gain momentum, and more and more people are drawn in.

Hardly Unique

Although Paula's experiences with Derek may sound so extreme as to be the only one of its kind, they are entirely characteristic of the traumatic and lasting effects factitious disorder patients have on their victims. A common thread running through accounts from victims is that they believed their experiences were unique until they stumbled upon a television show, Internet page, newspaper, or magazine and learned about factitious disorder and Munchausen syndrome. One man wrote about his isolation before coming across my work; he crossed paths bitterly with a woman who, like Derek, feigned cancer:

I was involved with a woman for almost 12 years who convinced not only me, but an entire group of friends and associates that she was diagnosed with terminal bone cancer. The woman in our situation has never been confronted. Rather, she has built a new life entirely, without past associations: new friends, a new job, and so on.

Until I read about your study I thought that I and my friends were entirely alone in our experience.

An anguished mother and father from the United Kingdom wrote of their desperation and befuddlement in view of their daughter's feigned cancer and pregnancy:

We as a family need help. Though our daughter was unmarried, we were ecstatic when she told us she was pregnant by a young man we knew and liked. We thought it would stop the constant chaos in her life—chaos on every front. But the pregnancy lasted 10 months before she seemed to realize that any pregnant woman would have delivered much earlier. She had moved away and cut off communication, so we were unaware of her location or the fact that the baby hadn't been born. She contacted us again to say that the baby had been born and was adopted on the spot.

She never had a baby. We contacted all the hospitals; she was on no one's books. In July of this year she told us she had breast cancer and was going to have an operation. The day came and went, with her saying she needed more time to save some money up, as they had told her she could be unable to work for 6 weeks. She has now missed the second date, saying again she needed more time. We went to the breast unit at the hospital to ask when she was listed for surgery. They didn't have and never had had a date for surgery for her. If she had, they would not have allowed her to cancel the date of the surgery. They mentioned the word "Munchausen" to us and we now realize that it is something we should have thought about.

Emotional Rape

Victims have, for the most part, silently endured the indignity, anger, pain, and embarrassment imposed upon them by factitious disorder without knowing the diagnosis even existed. No one is immune to such victimization. So believable are the stories of factitious disorder persons that even experienced professionals have been taken in. Persons in helping professions or those of a helping and generous nature are especially vulnerable. As we saw in the case of Libby (chapter 1), clergy are likely candidates for the co-dependent role because of the supportive and nurturing nature of their work. One minister told me about a parishioner whom he believed had faked accidents and injuries. She had staged an auto accident and even faked reports of brain cancer. Whenever the minister tried to get her to be specific about one incident or illness, she would evasively move on to the next. He said that he couldn't help but feel that he had been used.

The Story of Baillie and Jack

Jack reported that he developed an intimate relationship with a woman, Baillie, whom he met while vacationing in Canada. She turned up on his doorstep in the United States soon after he had returned home to Virginia, and moved in with him. She pretended to seek employment while accepting money and gifts of clothing and jewelry from him. After several weeks, when he began questioning her stories about jobs promised or lost, Baillie started spending more time at home with the excuse that she wasn't feeling well. Gradually, her minor complaints escalated into major displays of pain and exhaustion, and she began drinking heavily, which worried her partner and distracted him from work. She assured him that she was under a doctor's care, and when he pressed for details, she told him that she had a bladder infection that was being treated with antibiotics. She said that she was drinking to numb the pain, and that she would have to postpone her efforts to find a job because of her illness.

After several weeks, when her condition remained seemingly unchanged, Jack expressed doubts about her story. "I have a right to know if something is really wrong with you and, if you are sick, why you're not getting better," he insisted one evening during a heated argument. "I can't function properly because I worry about you day and night."

Baillie, who acted out her part with great flair, took him in her arms and confessed, "I didn't want to worry you over something we can't change, but I suppose you need to know. I have ovarian cancer."

Jack was overwhelmed with a sense of guilt. He begged for more information, talked about her seeing specialists, and offered to accompany her on doctors' visits and pay for her treatments. She told him to be brave and have faith, and to carry on as he had all along. She assured him that she was in good hands.

Months slipped by without any physical changes, and with her providing only sketchy details about her treatments. When Jack was at last financially and emotionally depleted and on the brink of losing his job because of his deteriorating performance, he once again began questioning Baillie's condition. "If I get fired, who's going to pay for your treatments?" he demanded to know. She told him that her doctor, who had also immigrated to this country, had taken pity on her because she had no roots and no means of income here, and the doctor was going to be treating her for free. She stonewalled him when he tried to check details of her story, and eventually he told her that he didn't believe her. She accused him of callous indifference and said that she couldn't live with a man who treated her so harshly. She promptly left.

In a desperate attempt to get at the truth, he contacted her uncle and learned that Baillie was alcoholic and frequently feigned symptoms to elicit pity and emotional and monetary support. She knew that he enjoyed traveling, and after realizing that Jack now knew the truth about her, she waged a campaign of terror via the telephone, threatening to kill him if he returned to Canada.

Danger to Others

I believe that this woman posed a serious threat to her victim. Her actions, like Derek's, appear to have reflected an antisocial personality disorder. Her web of lies went beyond a reckless disregard for the truth; there was a willful focus on being dishonest at every possible opportunity. Neither Derek nor Baillie acknowledged that there were victims to their deceptions. They were neither remorseful nor did they want to move on and make their lives different.

Baillie's homicidal threats are not typical even of the hardcore Munchausen patient. Most of them have antisocial traits, but they aren't particularly violent or threatening. This was an extreme case in which the woman's personality disorder eventually emerged in full force.

Family Involvement and Adaptation

The scope of the negative influence factitious disorder patients have on the lives of others varies with the magnitude of their deceptions. Most families suffer in silence, unaware of what they are dealing with, and knowing only that it is destroying their lives.

With guidance from counselors, families may contribute to the treatment of factitious disorder patients, but, for various reasons, most of them never become that involved. There is a surprising lack of information concerning the families of origin of these patients. The patients hit the hospital ward, cause tremendous uproar, and then disappear once the staff members discover they have been had. Even many of those who have accepted treatment on psychiatric units won't allow contact with their families. Only a small percentage permit their families to get involved in their treatment, inevitably reluctantly.

Still, it makes good sense to try to contact families whenever possible, even if just to build an accurate medical history. Once the boiling rage many of them feel has been reduced to simmering, they may provide help by fleshing out the possible motivations behind the ruses.

If the rage and frustration of victims do subside, a sense of aloneness arises, along with the feeling that one must have been stupid to have been duped this way. Victims of factitious disorder patients need counseling and adjustment time. They must first acknowledge the problem and not be reluctant to turn to mental health professionals for personal advice and support.

If you suspect that you know a factitious disorder patient, first talk to someone who can objectively listen and has enough medical knowledge to know whether factitious disorder is a possibility. You may want to confront the person you suspect of the factitious illness by saying, "This is what I believe is going on and you must seek help to continue a relationship with me." The next step, depending on the seriousness of any financial consequences endured by the victim as a result of the portrayal, sometimes involves contacting an attorney. (You will find much more on the legal issues in the following chapter, and much more on intervention and treatment in chapter 16).

As a victim, your own therapy might focus on fully letting go of the other person. Although it may sound harsh, especially when you've been so close to a person, your own well-being may depend upon ending the relationship and determining how to protect yourself. You may not be able to change the other person, so you will have to focus on how to distance yourself from the problem and carry on a healthier life.

Victims must remember that most factitious disorder patients are very glib. They tend to say what people want to hear and have been known to talk family members out of believing that any ruse occurred. A victim, or the person who regards himself or herself as a potential victim, has to be steeled against further manipulation by focusing on objective evidence.

Some victims, however, are as immovable as the patients when it comes to making attitudinal and/or behavioral changes. They feel a need to take care of sick people as much as factitious disorder patients need to be taken care of. For these people, acknowledging that the illness is a hoax is extremely difficult. The duty to take care of the sick is drummed into all of our heads throughout our lives. Traditional wedding vows obligate spouses to care for each other "in sickness and in health." But if your spouse *makes* himself or herself sick, should the obligation be called into question? I assert that it must be redefined to take into account the fact that a factitious disorder patient is indeed sick—albeit mentally—and still deserves care. That care, however, must usually be taken over by mental health professionals so that the victim can focus on his or her own much-deserved care and recovery.

Recovery for the victims begins with information about the disorder. Information is liberating. So say all the affected people with whom I have talked. The single most curative event for most was simply finding out that there is a name for this disorder. In sharing experiences about this bizarre psychological disorder, people have stated that they feel as if a great burden has been lifted from their shoulders. They no longer feel foolish or ashamed about having fallen for a false illness once they realize that they certainly are not the only ones who have been misled in this way. Most feel comfort and relief in learning that they have been dealing with a recognized disorder.

14

Conscience, Ethics, and the Law

In spite of clear evidence that Millie's wounds were self-inflicted, Millie's estate sued her physicians, charging them with responsibility for her death. Although the suit was thrown out after four years of litigation, Millie's case points to the troubling legal issues surrounding factitious disorder, Munchausen syndrome, and malingering. Factitious disorder patients put themselves at huge medical risk, create staggering costs for hospitals and insurance companies, and increase the possibility of malpractice suits for physicians. Nevertheless, ethics and the law allow these patients to be exposed only under narrowly defined circumstances. This chapter examines the issues of malpractice and patients' rights as applied to informed consent, secret searches, entrapment, and confidentiality. I discuss the pros and cons of various tactics, allowing that personal conscience may dictate the need for disclosure, regardless of the law or prevailing ethics.

Challenging legal and ethical questions swirl around factitious disorder, muddying the already darkened waters through which health care professionals must tread. As cases in this book have illustrated, medical personnel have made bold moves that in some instances were ethically and legally questionable. They felt that they had no other alternatives if they were going to detect, diagnose, and/or treat factitious disorder patients. But such actions are dicey at best, because they simultaneously expose doctors, other caregivers, and the health care facilities at which they practice to various risks. Salient among them are accusations of misconduct because of deviations from accepted standards of care.

Malpractice

Merely confronting a patient with suspicions can lead to the foremost legal consequences for doctors who encounter factitious disorder patients: the danger of being sued for malpractice. Doctors may feel safer in a case that turns out to involve factitious disorder than in any other case. They think that consequences befalling a deceptive patient (including permanent disfigurement or even loss of life) are entirely the fault of the deceiver, and that any jury would agree. Most physicians with whom I've discussed the matter view it as inconceivable that they could be sued in a case involving factitious disorder. But they're wrong. Factitious disorder patients can and sometimes do bring malpractice suits against doctors and others, no matter how unfair it seems.

The Case of Millie

I was an expert witness in a civil lawsuit involving a woman I'll call Millie. Millie had severe facial rawness and scabbing she attributed to an allergic reaction to a chemical agent used by police during an altercation. Redness, bleeding, and scabs were evident over her entire face, though the areas around her eyes were neatly spared. This sparing was odd because Millie claimed that the chemicals hit her eyes first. Over the next several years, Millie was treated continuously for facial rawness and infections. The infections failed to respond to multiple antibiotic trials, resulting in repeated hospitalizations. Partial facial healing in the hospital was followed by deterioration in unsupervised settings.

No satisfactory explanation for Millie's course was offered, despite testing and treatment by a large number of generalists, specialists, and subspecialists. At various times, unexplained abrasions appeared on Millie's face, and she was observed to remove dressings, touch her wounds with dirty hands, and scrub her face excessively while denying she had done so. She responded with outrage whenever it was suggested that she might be contributing to her own injuries. In the meantime, she filed suit on the basis of the incidental chemical exposure, having been urged by relatives to "seek justice." In reality, she pursued the litigation as a "cover" for facial problems stemming from factitious disorder. She delighted in wearing her mummy-like facial bandages at the supermarket and mall, knowing that all eyes would focus on *her*.

Millie eventually went much further. She showed up in an emergency department with a circular wound above the left eyebrow. She admitted that she had drilled into her own forehead with an electric drill, using three different drill bit sizes. She then had sprayed saliva and week-old urine into the wound. Initially, she admitted to having harmed herself this one time to create harsher and more dramatic skin problems that doctors would take more seriously. Later, she confessed to having chronically irritated her skin. She said she had picked at scabs and created facial infections with saliva and urine in the past. Once the medical emergency was over, however, she firmly retracted the confessions and continued the behavior. At all times she was fully in touch with reality, even as she made these profoundly self-damaging choices.

Millie continued her lawsuit due to claims about the chemical exposure and incompetent medical care, insisting that doctors were responsible for the persistence of her dermatitis and—somehow—the hole in her skull. A review of her medical records disclosed over two decades of continual, persistent, and wide-ranging medical complaints that were rarely validated. However, physicians had commonly complied with Millie's demands for tests and invasive medical interventions because of the intensity of her complaints and the fact that she withheld information about medications already prescribed. The patient eventually died from the 21 medications she had been prescribed by various doctors; she did not overdose on any, but simply took all 21 as prescribed, leading to organ damage culminating in death. The lawsuit, carried forward by her estate despite the clear-cut evidence of simulation, was finally dismissed—four full years after it was filed.

Only very infrequently are judgments rendered against the physicians or other defendants who were involved in factitious disorder and Munchausen syndrome cases. But, to some degree, whether damages are awarded in the end is the least of the issues involved in a malpractice case. Of greater importance is what the lawsuit does to the defendants and their families as it drags on for months or even years, as such cases often do. Even though such legal efforts usually prove unsuccessful, they can be lengthy and very frightening experiences for the health care professionals who stand accused.

Harvard's Dr. Don Lipsitt wrote about one situation in which a young woman who feigned cancer later sued 35 physicians collectively for $14 million because they had failed to recognize and treat her for factitious disorder, instead treating her for a disease she never had. Rather than face a battle, the insurance companies settled out of court for more than a quarter of a million dollars. This case underscores the message that health care professionals must recognize factitious disorders as early as possible.

Vicki's Travail

I served as an expert witness in another case, this time involving Vicki, a nurse's aide. Vicki was suing an insurance company that had stopped paying her medical expenses because it was concerned that she was not complying with treatment. They retained me to see if her noncompliance went further—into the realm of Munchausen syndrome.

The records I was to review arrived in two mammoth footlockers. Though it took over a month to read them page by page, this assiduous review showed a stunning pattern not only of noncompliance but of willful self-infection and interference with wound healing. What had begun as an accidental injury to her thumb on a door jamb had progressed over a period of eight years to swelling of the hand, the opening up of weeping lesions on her hand and wrist, and redness and raw areas over her forearm. Doctors often swabbed the wounds to try to see what bacteria were causing the obvious, unremitting infections, and typically fecal bacteria grew out on culture. The records, which Vicki was forced to provide because she had filed suit, also showed pathological lying to health care professionals and others; massive doctor-shopping in states all over the country that was unknown to most physicians; and—most troublesome to me as a physician—a readiness on the part of most doctors to accept any claim Vicki made, perform any test she desired, and write out any prescription she sought. Eventually, her hand and arm were so deeply infected that she underwent an amputation below the elbow—an outcome she had predicted years earlier and then ensured came true. When even the infection-free stump mysteriously failed to heal, a revision to the amputation—this one raising the amputation level to above the elbow—was performed. Not surprisingly, that stump was now show-ing signs of breakdown of the healing process.

Nurses documented then, as they had in the past, that her bandages were routinely askew, as if she had removed them to gain access to the raw tissue. All along, both doctors and nurses had noted torn sutures, scratches to the wounds, opening up of wounds, and other evidence that Vicki was creating and then exacerbating her ailments. Several doctors documented the possibility of Munchausen syndrome, but the few bold enough to question her accepted her denials even when they detected flagrant lies about her personal history. Some had even observed an indention circling her upper arm that was, at least in ret-rospect, evidence of Vicki's having applied a tight tourniquet at times to cause her lower arm and hand to swell. I ascertained that the origi-nal injury, had it been left to heal, would have resolved in perhaps a week.

Later, I underwent a lengthy deposition with Vicki's attorney. He was attempting to impugn each of my findings, but suddenly ended the deposition. Off the record, he told me that my report was over-whelming and he now accepted that Vicki had Munchausen syn-drome. He said he intended to end the action against the insurance company. However, he added (to my chagrin, as a colleague) that he was now going to turn his attention to the physicians who performed the amputation and its subsequent revision, and encourage Vicki to sue them for malpractice for performing unnecessary surgery.

Fraud

Another critical legal dilemma involves satisfaction of debts incurred by these patients. This conundrum has hospitals and health care professionals grappling with the question of whether factitious disorder patients are guilty of criminal fraud. Many factitious disor-der patients rely on private insurance carriers, the Veterans' Adminis-tration, Medicare, Medicaid, or other payers to absorb their medical costs. Others, who have no funds and no medical insurance, simply don't pay their bills. Some doctors believe that all factitious disorder patients should pay for their medical care with their *own* resources; otherwise, they say, they are guilty of fraud. In some states this think-ing is supported by the law. In North Carolina and Arizona, for example, it's a crime to seek medical care under fraudulent circumstances. I am aware of only one case involving actual criminal prosecution, however.

Ashley's Trial

Ashley, a 31-year-old woman, was indicted in Arizona on three counts of fraud. She was charged with having knowingly obtained uncompensated health care under false pretenses. Review of her background showed that, a year earlier, she had been attending high school while claiming to be of high-school age. School officials eventually discovered the ruse and removed her, but she was not charged with any offense.

The actual indictment involved allegations that, for two years, Ashley had presented a contrived history to numerous medical, psychiatric, and dental practitioners and facilities to obtain unwarranted or misdirected care. She had repeatedly impersonated an insurance company representative promising reimbursement to the health care providers, but payment was never forthcoming. Eventually, the misrepresentation became evident and she was reported to the county attorney.

An independent psychological examination was ordered by the court. The consultant identified Ashley's fraudulent behavior as compulsive; however, the prosecution's psychiatric expert indicated that he would testify that the factitious behavior was carefully planned and in no way irresistible, as the word compulsive implies.

Before trial, Ashley pled no contest to two counts of Fraudulent Scheme and Artifice, a felony. She was sentenced to seven years of probation, and also ordered to perform 1,000 hours of community service and undergo mental health treatment (paying as she went). Finally, she was ordered to pay restitution of more than $100,000—but at a rate that will require 178 years to complete!

Commitment and Competence

Another important legal issue for psychiatrists is whether factitious disorder patients can be committed for involuntary psychiatric hospitalization. In medicine in general, the only time that we can force people to make themselves available for treatment is through commitment, a serious matter involving adjudication through probate courts.

Commitment does not mean that we can force treatment, only that the patient will be available for it. An individual can be committed and refuse medications, individual psychotherapy, group therapy, and all other treatments. Unless exceptional circumstances exist, we are legally bound to respect their refusal. If we feel that a person doesn't have the intellectual capacity to make the decision to refuse treatment (or accept it, for that matter), this situation would convert into a question of competency to make medical decisions. This question must also be decided by a judge.

In chapter 4, I described my frantic chase after a woman who had bolted from the emergency room. Her life was in jeopardy, a fact she was refusing to acknowledge. Just as I had to recognize my legal limits, clinicians often find themselves in the frustrating position of believing they have the ability to help, but knowing their hands are legally tied. These restrictions are essentially the same in all states, though the specific laws and thresholds for commitment vary. Health care professionals, including physicians, have to recognize the limits of their authority. People have the right in our society to make unfortunate decisions about their lives.

In most states the only criteria for commitment are, first, acute mental illness and, second, imminent suicidal risk, overt danger to others, or the incapacity to care for one's basic needs, such as food, shelter and clothing. Factitious disorders do not fulfill those secondary requirements. Not surprisingly, then, there are very few cases in the United States in which a patient has been committed solely on the basis of factitious disorder. In one instance, a patient had come to a hospital with factitious hematuria after she catheterized herself and injected herself with her own blood to simulate bloody urine. Although her behavior wasn't suicidal, a judge found that she was nevertheless placing herself in serious medical danger that might well result in her death at some point, and he bent the requirements a bit and committed her for psychiatric treatment. Unfortunately, she was released only one week later by a psychiatrist who said that he viewed all Munchausen patients as untreatable. It requires a leap for judges and lawyers, and for doctors such as this one, even to view factitious disorder as a mental illness. In cases of commitment, they're usually considering disorders such as schizophrenia with violence or intense suicidal depression.

In a case in Oregon, the judge developed a creative alternative to commitment. He set up a medical conservatorship in which one person was appointed to make all medical decisions on behalf of the patient. This approach is eminently reasonable and other states might consider amending their laws slightly to permit such actions in cases involving factitious disorder patients.

Secret Searches

Other legal questions that involve individual rights have resulted from secret surveillance and surreptitious searches of patients' property and rooms. Sometimes these searches, whether conducted on an inpatient or outpatient basis, have yielded evidence used to confirm factitious illnesses. Such actions were seldom questioned in the not-too-distant past, but today they are considered blatant invasions of privacy unless the patient has agreed to them or there is serious suspicion of Munchausen by proxy abuse (see chapters 10 and 11).

The issue of privacy arose in a case in which a woman was suspected of inducing vomiting to cause an electrolyte imbalance. Doctors secretly performed tests (not explaining what they were really for) to monitor serum and urinary electrolytes, which are among the most important fluid components in the body. They were able to determine that the electrolyte loss was occurring through vomiting. Was it ethical for doctors to perform that kind of diagnostic study without telling the patient what they were doing and why? The matter can be debated, but currently most legal and medical professionals would answer "no."

Informed Consent

Another dubious practice regarding the management of factitious disorder cases is the *medication-assisted interview*. This technique involves interviewing patients while they are under the influence of so-called *disinhibiting* medications. Such medications, administered intravenously, deeply relax patients and make it more likely that, under questioning, they will admit to their ruses. It is unlawful to administer a chemical without informed consent, and the technique would obviously be refused by factitious disorder patients notified that it is being performed only for the purpose of trying to extract the truth. Regardless, often the methods are ineffective; a patient who is highly motivated to maintain a deception can resist the effects of such a drug, so such interventions don't really force truthfulness.

Some doctors have argued that there is a therapeutic privilege that allows them to forego the conventional process of getting informed consent before administering such substances, but I don't agree. Even procedures of low risk are not entirely without risk. Imagine the scenario of a doctor's administering a drug without informed consent and the patient's having a life-threatening reaction. Civilly, it would be considered malpractice; criminally, it would constitute assault and battery. Doctors cannot practice with that kind of disregard for potential liability and individual rights.

Other doctors say that diagnostic maneuvers such as room searches might be legally and ethically justifiable if a patient's life has been endangered by a factitious illness. If a true medical emergency exists, such thinking has some foundation. If the danger is not of life-threatening proportions at that moment, however, it probably does not. Unless the patient is informed and accepts the possibility of room searches as a precondition to admission—which has indeed become a common pre-admission requirement—the days of such actions are long gone. When a man or woman enters a hospital today, even a psychiatric hospital, he or she does not give up any civil rights. Hospitals are even required to post a patient's bill of rights on every unit. Also, informed consent technically should be obtained for every procedure and medication of at least moderate risk. There is no blanket form that allows doctors to do to the patient whatever they deem necessary, without regard to the patient's rights or preferences in that situation.

Acceptable Options

Doctors still do have some options for catching disease forgers, and one is to incorporate the informed consent process into testing. For instance, a doctor who suspects a patient of feigning an illness can sit with him or her and explain, "I don't know what's going on with you yet, but one of the possibilities is that you are producing this disease yourself. Because I'm considering this among the diagnoses, I need to do a series of tests that will rule out that option as well as other possible diagnoses. I'm telling you beforehand to ask your permission to go ahead with the diagnostic workup." This statement is very hard for doctors because it immediately strains the doctor/patient relationship. If the patient does have a factitious disorder, he or she may find an excuse to check out of the hospital and slip off to another hospital to perpetuate the same behavior. But the direct approach could make a big difference in helping to identify selected cases of factitious disorder and perhaps result in proper treatment for some patients.

As I pointed out earlier, using video cameras as watchful eyes can be very helpful in diagnosing MBP. Videotaped documentation of abuse should be made part of the child's permanent medical record for review by protective services personnel, the lawyers on both sides, and the courts. The mother's attorney will inevitably insist that the monitoring was an invasion of privacy resulting in illegally obtained evidence, but such challenges routinely fail due to Federal law and legal precedents. Still, to be safe, as soon as doctors become suspicious, they should contact the hospital's attorney and administrator. They should also consult the hospital's risk management office on any proposed detective work. The arguments in favor of video surveillance should be enumerated to these hospital personnel: for instance, performing CVS can save a child's life and provide dramatic proof of abuse; it can be shown in court; it can help exonerate an innocent mother who is under suspicion; and, unlike a hotel, there is no reasonable expectation of privacy in a hospital room. (Of course, mothers suspicious of surveillance can avoid abusive behavior during the observation period and try to claim that the problem-free parenting on the tape disproves all allegations.) If the worrisome behavior is occurring outside a hospital, a doctor should contact his or her attorney or a legal advisor with the American Psychiatric Association or American Medical Association.

In cases of possible MBP, doctors in the United States must, by law, share their suspicions with the proper authorities. (This requirement is absent in many other countries in the world, including England.) With reporting comes immunity from any type of prosecution or lawsuits for defamation, as long as the report was not filed with conscious malicious intent to injure a person. In contrast, failure to report is a misdemeanor punishable by incarceration and/or a fine.

Doctors who recognize factitious disorder in any patient find themselves in an ethical quandary that pits their desire and commitment to heal against the often-aversive nature of these patients. The actions physicians must take are largely determined by the laws and standard professional practices. A physician can't unilaterally terminate active care, for instance, suddenly saying, "I think you're faking and I'm not going to see you or treat you from this moment on." A physician must in some way provide warning to a patient that, on a certain date, he or she will no longer offer care. There also has to be some reasonable hope that the patient can obtain other medical care to the extent that it is needed, and the physician may be required to assist in getting the patient that care.

Sharing the Secret: Telling Others about the Deception

Legally and ethically, physicians must respect the confidentiality of the patient and abide by a host of other professional requirements. But if a patient is not playing by the tacit rules of the doctor-patient relationship, does the physician have to play by them? Except under certain conditions, the answer is yes.

Those conditions are of paramount importance to medical staff members who, almost certainly against the patient's wishes, want to disclose the diagnosis of factitious disorder to others—to help end the medical merry-go-round, for instance. According to the landmark book *The Clinical Handbook of Psychiatry and the Law*, disclosing information without a patient's consent may be legally justified, or even necessary, in a number of circumstances, including:

- *Responding to emergencies.* When a patient is in a state of emergency, physically or psychiatrically, a doctor or therapist, acting in the person's best interests, may deem it necessary to disclose appropriate information about a patient. He or she can do so without the patient's explicit consent and can discuss the diagnosis of factitious disorder and other vital matters, such as medications prescribed or illicit drugs used. To forestall subsequent second-guessing, it is a helpful legal protection to have a second clinician evaluate the situation and document his or her agreement that an emergency is occurring.

- *Responding to incompetence.* If a clinician believes that a patient is not legally competent to give or withhold consent, he or she should consult an appropriate guardian or relative. This situation arose in the case of Millie, who became incoherent weeks before her death, probably as a result of the self-injury to her brain and the medications prescribed. In the absence of such a person, the clinician can release information that will serve the patient's best interests. A formal adjudication of incompetence and appointment of a guardian may need to be pursued if the incompetence is expected to persist.

- *Acting to hospitalize or commit a patient.* When information (such as overt suicidal or homicidal behavior) is needed to involuntarily hospitalize or commit a person, such disclosure is permitted in most states. There are restrictions, however, in some parts of the country that should be explored with local authorities.

- *Acting to protect third parties. The Clinical Handbook of Psychiatry and the Law* notes that, in the past, psychiatrists' obligations to protect others from patients' violent acts were limited to hospitalizing such patients, and then ensuring that they did not escape and were not prematurely released—duties that did not require breach of confidentiality. A 1976 decision by the California Supreme Court, however, recognized the duty of all mental health professionals to "take whatever steps are reasonably necessary" to protect their patients' potential victims. In the decision, the court recognized that warnings might have to be issued to the victim and/or the police. Most states have rendered similar decisions and/or issued statutes governing such situations. Such concerns rarely arise in factitious disorder cases, though they can be paramount in those involving MBP.

- *Acting in conformance with reporting requirements.* Mental health and other professionals, physicians, and sometimes nurses, educators, and others are required by law to report situations such as MBP abuse. Though the precise wording of the statutes varies from state to state, all 50 states do mandate the report of suspected child abuse. It is crucial for health care professionals to be aware of local statutes and laws pertaining to these issues.

- *Consulting with supervisors and collaborators.* According to the Handbook, it is not considered a breach of confidentiality to disclose information to professionals who are assisting a primary caregiver in a patient's care. These professionals may include supervisors, members of a hospital's nursing staff, and colleagues. Once taken into a primary physician's confidence, however, they are obliged to maintain the same confidentiality as the primary caregiver. Thus, a clinician inexperienced in factitious disorder can feel free to consult with an expert colleague about matters such as diagnosis and treatment, though the expert must not share any patient-specific information with others.

The Risks of Disclosure

These legal requirements and restrictions are clear, but they are becoming even more stringent in some cases. New federal privacy regulations governing health care records make outside records very difficult to access without full patient consent. Also, the regulations allow patients to request alterations to their medical records, and the effect in cases of medical deception remains to be seen.

What about matters of conscience in cases of factitious disorder? Can doctors who are genuinely worried about the factitious behavior of a patient warn each other, hospitals, or insurance carriers simply because they are desperate to help their patients preserve their health? They should be prepared for a range of unpleasant consequences if they do. A lawsuit for breach of confidentiality is an almost inevitable outcome. But less predictable outcomes can befall the reporting professional as well. For example, one doctor tried to alert his colleagues to a woman whom he had seen as a patient and was sure was suffering from a factitious disorder. Feeling concerned about her well-being and also feeling obligated to warn his fellow physicians, he contacted a number of doctors whom he had learned were seeing this patient. He was offhandedly dismissed by every one of them. He was shocked by how willing his colleagues were to disbelieve him and accept the compelling tales of his former patient.

Many health care professionals have sought to sidestep the legal constraints and enhance reporting by arguing in favor of a national registry of factitious disorder patients. The rationale is to help monitor and curb the activities of these patients. Although registries exist in some countries, I believe this idea is unacceptable. There are myriad problems with generating a list of these patients and sending it to every hospital, clinic, and doctor's office in the country. A primary concern would be that every person on that list could never become authentically ill because they probably wouldn't receive treatment. As Wendy Scott showed us (chapter 7), disease portrayals can end at any time. In many cases, once a person's emotional needs are met, the portrayals seem to end and the individual moves ahead with his or her life. Moreover, it's likely that everyone on the list would promptly and permanently be denied health insurance.

Other less formal measures have been suggested to try to track and identify factitious disorder patients, including posting their pictures on hospital bulletin boards and circulating flyers about them to emergency rooms. However, access to bulletin boards and flyers is uncontrolled and so these measures would involve breaches of confidentiality. In *General Hospital Psychiatry*, Dr. Frederic C. Kass postulated that to strike a happy medium, physicians should consider each individual case when deciding whether to publicly expose a factitious disorder patient. He recommended taking into consideration such factors as the frequency of the disease portrayals, the jeopardy in which a patient is placed based on the severity of the factitious illness, and the nature of the disease which is being feigned. While I appreciate his well-meaning effort at compromise, it would create a slippery slope in which severity is in the eye of the beholder and patients may be unnecessarily, and illegally, denied treatment or even openly maligned.

Despite these cautions, a number of articles have been written for professional journals with the intention of disclosing the identity of a particular patient. In this way, other professionals would become aware of his or her existence. For example, a dental journal carried an account of a patient with Munchausen syndrome who received treatment from at least 25 dentists in the New York metropolitan area. The characteristics of the patient and the syndrome were described to alert the dental community to this patient, who was believed still to be living in the area. Some older papers written by psychiatrists, especially in Europe, have contained actual patient names. Or they contain accurate initials and so many specific details that it would be easy to identify the particular patient. Physicians have become more and more careful over time about engaging in that sort of disclosure, and professional journals will not accept manuscripts that might lead to identification of specific factitious disorder patients.

But physicians are resourceful, and ideas for circumventing confidentiality still emerge. Some physicians suggest that confidentiality is not breached if, for example, they merely drop blatant hints that there is a story behind a patient that can't be told. Some suggest writing a letter to a referring physician about the patient in question, noting, "I have been forbidden to comment on whether this patient has factitious disorder." However, such techniques merely finesse the ethical and legal issues and do not directly confront them. Such actions are no different from other breaches of confidentiality.

Yet, even more arguments have been offered to support limits on doctor/patient confidentiality when factitious disorder is involved. A person is stealing if he or she goes to a medical office pretending to be ill and uses time and services without paying. However, because he or she presented as a patient, clinicians are under a variety of ethical and legal constraints, not the least of which is confidentiality. If someone walks into a store, however, and takes merchandise without paying for it, there's no expectation that confidentiality will be preserved. Yet both situations are thefts. This argument is compelling, but, once again, the bottom line is one that physicians—so used to calling the shots—find abhorrent: These patients have an unfair advantage over doctors. They don't have to play by the rules of being a patient, but doctors must play by the rules of being a physician. In almost every case, the factitious disorder patient can deny the doctor the right to impart any information to anyone about the ruses.

One way to change this situation is for the American Medical Association and/or other professional organizations to take positions on these issues and say publicly, "In terms of our code of ethics, there are certain circumstances in which confidentiality no longer holds. These include situations in which patients have been fraudulent in producing information and/or have surreptitiously produced their own diseases. As a result, it may not be necessary for the physician to maintain the standard level of confidentiality with these patients." Legislators would need to develop similar statutory language, and judges would need to affirm its legality. Historically, however, almost every conceivable issue has taken priority over consideration of medical deception. I fear that even the first step—a formal policy statement from an established medical organization to help guide physician conduct—will be a long time in coming.

Concluding Points

Other factors that keep the legal and ethical pot boiling are the subtle differences between malingering, with its criminal overtones, and factitious disorder or Munchausen syndrome. According to diagnostic criteria, the only way that a physician can distinguish between malingering and an established mental illness such as factitious disorder is by apparent motive. But can a doctor read the mind of his or her patient to determine whether the patient's primary motive is the sick role itself or some external gain? What about the fact that various motives can co-exist or change over time? These questions are rhetorical because the professional community has no answers, nor has it convened a consensus panel of experts to advise clinicians in daily practice.

Regardless of these hazards and limitations, a well-coordinated, multi-disciplinary approach is always crucial for health care professionals who are trying to treat factitious disorder. It is essential whether a parent is harming her child (abuse) or an adult is poisoning himself (mental illness), because once suspicions are voiced, the burden of proof rests with the accusers.

To date, I know of no civil cases instigated against factitious disorder patients by family members, friends, professionals, or health care facilities. Lawsuits would be one way to turn the tables on factitious disorder patients when they have done damage, financial or emotional; such patients would inevitably argue that they were the helpless victims of a mental disorder. Nevertheless, the odds are good that someday a precedent-setting civil case against a factitious disorder patient will be waged and won by a person, organization, or facility that has been deeply affected.

15

Detection and Diagnosis

This chapter shows how factitious disorder is widely prevalent but remains underdiagnosed and undertreated for a variety of reasons. Most medical professionals receive little training in factitious disorder. They rarely spot the warning signs and, even when they do, they rarely know how to intervene. Payment systems, fear of legal reprisal, social stigma, and lack of communication among medical professionals also inhibit accurate diagnosis. This chapter presents a list of warning signs that signal the possibility of factitious disorder, such as bodily scars with peculiar shapes that appear within easy reach of the dominant hand. The chapter also discusses tactics physicians can use to confirm their suspicions.

Being able to prove that someone has a factitious disorder, whether in a hospital or a court of law, is unquestionably one of the most daunting tasks any clinician can ever face. Most professionals will never find themselves in that position, however, because the majority of factitious disorder patients are falling through cracks in the health care system—cracks that have been created by lack of knowledge, lack of communication among health providers, fear of litigation, and in some cases, indifference. A number of physicians have wagged fingers at their colleagues, scolding them for letting factitious disorder patients slip by them without detection. Sometimes, the true diagnosis has been apparent for years but was flatly ignored by the medical staff, and mine has been one of the scolding voices. Scores of cases involve the removal of healthy organs and repeated exploratory operations and invasive procedures in attempts to isolate the causes of what ultimately proved to be feigned illnesses. Too often, doctors have prescribed medications and other treatments for factitious disorder patients even when costly tests proved negative time after time. People who engage in medical deceit of all kinds are woefully undercounted. The reasons are manifold:

- Medical and psychological professionals receive little training in the treatment of medical trickery and seldom spot their red flags. I, for one, never heard the terms "factitious disorder" or "Munchausen by proxy" (MBP) during my four years of medical school and four years of psychiatric residency at esteemed institutions. I learned the difference between factitious disorder and malingering only when the editor of a medical journal spotted my confusion in an article I had written and then gently corrected me.

- When professionals spot people with factitious disorder or even MBP, they rarely know how to intervene, enabling the patients or perpetrators to move on to other doctors and medical facilities.

- When health caregivers detect disease forgery, they sometimes deliberately avoid providing an accurate diagnosis. They know their clients don't like the stigmatizing label, and confrontation is exceptionally difficult and anxiety-producing for all involved. Even when they have substantial proof, professionals may fear that the patient will sue for malpractice, slander, or libel to divert attention away from the illness ploys and silence the worried whistle-blower.

- The payment system actually works against accurate diagnoses of disease forgery. Instead of rewarding informers who present a strong case, insurance carriers and others who should foot the bill generally refuse to pay for care that results from health problems the client has feigned or induced. Doctors have no incentive to fill in forms with diagnoses such as factitious disorder for which they are guaranteed nonpayment. In a parallel way, the family members of patients who commit suicide often receive no life insurance benefits, and some well-meaning coroners and medical examiners may list "cause undetermined" rather than "suicide" for that reason.

Damage or death from self-harm vitiates payment in all sorts of policies.

- Because the medical and psychological communities don't fully understand medical and psychological ruses, professionals have mistakenly undertreated real patients assumed to be faking. Cautionary stories like that of Wendy Scott (chapter 7) may have contributed in a small way to a defensive underdiagnosis of factitious disorder and related phenomena.

- Almost all patients with factitious disorder, and almost all perpetrators engaging in MBP, avoid coming forward due to fears of social stigma and/or legal reprisal—even in those infrequent cases in which they want help in ending the deceptions.

- No government association or health care organization disseminates information—online or otherwise—about factitious disorders, Munchausen syndrome, Munchausen by proxy, or malingering.

- Perhaps most importantly, patients and perpetrators can be as nimble as circus acrobats in evading discovery.

One of my former patients provided her personal account about how so much misdirected medical intervention can occur. Hers is also a hopeful story, in that she was able to be entirely cured of her Munchausen syndrome.

Nellie's Words

The stark truth is that I have spent many years of my life making myself sick. I have been hospitalized 30 to 40 times, had innumerable surgeries and diagnostic procedures, and been prescribed literally hundreds of medications by physicians who never suspected that I was the cause of my own illnesses. It started in my teens when I secretly caused chemical burns on my arms with oven cleaner and drank juice mixed with kitchen cleansers. Over the years, I moved into even more hazardous behavior and wound up causing damage to my body that confronts me every day. It saddens me to realize that I will have to live with these scars for the rest of my life.

I know that my actions seem utterly inexplicable, and yet I just didn't seem to have any other options. Strangely enough, my harming myself was my only means of survival. My goal in being sick was not to cause myself pain or create permanent injury. These outcomes were just the necessary inconveniences along the road to my real destination—receiving that little bit of caring from the hospital staff that would energize me and enable me to go on with my life. I would get sick, be hospitalized, and get better...over and over.

For a long time, I had felt as if I were indestructible. But when I had to have my bladder removed due to my self-injuries, I realized I was not indestructible. I now had a permanently placed external urinary bag to remind me of how far I had taken things, but by this time, being sick had become a way of life and I was unable to stop. The rewards were just too great. I also had to declare bankruptcy because of the medical expenses that were incurred during the times I had no insurance. A conservative estimate of the costs of my inpatient services, outpatient care, and medications would be $400,000, and I will continue indefinitely to need around $200 a month in medication and medical supplies.

I initially engaged in factitious behavior to avoid the abuse I endured as a young teenager. When I was sick, my abusers would leave me alone. It wasn't until I was 18 and hospitalized after a car accident that, by chance, I fully discovered the love and caring to be gained by being hospitalized. It was after this experience that I began to make myself sick for the express purpose of hospitalization. Though I eventually received my college degree, I had to drop out from time to time because I was so busy being sick. After I graduated, I spent a year working only sporadically due to frequent inpatient stays.

Throughout the years, nobody suspected what I was doing. I might fake having a symptom such as abdominal pain, add blood to a urine specimen to cause abnormal results, or self-induce actual ailments such as frostbite and infections. Then I experienced a turning point of sorts. As I had many times in the past, I injected bacteria into my bloodstream but this time I ended up in the intensive care unit (ICU) with signs of septic shock. For the first time, I found myself really scared that I might die. During the previous several months, I had started visiting a doctor who spent a lot of time with me, and I decided in the ICU that if I recovered from the sepsis, I would finally tell her the truth about what I was doing. I guess I thought that telling her—sharing the secret—would provide me with some accountability and enable me to stop.

Miraculously, I did recover, and I did tell my internist. Instead of reacting with anger at having been misled, she was surprisingly supportive and understanding. She stuck with me even though I was not able to stop my factitious behavior immediately. When word spread in the medical community about me, however, no one else would see me—not even the psychiatrists to whom my doctor tried to refer me. It seemed that other professionals were disgusted by me, afraid of me, or just didn't feel qualified to see me. Though I was disappointed, I can totally understand their feelings because I often have the same feelings toward myself. Though I don't deny my past, I am ashamed of it.

Ultimately, I became convinced that, if I were to get a second chance in life, I needed to move to another part of the country. The thought of moving was frightening because I knew that, in doing so, I would be giving up what little security I did have at home. I was also worried that, if I slipped up and went back to doing what I had done in the past, I would never be able to tell anyone the truth: I would feel that I couldn't live through the shame and humiliation yet again. Still, as I started to make plans for the move and visited potential towns, I did realize that without therapy I'd probably fail as I had failed before. I finally selected my new home in large part because I knew that therapy would be available for me there.

Now I have indeed made a new life for myself: I am employed full-time with an excellent work record and have just completed an advanced degree. I have a relationship with a new internist who is nonjudgmental and whom I see on a fixed schedule. I am and have been healthy for several years now, and I am determined to share my story.

I want other patients with this disorder to know that when I was engaging in factitious behavior, I thought that I was hurting no one but myself and that I would be able to stop after just one more hospitalization. But things worked out differently. First, others are inevitably affected. I lost the support of nearly all my friends and family when they realized I had deceived them. Second, I was unable to stop my factitious behavior by sheer willpower. I didn't stop until I realized, through therapy, that there were reliable and safe ways to meet my need to be cared about. I used to think that my ruses were the answer to my problems. Now I realize that they only created more problems and solved nothing.

At the same time, I want physicians to realize that my goal was not to deceive them but rather to gain hospitalization. Within this context, physicians were, simply put, a conduit. When I finally gained insight, motivation, and a consistent relationship with a single caring doctor, I soon ended my deceptions because my need to be sick lessened dramatically.

What continues to trouble me, however, is that so many patients trapped in the cycle of factitious illnesses will never experience this kind of emancipation. I wish I could tell people with factitious disorder and their doctors that substitute supplies of care and concern can be easily found and that therapists feel secure in their ability to help because consistently effective treatment approaches are at hand... but this is a situation that doesn't yet exist. I hope and believe that some day it will.

I spoke to Nellie 6 years after the end of my work with her, and she had not engaged in a single episode of self-harm during the intervening years. She had her annual physical with the same internist she had seen for years but had no other doctor visits, and she was upbeat, productive, funny, focused on making the most of her life, and entirely healthy.

Unlike Nellie, most patients do not acknowledge their deceptions and ask for help. Thus, identifying factitious disorder and Munchausen patients depends upon two supremely basic yet critical factors: proper training and teamwork. Obviously, the burden of accurately diagnosing all patients rests with their health care providers, who must act in tandem with the other providers attending to these patients. The goal of the team must be to confirm or discard diagnostic suspicions and then to take proper action. As simplistic as this path sounds, it is not being followed on a large scale. In the United States, for instance, physicians tend to follow a different path—one of rigid individualism in which they look after patients without even finding out whether they are seeing other doctors. Those who do ask may find it hard to get copies of outside records or even chat by phone with other professionals. Clinicians cannot access a central repository of medical data about a patient. Facing busy schedules, they may even ignore it when patients let it slip that they are seeing others and oddly decline to sign releases to allow communication among them.

Awareness that factitious disorder, Munchausen syndrome, MBP, and malingering exist and that they follow consistent patterns is key to diagnosing them accurately. There's an old saying in medicine that the first step in diagnosis is a high index of suspicion. If you're not aware of a particular disorder or don't know about its characteristics, you're not likely to have very much suspicion about it and the diagnosis is not likely to be made.

The daughter of one deceased Munchausen patient wrote about her intense anger that her mother's deceptions were not detected and confronted by doctors during her mother's life. Several doctors did have suspicions, but none collected the medical records or interviewed any family members to help substantiate—or disconfirm—their beliefs. Instead, they proceeded with making diagnoses and administering treatments based only on the patient's constant, changeable reports of decades of terrible symptoms throughout her body. The diagnosis of Munchausen syndrome became unmistakable only after the patient's death, when her daughter assembled all of the records and consulted with an authority on the subject.

Heather's Recollection

I find myself angry and frustrated at the fact that so many doctors and nurses apparently went along with my mother. The wall of silence that they created in collusion with my mother was extremely harmful to me and my family as a whole—and ultimately to her. It seems to me that many medical personnel actually went against their ethical commitment to prevent harm. Why would all these medical personnel have gone along with her and never confronted her about her psychological problems? Why would they have assented to putting her through surgery after surgery—some of which were life threatening? With no exceptions, every single surgical procedure she went through was elective. I simply find this fact in and of itself amazing and angering, in part because of the negative impact these actions had on my own life.

At her death, Heather's mother was taking 17 medications and had failed to respond or described herself as allergic to another 50. She had undergone surgery 19 times, had 22 additional hospitalizations at an assortment of hospitals, and self-identified 33 active medical problems that were being treated by a broad assortment of physicians, though essentially none was confirmed on autopsy. Indeed, though there were no supporting findings on autopsy, the coroner wrote that this woman had died of "congestive heart failure due to idiopathic restrictive cardiomyopathy"—jargon in lieu of the more honest statement, "cause undetermined" or maybe even "cumulative effects of medications and surgery resulting from Munchausen syndrome."

Some of Heather's rage does stem from the utter clarity of hindsight. She attributes to professionals knowledge they had not had at the time they treated her mother. She even accuses them of collusion. Instead, I believe they acquiesced to the patient's demands because they were unfamiliar with the indicators of feigned and induced illness. If the doctors are to be faulted, and I believe some are, it was for failing to insist that the patient sign blanket releases to talk to her children and to obtain records from other hospitals. They also considered diagnoses much more uncommon than factitious disorder itself. Importantly, a proper diagnostic process calls for doctors to proceed from the most likely (or common) diagnoses to the least likely, and not skip over factitious disorder. In fact, the characteristics of full-blown Munchausen syndrome had been evident for decades. They included pseudologia fantastica, with the mother's making bizarre, attention-getting claims to fellow church congregants. One was that Heather attempted to murder her during one hospitalization and that, during another, a surgeon had beaten her up and tried to kill her. It is dispiriting that even after the diagnosis of Munchausen syndrome had become obvious after the mother's death, the doctors whom Heather contacted discounted or refused to discuss it. Perhaps they feared malpractice liability, but their reticence only fueled her anger and impeded closure of this bedeviling aspect of her past.

Education about factitious disorder is important for all people involved in medical care, not just doctors. Since nursing and other front-line staff members generally have more contact with patients than doctors, they too must be knowledgeable about this particular diagnostic group. If they're not educated about it, they won't have the information to communicate to doctors. Good medical care, irrespective of whether an illness is factitious or not, involves good communication within the entire multidisciplinary team.

The "Red Flags" of Factitious Disorder, Munchausen Syndrome, and Malingering

There is no doubt that careful reviews of medical charts and personal histories can help alert professionals to patients with factitious disorder and its extreme variant, Munchausen syndrome, as well as those who malinger. However, clinicians must know the warning signs or "red flags" of medical/psychological deception or else examination of this information will be of little use. (The warning signs of MBP were covered in chapter 10).

When a history is unusual or when there are no positive findings for a disease the patient claims, providers should—as suggested—make every effort to track down records and speak with others who have, or supposedly have, treated the patient. Some physicians, including me, have even suggested that continued hospitalization should be contingent upon the patient's providing accurate information and signing release forms that can lead to the compilation of complete histories. Medical records are enormously useful in detecting factitious disorder. Research shows that patients using a high number of medical services often have a psychiatric condition that warrants treatment. High utilization does not prove that a person has a phony disease. It is, however, a major clue that something more than a physical ailment is wrong with the patient. For example, people who are depressed as well as physically diseased utilize two to three times the medical care of people with the same disease who aren't depressed. Concurrent anxiety jacks up medical utilization as well. Somatization disorder (see chapter 2) increases medical expenditures to six or eight times the norm. Hefty use of medical services means that the physician, nurse, or other caregiver should be highly suspicious that the patient has a psychiatric diagnosis. These considerations should include factitious disorder.

Factitious disorder (including Munchausen syndrome), MBP, and malingering are not personal characteristics that can be elicited or disconfirmed during an interview. Clinicians as a group, including highly trained psychiatrists and psychologists, do no better than the general public in determining during an interview whether someone is telling the truth (though they are often supremely confident about their own judgments, even when completely wrong). In fact, the only occupational groups that do better than the general public in ascertaining truthfulness in face-to-face encounters with others are the Secret Service and professional poker players. The reason seems to be that both have learned to ignore the content of what is being said and rely instead on nonverbal clues, such as excessive blinking and a tendency to avoid eye contact.

Except in cases of feigned memory defects such as those in dementia or amnesia, psychological testing or structured personality profiles cannot reliably establish or disprove trickery. Instead, deception usually is deduced by examining a broad range of factors, and it does not depend upon the absolute number of factors identified in a given case. Over my career, I have developed a list of such potential red flags. Most of these warning signs can be used by family members, friends, and associates such as co-workers, not just health care providers, as aids to the diagnosis. They follow in no special order.

1. The signs and symptoms do not improve with medical treatment. There is continual escalation, or improvement is reliably followed by relapse, or new complaints are elaborated—all in the service of keeping caregivers engaged.

2. The magnitude of symptoms consistently exceeds what is normal for the disease and/or there is proved medical dishonesty.

3. The individual demands hospitalization and becomes more vociferous, even threatening, if doctors appear ambivalent or dissuaded.

4. Some findings are determined to have been self-induced, or at least worsened through self-manipulation.

5. There are remarkable numbers of tests, consultations, and treatment efforts to no avail.

6. The individual is unusually willing to consent to medical or surgical procedures, including painful and risky ones.

7. The individual disputes test results that do not support the presence of authentic disease.

8. The individual accurately predicts physical deteriorations.

9. The individual's condition regularly worsens shortly before or after discharge from the hospital, emergency department, or doctor's office.

10. The individual "doctor shops" and has sought treatment at numerous facilities.

11. The individual emerges as an inconsistent, selective, or misleading source of information.

12. The individual refuses to allow the treatment team access to outside information sources, such as family members or other physicians.

13. There is a history of medical treatment for secondary problems, such as falls or traffic accidents, that creates the impression that the individual must be astonishingly unlucky.

(I call this the "black cloud" phenomenon, in which the individual reports so many mishaps that it strains credulity to the breaking point.)

14. Deception is explicitly considered by at least one health care professional, if evidenced merely by a brief chart entry.

15. The individual does not follow treatment recommendations and/or is disruptive on the hospital unit or in the outpatient setting.

16. The individual focuses on his or her self-perceived "victimization" by medical personnel and others.

17. There is consistent evidence from laboratory or other tests that disproves information supplied by the individual.

18. When suspicions arise or the patient feels challenged, he or she leaves the hospital or emergency department against medical advice.

19. The individual is socially isolated, receiving no visitors in the hospital.

20. The individual has had exposure to a model of the ailment they are falsifying (e.g., he or she grew up with a grandparent with severe leg pains from diabetes).

21. The individual engages in gratuitous lying, if not frank pseudologia fantastica.

22. Even while unceasingly pursuing medical/surgical intervention, the individual vigorously opposes psychiatric assessment and treatment.

23. During interviews, the individual makes statements to strengthen his or her case that nevertheless contradict the records. Alternatively, he or she fails to recall incriminating findings and events. (This behavior may reflect the individual's efforts to keep the previous medical ruses concealed, or represent a new effort to maximize the chances of successful litigation).

24. There is evidence for external incentives for illness or incapacity (i.e., malingering).

25. There is evidence for internal incentives for illness or incapacity (i.e., factitious disorder and Munchausen syndrome).

Obviously, not all red flags are evident in every case, but any combination of them can be telling. The warning signs just listed are usually elicited upon review of the medical records. In the clinical setting, as professionals interact with the patient, other clues are obvious once health caregivers know what to look for. For example, old scars in unusual patterns often betray self-administered wounds. Self-inflicted lesions are produced on the body within easy reach of the dominant hand, usually have bizarre shapes, and have neat, linear outlines. Another important clue to self-inflicted wounds is that they heal quickly in hospital settings when a patient is being watched.

A startling number of scars on a patient's body can also indicate that he or she has undergone multiple exploratory surgeries because of vague symptoms. The surgeries may have been performed in response to the patient's expressions of wrenching pain "somewhere" in a region of the body. For instance, Wendy Scott's pain complaints resulted in 42 abdominal operations. It was impossible to tell where scar tissue ended and healthy tissue began: Her abdomen was one colossal scar.

Other overt signs have been discussed elsewhere in this book. Remember that these people have a fascinating knack for being able to divide the staff and create tension and hostility among caregivers. Health care professionals should also remember that these patients usually go to extremes to ensure that they will receive treatment and/ or hospitalization; thus, any exotic case should be carefully reviewed. Hospital, emergency department, or clinic employees may discover concealed syringes or drugs in a patient's room. The medical staff may discover evidence on drug screens of surreptitious use. Other findings that may be seen but do not rise to the level of red flags are a history of drug or alcohol abuse; a background of considerable travel; medical savvy; and a noticeable tendency to try to manipulate others, sometimes including fellow patients. They often show up at emergency rooms late at night or on weekends, when less experienced staff members, including young interns and residents, may be working and when insurance and medical data are more difficult to verify. Other clues to factitious disorders can be even subtler. Intuition stemming from knowledge and experience can be extremely helpful.

Provoking a Response

At times, doctors employ special tests or maneuvers to try actively to separate the medical wheat from the falsified chafe. One example is to obtain continuous and simultaneous videotape and electroencepholographic (EEG) recordings in patients who may or may not have certain neurologic problems. Ailments such as epilepsy have found their way onto the list of diseases of choice for factitious disorder patients because they draw such swift responses from doctors and because signs can sometimes be difficult to prove as fraudulent. False seizures (or *pseudoseizures*), for instance, are often seen in factitious disorder patients, but not all false seizures are factitious. Some patients with genuine epilepsy are chronically concerned about having a sudden epileptic fit and develop pseudoseizures as a result of their anxiety. Others with genuine epilepsy have learned that seizures are a powerful means of eliciting responses from others and enact "seizures" when they are needed. It takes a keen and creative observer to distinguish which seizures are real.

The Case of Julius and Sharon

Julius was a man whose grand mal (or total-body) seizures occurred at seemingly selected times. In addition, his body movements weren't rhythmic, nor were his limbs coordinated, which made his seizures less than convincing. During one of his alleged seizures, I told Julius that if he opened his mouth the seizure would stop. He opened his mouth and the seizure did indeed suddenly end. Had Julius been in the throes of a real seizure, he would never have had such excellent control over his body.

I participated in another technique to unveil Sharon, a patient whom I was quite sure was feigning neurologic illness. Sharon was hospitalized for what appeared to be epilepsy, but the history was highly suggestive of factitious disorder. Her neurologist also believed that she was faking seizures but wanted to be certain. To treat her properly, we felt it was imperative to confirm the authenticity of illness. We told her that, in order to test the intensity of her seizures, we needed to administer a liquid that would precipitate a seizure in a controlled environment. We also assured her that we had another medication available, an antidote. In reality, all we had was a salt water solution that would have no ill effect on her whatsoever—and certainly wouldn't induce a seizure. Sharon readily agreed to let us give her the liquid, and as the saline started flowing into her arm, the neurologist said, "In about five seconds you're probably going to have a seizure." Moments later, her head tipped back and her eyelids started fluttering. She enacted a full-blown seizure. She instantly "came out" of it when we gave her the so-called antidote, which was more saline.

Luther

Luther, the teenager described in chapter 6 who feigned asthma attacks, recounted a similar experience:

I went to see an allergist who gave me a placebo and proved that some of what I had displayed was false. He was a very bright man, but my initial impression of him was that he was a little spacey. So I faked an asthma attack with him. He was a lot better doctor than I gave him credit for. As I was sitting there, wheezing and pulling for air, he gave me a shot and told me that it was adrenaline. I knew that adrenaline should make my symptoms end very quickly, so I very quickly got better. And he said, "Okay, take care, I'll see you in a week." Well, that night I figured the adrenaline should have worn off, so I started wheezing again. My mother paged him at a rock concert, but he called us back and asked to speak to my mother alone. I saw her face drop. She hung up the phone and said to me, "Well, the doctor didn't give you adrenaline, he gave you sugar water." I was livid that I had been duped.

Doctors Employing Tricks of Their Own

Doctors have employed ruses of their own—from the passive withholding of information about a procedure to more active deception—to ensnare patients whom they believed were creating their own illnesses. In one instance, a 23-year-old woman was admitted to a hospital for chronic diarrhea and weight loss, but a resident suspected that she was guilty of a hoax when no cause for her illness could be found. Though she denied using laxatives, the doctor performed a test: he placed sodium hydroxide on a sample of her stool, and the color turned pink. This indicated that she had indeed used the type of laxative found in products like Ex-Lax.

One of the studies ophthalmologists routinely perform when a patient says he or she can't see is to test the *visual fields*. The patient is shown a chart and asked to draw everything he or she can see. The patient is then told to step back and draw the visual field again. Factitious disorder patients mistakenly believe that if they move back, they will be able to see less; therefore, they reproduce less of the chart. In reality, however, if you move back, your vision becomes broader. Doctors also sometimes test people who claim to be blind by throwing a foam ball at their faces without warning. Blinking and protective movements give away sighted people.

Some classic techniques to elicit evidence for medical deception appear in a book by Sir John Colie— enormously valuable today though it was published almost a century ago. Dr. Colie's observations, amassed from the tens of thousands of physical examinations he had performed, still apply to patients in whom the diagnoses of authentic and fabricated illness appear hopelessly intertwined. Some examples from Dr. Colie's "hands-on" practice, which mostly targeted pain and neurologic syndromes:

- Patients claiming to be unable to walk unaided forgetfully leave their crutches or canes behind in the exam room.

- Individuals barely able to move their arms and hands briskly get dressed after the physical.

- Patients' medical signs (e.g., contorted faces with every movement due to excruciating pain) miraculously improve when they are unaware of being observed.

- They may be found in incriminating postures (e.g., tying a shoelace while claiming to have unyielding back pain) if the doctor walks into the room unannounced.

- A nonhealing wound on an arm or leg promptly heals after being placed in a cast that prevents the patient's engaging in medical mischief. Removal of the cast results in recurrence of the wound.

- Patients are unable, with their eyes closed tightly or blindfolded, to point reliably to the sites of greatest pain or, alternatively, trace the area of loss of sensation. These sites and "maps" may vary by many inches as the test is performed several times during the course of the exam.

- A doctor's quick pinch of areas of supposed loss of sensation, performed while the patient is distracted or (in the hospital) asleep, results—inconsistent with the claim—in instant startle or awakening.

- Patients complaining of chest pain may howl when their ribs are directly pushed by the hands of the examiner, but remain undistressed when undergoing a lung or heart exam during which they are pressed just as forcefully by the stethoscope.

- Forcibly moving a painful limb may result in protests, but not the increased heart rate or pupil dilation seem when people are in genuine acute pain.

- With eyes closed or blindfolded, patients unintentionally reveal that they can feel a sensation even when they claim the body part is totally incapable of feeling. For instance, they may promptly answer "no" when asked if they can feel a pinprick or light touch to an area of allegedly lost sensation. If they truly had no sensation, they wouldn't even have known that the stimulus had been applied when it was; they would have said nothing. Thus, they betray their true capacity to feel.

Such procedures and observations, ignoble though they may seem, can neatly demonstrate that a sign or symptom is at least partially psychological. Still, they do not necessarily indicate whether the initiation of the symptom is conscious (factitious or malingered) or unconscious (conversion disorder).

Unmasking Factitious Psychological Disorders

Subtle calls are almost always required when diagnosing factitious disorder with psychological symptoms. A tip-off occurs, however, when the patient's overall clinical appearance is uncharacteristic of any recognized mental disorder, and psychological tests (which are often refused) reflect a layman's concept of a mental illness as opposed to consistent evidence for a specific disorder. Doctors must also watch for approximate, vague, overemphatic, or random answers. When attempting to assess the legitimacy of a given case of multiple personality disorder (MPD), doctors should be mindful that fakers have difficulty maintaining different personalities over time, often confusing or forgetting details and characteristics. Patients who are suffering from true MPD also tend to downplay the disorder, whereas people who fake this mental illness tend to dramatize it. Factitious disorder patients with psychological symptoms may fail to respond to medications that would have been expected to help in genuine illness or they may show improvement with medications not expected to be beneficial. The red flags listed above apply in factitious psychological cases as they do in physical ones.

In sum, a host of challenges is associated with detecting and diagnosing factitious disorder, not the least of which is the cleverness these patients display in creating and mimicking symptoms. However, medical knowledge, when properly applied, can prevail most of the time in detecting disease forgery and making the appropriate diagnosis.

16

Healing:
Intervention and Treatment

For reasons explained in the Foreword, professionals willing to try to assist have had to rely not on a rich, solid research base, but on instinct and the limited anecdotal data in published accounts. Only rarely will they have accumulated relevant patient experiences to shape their treatment approaches when these desperate patients or families finally reach out for help. Revealing the suspicion and diagnosis of factitious disorder, Munchausen syndrome, and malingering involves a number of complex considerations. This chapter weighs the approaches of hard-hitting confrontation, supportive confrontation, and indirect suggestion. Several case studies of patients who successfully recovered from factitious disorder and Munchausen syndrome are presented, including the case of Wendy Scott, whose own recovery was triggered by the adoption of a kitten. This chapter also looks at the controversy of whether factitious behavior is a compulsion or an addiction and how 12-step programs can fit into the treatment plan.

Immediate gratification. Control over life. An abundance of warmth and nurturance from loving, caring people. These are the goals of men and women who are plagued by factitious disorder. Simply put, factitious disorder patients want nothing more than the rest of us. The problem for factitious disorder patients is that they don't know how to achieve these ends in healthy, socially acceptable ways.

Thus, they find themselves on urgent quests which become bizarre and convoluted and usually end up causing physical harm to themselves and emotional travails for their caregivers and loved ones.

To Confront or Not to Confront?

Revealing the suspicions and diagnosis of factitious disorder is unlike any other revelation that can occur between a physician and patient. How this information is presented to the factitious disorder patient is crucial. It is the pivotal point when a patient either denies the statement and recoils or concedes and possibly accepts treatment. The clinician has a number of choices in how to handle confrontation. The approach can be harsh and direct, gentle and persuasive, or so subtle that the patient's perceived control is never threatened. Ideally, a treatment team will be in place to decide together which method is likely to achieve the best results, taking into account risk factors such as patient flight and escalation of behaviors. In reality, the choice often reflects the clinician's beliefs about and attitudes toward factitious disorder patients.

The Hard-Hitting Approach

Some doctors advocate a strong confrontational approach. This approach essentially entails telling patients that the curtain has come crashing down on their acts and everybody now sees through the disguise. It may involve displaying illicit syringes or medications that have been discovered by the staff, brandishing lab reports with discrepant or medically impossible findings, and/or presenting exhibits similar to those a prosecutor might show a jury to discredit and incriminate a person on trial. Physicians who use this method may be subtly sarcastic, if not openly irked, during such no-holds-barred confrontations. Indeed, animosity toward the betraying patient usually plays a role in their selecting this unquestionably direct approach.

In a review of 12 patients with self-induced infections who had been directly confronted by their physicians, only one patient admitted to the factitious disorder. However, five of the other 11 patients stopped producing their symptoms even while denying their involvement in them, and two of these five had not repeated their factitious behavior after two years (Researchers could not keep track of the others.). These findings are encouraging, but they run counter to a host of other papers and my own experience, which suggest that highly confrontational approaches lead patients to move on to new medical audiences and ply ruses for which they have greater talent. They also learn not to commit the same mistakes made so evident through the hard-hitting approach.

Supportive Confrontation

Physicians who consider factitious disorder to be a protective defense find great merit in a *supportive or therapeutic confrontation*, in which the primary physician and a consulting psychiatrist approach the patient in a non-condemning but firm manner. At the same time, they convey a wish to help and extend an offer of psychiatric treatment and ongoing medical evaluation that might include hospitalization. The psychiatrist can also assist the members of the professional staff, who may be outraged, by explaining the nature of the disorder and the psychopathology involved.

A typical supportive confrontation might involve a caregiver's saying, "We have discovered that you do indeed have a serious problem. However, it isn't the medical problem you wanted us to believe you had. Instead, we now realize that your primary problem is an emotional one, because you must have been very distressed to go so far as to fake or produce your medical ailments. For this type of problem, we recommend that you get help from the psychiatrist who is here and who has the skills to help you deal with emotional matters." In this way, doctors attempt to renegotiate the therapeutic contract and redefine the diagnosis rather than simply expose, embarrass, or get rid of the patient.

Sadly, even in a supportive confrontation, the patient will typically say, "Doctors, you're crazy. I don't know what you're talking about, and if you continue to talk this way I'm going to sue you." If the impasse can't be broken, the primary care physician must be prepared to say, "I cannot be forced to commit malpractice by pursuing tests and treatment which are not medically sound. Therefore, I am letting you know that, effective in 30 days, I can no longer be your doctor." In short, the doctor explicitly recognizes the limits of his or her authority over the patient and the primary Hippocratic dictum "Do no harm." The physician should send the patient a certified letter (or have one hand-delivered with receipt), restating this information and offering recommendations for follow-up treatment and potential providers of that care. The door should always be left open in case the patient changes his or her mind and chooses to accept the physician's treatment recommendations.

I will illustrate supportive confrontation with a case especially close to my heart because it occurred early in my career.

Colleen's Story

Colleen was unremarkable in every way. Her quiet and unassuming presence made her all but invisible to the people she saw every day. She was a secretary for a manufacturing firm, and had earned a reputation for being dependable and efficient even if she wasn't ambitious. These characteristics contributed to her unassuming presence. She hadn't developed strong personal relationships at work, but 35-year-old Colleen didn't seem to miss that kind of camaraderie, looking instead to her after-five existence for comfort, companionship, and security. She lived with the man to whom she had been engaged for more than a year, had a small circle of casual friends, and periodically saw her mother, who lived in the same Western city. Week in and week out, Colleen's world seemed never to change, until one day it suddenly, quietly, fell apart.

Without any warnings that had been evident to Colleen, her fiancé announced that he was breaking their engagement. She needn't grope for solutions, he told her. The relationship was over and Colleen would have to move out of his apartment.

Colleen reeled from the prospect of having to live without this man. She blamed herself for the breakup even though she didn't know what she had done to cause it. Bewildered, Colleen surrendered the relationship amidst tears and pleas for answers, but without a fight. With nowhere else to turn, she went to live with her mother, a workaholic elementary school teacher whose prescription for coping was "keep busy."

After months of functioning under intense emotional strain, Colleen went to work one day and confessed to everyone there, "I have terminal breast cancer." She discovered that the lie had extraordinary power. In telling it, she became an instant "Somebody," the object of sympathy and attention from people who never noticed her before. Suddenly co-workers became best friends. Everyone rallied to her support. People were willing to change their own lifestyles to accommodate Colleen. They offered to include her in car pools to cut down on the amount of traveling she had to do, and to share her work load, even though that meant that they might have to work overtime without compensation. But Colleen declined their offers, saying that she wanted to carry on as she had before in spite of her illness. Her co-workers were moved by her spirit.

Colleen was rewarded with the kind of nurturance and support she had been craving. She had watched a neighbor suffer and die of breast cancer and knew how a woman would look as the disease progressed. Gradually, she, too, lost her hair. She seemed to lose any incentive to wear makeup that would help to hide her haggard appearance, and her already slight figure reflected drastic weight loss.

As her hair disappeared (and was later replaced by a wig), as she lost 50 pounds and looked more gaunt and pale each day, Colleen's life was, ironically, transformed into that of someone "special." Emotionally she was finally fulfilled.

Several months after breaking the news about her illness at work, Colleen enrolled in a weekly hospital support group for women with breast cancer. She became a diligent member, never missing an opportunity to be with the caring group of cancer victims and the social support team from the local cancer center. The complaints and tribulations of the other women in the group mirrored Colleen's own descriptions, appearance, and worries.

Although some people wondered about Colleen's ability to report to work every day, there was surprisingly little questioning from her co-workers and supervisors, despite her failure to file insurance claims. It wasn't until her support group leaders tried to gain more information about her medical status that suspicions arose.

Colleen provided the group's leaders with the names of doctors who had treated her, but it seemed that she was sending them on one wild goose chase after another. After chasing Colleen's dead ends, the group's leaders became convinced that she was lying.

I first became involved when the leaders called me and let the whole story come spilling out. I knew relatively little about factitious disorder in those days, but shared the knowledge I did have. I told them to avoid being harsh or judgmental, but still to maintain their position and to beware of the denials that Colleen would surely issue. I advised them to let her know that she was not somehow "in trouble" and that there was immediate help for her if she would accept it. I agreed to make myself available to treat Colleen, never guessing that the chance to work with her and learn from her other caregivers would determine the course of my research and writing interests. Colleen's initial reaction to the confrontation was the same as most sufferers of factitious disorder when they are discovered: She vociferously denied having lied about anything. The group's leaders used a highly supportive confrontational approach, remaining firm but compassionate and assuring Colleen that she would not be abandoned. Colleen collapsed into a chair, admitting to her ruse in a flood of tears.

The counselors assured her that now that the truth was known, help for her emotional problems was available, and they recommended that she accept psychiatric counseling. Before the episode was over, Colleen made two enormous promises. First, she agreed to see me. Second, she promised to tell others that she had concocted the entire story and, when she lived up to that second promise, she felt the repercussions of her actions. Colleen sheepishly returned to work and confided in her supervisor, a no-nonsense woman who had lightened Colleen's work load because of her "illness." The supervisor was enraged by Colleen's tearful confession. She chastised her for all the pain and anguish she had caused her co-workers. As word of Colleen's ruse became general knowledge at the office, many of Colleen's co-workers wanted more information about her, contacting me themselves. When I refused to violate my patient's confidentiality, some took their anger out on me, demanding that Colleen be given no consideration in view of what she had done. They felt she should be punished in some way for her deeds.

When Colleen came to see me, she was teary, sad, and remorseful. But I didn't know if her sorrow was over her having feigned the cancer, or if it reflected a deep depression that had led her to behave in such a desperate way. There are certain signs exhibited by people suffering from depression and Colleen was exhibiting many of them: a sad mood, lack of energy, an inability to concentrate. She wasn't sleeping, was feeling helpless, and obviously wasn't eating well.

Part of Colleen's fantasy surrounding her cancer portrayal was that her ex-fiancé would hear about her "illness" and rush to be with her. But they ran in such different circles after they broke up that he never even knew she was carrying out the deception. He had chosen to make a very clean break and move on with his life, while Colleen remained devastated by the separation.

After spending time with Colleen, I knew that she had to be treated for depression. I came to realize that Colleen had feigned cancer in order to feel in control. For some patients factitious disorder becomes an elaborate form of denial, a way of avoiding painful emotions by focusing their attention on their bodies; they also avoid others' sympathy for the emotional trauma because it would be too hard to accept it and still move on. I thought that with her sources of support suddenly gone, Colleen was potentially suicidal, so I suggested hospitalization and she agreed to it.

I worked from the premise that Colleen also had a personality disorder that prevented her from having adequate coping skills and a clear-cut image of who she was. Colleen responded surprisingly quickly to medication for her depression, while continuing to address the factitious disorder in therapy. Colleen also received self-relaxation training from a psychologist that I believe hastened her progress. The psychologist tried to teach her to relax as part of her becoming more self-reliant. These were skills she could utilize whenever anxiety and pressure built up, instead of resorting to drastic measures to deal with stress.

Colleen reached a major turning point in her recovery when she was able to talk with other patients and hospital staff about her ruse and found them open-minded and accepting. As part of Colleen's treatment, I asked her to call her father, who was divorced from her mother and living in New Mexico, and tell him about her illness. She thought that he was going to be hostile and punitive but instead he wanted to know how he could help her.

Colleen agreed that it was important to talk about her behavior and share her feelings with her father. In a series of visits facilitated by the ward social worker, he visited her in the hospital and his presence and keen interest in her condition implied that a support network was going to be in place for Colleen after her hospitalization. That likely support improved her prognosis remarkably. It was important that she not have to go it alone.

Although antidepressant drugs can take as long as eight weeks to make a significant difference in a patient's condition, Colleen showed marked improvement after only three weeks. When Colleen turned the corner, she turned it at a 180 degree angle and was doing 90 miles an hour in the opposite direction. I think the key was a combination of the medication and behavior therapy, plus the nonjudgmental, caring way in which she was treated by the skilled hospital staff and by her father. I have never felt as confident about a factitious disorder patient's recovery as I did about hers.

As Colleen's case demonstrates, the psychiatric examination following therapeutic confrontation should be non-accusatory and impartial. The physician or other caregivers should remember that discovery has already weakened the patient's defenses and he or she may act rashly to preserve what little is left of the façade. If a clinician can approach the patient in a supportive fashion, he or she will to some degree obviate the need for the symptoms to recur. These are such fragile people that they will accept concern from almost wherever it comes, and it is an advantage if it can come from within the confines of a therapy session.

Non-Confrontation: Saving Face

Face-saving techniques have been advocated by experts such as Stuart J. Eisendrath, M.D., and have shown very promising results. Here, the patient is given the gentle, even subconscious message that the doctors are wise to the deceptions, but given the chance to abandon the factitious behavior without any confrontation at all. In short, the patient is allowed to save face in front of the doctor. The patient might be told that, "If the next treatment fails to work [and the treatment may be almost anything at all], we're going to be forced to conclude that you are the source of your own illnesses." The treatment (e.g., fake hypnosis, massage, or a benign, mild medication) is then applied, and a surprising number of patients will undergo miraculous improvement—rather than being exposed as frauds. In one case, a woman feigning deafness began to report normal hearing following the face-saving maneuver of being given a "new and better" hearing aid (one that was actually equivalent to the old one). Its power was doubtless enhanced by its being presented at an impressive, internationally known facility for the deaf, where the patient had managed to get herself admitted.

In another face-saving variant, the doctor makes up a baseless but scientific-sounding explanation for the patient's behaviors. The doctor tells the patient "Now that we understand the psychological conflicts that led to your medical problems, your problems will disappear and your health will be restored." The patient is eager to convince the doctor that her medical problems were real. Confronted by the doctor's insistence that the problems will vanish now that the cause is known, the patient must abandon her factitious behavior in order to remain credible.

These techniques may spawn a type of *placebo effect* even for the most refractory of factitious disorder patients. For instance, doctors spoke with a patient who had been secretly taking a medication that lowers blood sugar, but she offered an emphatic, hostile denial. To avoid antagonizing her further, the doctors said, "You know, you must have been taking it in your sleep." She replied, "I guess *that* was the explanation for it." Afterwards, her behavior changed and she no longer took the medication.

A further example of non-confrontation—one that nevertheless involved *aversive therapy*, or the administration of a noxious stimulus, which is a technique no longer allowed in most clinics and hospitals—is provided in the following case. This patient's fraudulent illness involved paraplegia. Treatment included a physiotherapy machine that utilized electrical current to deliver a painful massage. The discomfort was intended to convince the patient that she was receiving powerful treatments for her useless legs, ones that would "increase circulation and stimulate nerve endings." The machine turned the skin a rosy hue, which was pointed out to the patient as a sign that it was working and that recovery was possible. The patient was told, however, that if goals weren't reached, the massage would be extended by one minute. Conversely, the treatments would end as soon as she recovered function of her limbs. The patient's caregivers, Carol and Leslie Solyom, noted that their strategy was simple: They told the patient that they had accepted her illness and were going to treat her for it. After the first painful "treatment session," the patient was advised that the second session would occur the next day. Three hours later, she was walking! This patient remained in follow-up care for one-and-a-half years and, though she tried to be rehospitalized, her efforts were rebuffed. The Solyoms wrote, "There are people whose vitality thrives on untruthfulness both towards themselves and the world at large. We must, therefore, consider all the more carefully what cure means and what the limits of psychotherapeutic effort are."

One research report found that, after such non-confrontations, roughly one-third of the patients ended their hoaxes. They may have vigorously denied what they were doing, but, if the doctors somehow allowed them to save face, the behavior stopped, at least for a period of time. The embarrassment of discovery was avoided in this substantial minority of patients.

Acceptance of Treatment

Even if patients admit to some or all of the deceptions, most will continue to engage in them. Clinicians will then have to recognize the difficulty in motivating them to accept mental health interventions. Referring to therapy as "stress management" or "tightening the mind's control over the body" may help ease patients into the mental health system. If a patient does agree to treatment, it must begin with the gradual development of the *therapist-patient alliance.* Through this consistent relationship, patients ideally learn that they don't need to use ostensive illness to elicit interest from others. Rather, they are now guaranteed a time and place when they can meet with a health care professional about matters important to them. They generally meet with their mental health clinician (typically a psychiatrist or psychologist) once or twice a week. In addition, one primary care physician should meet with and briefly examine the patient every three to six weeks for an indefinite period of time so that medical contacts are not contingent on the enactment or induction of illness.

When therapists consider the precise course of action to take when patients are willing to enter into therapy, they must consider how long the patient has been feigning illness, the nature of any early disturbances in personality development, and any crises that sparked the factitious symptoms. All weigh heavily in choosing the type of treatment and determining the patient's prognosis. Therapy generally involves exploration of alternative activities such as hobbies and other sources of accomplishment for which the person would be praised. Active discussion about the life problems that seem to precipitate factitious behaviors, such as conflict with other people, can further raise the threshold for renewed factitious behavior. Education regarding the connection between mental and physical well-being has proved beneficial for patients who will accept it. In addition, every individual has a "story," a way of defining oneself that is acceptable and appealing to others. For the factitious disorder patient, dramatic, intractable illnesses have become the story, with the individual's playing the role of brave or needy patient. The patient can be helped to understand that psychotherapy in all its forms will help him or her rewrite the story in a positive and healthy way.

The Benefits of Many Minds

Understanding that factitious disorder often serves the important function of providing self-esteem for individuals who otherwise have quite negative views of themselves may help clinicians to intervene with these challenging, often disquieting patients. The urge to resort to factitious disorder symptoms in times of stress means that more aggressive treatment is needed for some period of time. As I have suggested, ultimately these patients may abandon the sick role only when they have constructed alternative, healthier self-definitions.

All professionals involved in the patient's care should communicate clearly and regularly with one another. As illustrated in the case of Colleen, there is no substitute for the mélange of professionals from multiple disciplines bringing their own expertise to bear. In addition, this kind of partnering can counter the feelings of isolation, powerlessness, pervasive distrust, or therapeutic nihilism that regularly arise in work with factitious disorder, and especially Munchausen syndrome, patients. The ailments these patients have feigned or produced baffle the imagination, and I will again show the benefits of a multidisciplinary approach by considering an astonishing case involving feigned quadriplegia.

Sarah's History

Ten years after our medical school graduation, I heard from a talented classmate now practicing family medicine far away in Oregon. He knew of my interest in Munchausen syndrome, and called to discuss the fact that the diagnosis seemed to apply to his most mystifying patient. Hearing the story of this patient, a 24-year-old woman, I could confirm his suspicions and assist in establishing a plan of treatment.

The patient, Sarah, first went to my former classmate for treatment of a chronic cough. She described herself as a quadriplegic and used a motorized wheelchair. Her limbs were withered and her hands were frozen in position, but she retained enough movement of her arms to operate the wheelchair and take care of her basic needs. Sarah attributed her quadriplegia to a motor-vehicle accident at age 13. She had undergone a series of complex surgical procedures and had both a colostomy and urostomy due to dysfunction of her colon and bladder.

The cough resolved, but Sarah returned a year later with the main complaint of vomiting. Dietary changes didn't help, and after weeks of doctor's visits she was still malnourished and dehydrated. She was hospitalized, her condition stabilized, and a feeding tube placed. After discharge, however, frequent outpatient appointments continued as Sarah indicated that the feeding tube kept falling out. A new tube was placed surgically to ensure it would stay in place, but surprisingly, she stated that she was still vomiting feedings placed directly into her intestines. Plans were made to color the feedings to determine whether she was indeed vomiting such deeply placed nutrition, but when her physicians arrived in her hospital room to perform this test, Sarah pointed out that the tube had somehow "fallen out."

Sarah was next placed on nourishment through an intravenous tube running under her skin. A series of readmissions ensued, however, for infections of the tubing caused by bacteria typically found in fecal material. It was during this period that a nurse recognized Sarah and recalled having taken care of her after the car accident years earlier. The nurse remembered clearly that Sarah had been walking following the trauma and had had no lingering physical damage at discharge. For the first time, the diagnosis of Munchausen syndrome was considered.

Sarah was not confronted with this suspicion. Instead, she underwent extensive neurologic testing that affirmed that her spinal cord was intact and her arms and legs should have been functioning normally. In other words, her medical history and current appearance—taken on faith, as in most physician-patient interactions—was a fabrication. Her incapacity was willful, but had been so sustained that she had indeed lost much of her muscle mass through inactivity. She had also taken every opportunity to undermine her treatment through mechanisms such as removing or contaminating her tubing.

After talking with me, my classmate finally confronted her with the ruses, albeit in a kind and caring way, and in the presence of a psychologist. He did insist on permission to speak with her parents as a mandatory component of effective medical care, and it was finally granted. Sarah cautioned, however, that though her parents wanted nothing to do with her, they would deceive the staff into believing that they were supportive.

Sarah cancelled several proposed family meetings, but eventually a family session took place. Her parents welcomed the opportunity to meet, stating that they had always felt badly that Sarah discouraged their involvement. She had gone so far as to demand that they not visit her in the hospital; when they did nonetheless, she insisted that they leave before her physicians arrived. The parents confirmed that Sarah was physically normal following her accident, even playing high school sports. Only in her senior year, as she was preparing for college, did she begin to develop neurologic problems that defied attempts at diagnosis. Her incapacity progressed until she was no longer able to walk and became wheelchair-bound.

Sarah admitted that she had been told in the past that she needed psychiatric care, since there was nothing physically wrong with her. However, she was able to obtain care from new physicians, leading to the multiple surgical procedures. Confronted in the context of the family meeting, Sarah acknowledged that perhaps she had never had any physical pathology. She proposed that perhaps she had "acted quadriplegic" because her doctors had told her she was quadriplegic, a classic effort at saving face.

After the meeting, a team was formed that consisted of the patient's doctors, occupational therapist, physical therapist, and social worker, as well as a psychiatric nurse. The team met regularly and made it clear to Sarah from the start that the goals for her were nothing short of full recovery. Within this firm and expectant approach, she was discharged with follow-up physical and occupational therapy, psychological counseling, and regular medical assessment.

When I last heard about Sarah, she was in a manual wheelchair that she propelled herself. She could walk with leg braces and a cane. She was eating adequately, gaining weight, and required no further hospitalizations. She had briefly gone skiing using specialized sports equipment. Most importantly, she accepted the psychiatric nature of her illness and remained committed to full recovery.

Overall, Sarah's dramatic case of feigned quadriplegia illustrates the intensity of the psychological factors often underlying factitious disorder. She consciously sought two of the main elements of the sick role: the attention and concern of skilled medical professionals, and relief from life's responsibilities and expectations, such as establishing autonomy. Her case also shows that effective management of factitious disorder is contingent on each clinician's acting in tandem with the other members of the treatment team. Such coordination increases the chance that suspicions will be confirmed or disproved in an efficient way and that, as in this case, intervention will be successful.

Combining Treatments

Multimodal treatments, such as the approach utilized with Sara, have proved invaluable in many other cases. For example, researchers reported a case in the *International Journal of Psychiatry in Medicine* in which a 29-year-old woman was admitted to an intensive care unit for paralysis in her left arm and both legs. She had been diagnosed three years earlier as having multiple sclerosis and epilepsy. Watchful nurses noticed that her seizures increased in frequency when she was angry with hospital workers or with her parents. They also detected movements in her "paralyzed" arm. A psychiatric consultation, interviews with her parents, and a review of her records disclosed that, from the time she was a little girl, she dreamed of becoming a doctor. During her high school years, she began visits to doctors for vague complaints and when, as a college senior, she was rejected by every medical school to which she applied, her neurologic complaints began. Frequent hospitalizations characterized her life, and she once spent eight months in a rehabilitation hospital, where she was suspected of feigning illness. Factitious disorder was confirmed when she had a convulsion during a brain-wave tracing but the reading on the test didn't change as it would have during a genuine seizure.

Once she agreed to treatment, her therapeutic team devised a treatment plan and set goals which included increasing her sense of control and self-esteem; helping her to build better relationships; and promoting interests that were appropriate for her age. Treatment included co-therapy by two psychologists; biofeedback that was used to monitor tiny changes in muscle tension in her "paralyzed" arms and legs; and behavioral-conditioning procedures, such as telling her family to flatly ignore her "seizures." The woman was seen weekly for nine months and monthly for the following six. During that time, her most serious symptoms—such as paralysis, seizures, respiratory arrest, and loss of bladder control—almost disappeared; the number of days she spent hospitalized decreased; she entered a college that offered degrees in health professions; and she began to function socially in ways that suited her age.

Controversy: Is Factitious Disorder an Addiction or Compulsion?

Many factitious disorder and Munchausen syndrome patients persuasively describe their behavior as seemingly irresistible—in short, as *compulsive* or *addictive*. Patients often describe the powerful "high" or feeling of exquisite release and relief associated with successful deceit. Patients so affected state that they don't want to lie but can't seem to stop, even when the lying is ruining their lives. The medicines effective in obsessive-compulsive disorder and in some forms of addiction may prove to be useful, though research in this area is nascent.

Family members and others need to recognize their own roles in enabling the ongoing deceptions. The co-dependent provision of money without any accountability on the part of the patient is illustrated in the example that follows. *Enabling* and *co-dependency* are classic behaviors among the family members and friends of alcoholics and addicts, as they unwittingly abet the substance abuse through their tacit acquiescence. The terms seem as if they were invented for this case of Munchausen syndrome, which involved drug abuse as well.

Terrence's Ruse

Thirty-year-old Terrence had sustained the story for 5 years that he had cancer dotted by remissions and inevitable recurrences, side effects from chemotherapy, and the onset of unrelated medical problems to add to his woe. In doing so, Terrence exacted over $200,000 from his parents who, fearing their son's rejection, turned a deaf ear and blind eye to even the most transparent of Terrence's lies. They expected no accountability for the vast amounts of money they shoveled in Terrence's direction and they never spoke with even one billing department of a health provider supposedly responsible for Terrence's care. In reality, Terrence used the money on recreational drugs and on get-aways in which he took groups of friends to the fanciest restaurants and hotels in Manhattan, painting the town red as they watched Broadway shows from their front-row seats. The possibility of retirement for Terrence's aging parents had evaporated now that they had taken out three mortgages on their home. As they wrote,

Terrence has now informed us that everything was a lie. He
had told us he was dying from renal cell carcinoma. He had
told us that he had 6 months to live. He asked us not to get
involved with the doctors or the hospitals because he had
already lost control of his life. We respected his privacy. But
we know now that he never received treatments or had surgery of any kind. At the same time, he was telling others that
his mother was in a coma or had died, which is false. He told
us he was involved in clinical trials at Chicago, Sloan-Kettering, and Mayo Clinic, all lies. He told us of multiple surgeries
including partial lung removal, partial stomach removal, a
colostomy, the loss of both testes, etc.–false. His trips to
Sloan-Kettering were to see Broadway plays, not for surgery
or treatment. We spent a healthy sum of money buying him
canes, crutches, leg braces, walkers, wrist bandages, arm
slings, special walking shoes, and scarves to cover his bald-
ness none of which was needed. We become his constant
source of "props." We don't know where to go from here.

When they flew cross-country to meet with me, I provided education and counseling. I strongly advised them to end the focus on Ter-
rance's demands—through a complete severing of the relationship, if
necessary—and explicitly recognize his lies for what they were. They
needed to accept that they might be rejected by their son in turn, but
there was no healthier alternative. They needed liberally to use the
word "no," a concept that had been unthinkable to them. I have not
had contact with them since then.

The parallels with addiction can be found in the benefit some factitious disorder patients have found in 12-step programs such as Alcoholics Anonymous. Several patients, by themselves, have tailored and
"worked" programs to overcome factitious disorder (Factitious Anonymous and Munchausen Anonymous do not yet exist). Those who
also have substance addictions may find that attendance at Alcoholics
Anonymous, Narcotics Anonymous, or Cocaine Anonymous has a
secondary beneficial effect on their factitious disorder. Luther, the
teen who feigned asthma aboard an airplane, has been in recovery
from his factitious illness behaviors for over 5 years. He found a combination of a self-taught 12-step program, an antidepressant, psychotherapy, and ongoing attendance at Narcotics Anonymous to be the
key to unlocking his door to fulfillment. He is now a respected leader

in his community. Another patient whom I came to know especially well wrote about her recovery that, though tenuous, continues to hold.

Taesha's Perspective

I have had so much more control over my desire for attention since I started going to Alcoholics Anonymous. There is a destructive pattern repeating all through my life: anorexia, bulimia, injuring myself with knives or blades. Even a time when I simply couldn't find enough men to sleep with. It was debasing and it made me feel ugly inside and out, but each time a man left me I wanted to get another one because I was so desperate for attention. I never used alcohol destructively before I was forty, and then I quickly became dependent on it. Curiously, it was alcohol that saved me: My intoxication was so obvious to everyone and there was an answer at street level.

Taesha found that the support of Alcoholics Anonymous supplanted her need to continue her factitious disorder though, like her craving for alcohol, the impulse to feign or self-induce illness always lurks. For many patients, factitious disorder mirrors addiction in that recovery will be a lifelong process and continuing support will be needed to prevent relapsing into old behaviors.

Others have formed support groups over the telephone or Internet. Indeed, at http://groups.yahoo.com, there are several online support groups for people with factitious disorder and Munchausen syndrome, and there are still others for those who have been duped in ways small and large. Also, many patients find solace and improvement in directly e-mailing individuals who are in recovery from factitious disorder or Munchausen syndrome.

Although it remains largely untested, an *intervention* (another term used in addiction treatment) may be valuable. In the context of factitious disorder, it means that those who love and support the patient, but will not abide his or her continuing the ruses, meet ahead of time—sometimes in the presence of a therapist—to plan when, where, and how they are going to confront the patient. Those family members and/or friends who are ambivalent or enabling are left out. One technique is for everyone first to compile, in writing, evidence that the patient is faking. Then, the group must decide on the consequences if he or she doesn't submit to the plan of action. The plan might entail inpatient psychiatric treatment (for this reason, it is good to have an admitting psychiatrist identified ahead of time) and/or outpatient treatment. There might include a demand from the team that the patient write corrective letters to those who have been misled, that he or she meet immediately with selected individuals to tell them the truth, and that the patient do whatever else is relevant in the particular case. Someone then arranges for the patient to be at a given place at a given time, without letting on that the reason is an intervention.

During the meeting, the patient is confronted with the evidence and the consequences of the lies. If he or she refuses to continue the meeting or abide by any of the rules the rest of the group has set, the consequences are enforced. In some cases, it might mean curtailing or ending financial support or establishing a date by which he or she must find alternate housing. All involved must be aware, however, that factitious disorder patients may escalate their behavior, and threatened, attempted, or completed suicide is possible. For that reason, if hospitalization doesn't occur, the patient may need continual observation until the members of the intervention team believe he or she is safe.

The intervention itself can be stated in a face-saving way. For instance, the patient might be told that the group has accumulated incontrovertible evidence that he or she is not sick, but that he or she may have misunderstood a doctor or overinterpreted some normal physical sensations, ending up on a misguided path.

Caring for Caregivers

Therapy should not be reserved only for factitious disorder patients. Professional caregivers who have been caught up in the patient's web of deception may also need therapeutic support. To this end, a mental health consultant can offer assistance to the staff while the patient is still on the ward or in the emergency department—and long after he or she has left. Even if a patient entirely refuses therapy, a mental health consultant still has a role to play with the staff. As described, professionals commonly feel some anger, betrayal, and even contempt toward these patients. The staff has to be shown how to manage those feelings so that they don't get in the way of patient care. Offering staff education and support is critical both during and after an encounter with a factitious disorder patient. Everyone must be given an opportunity to discuss the emotions that are evoked. Because the nursing staff spends so much time with patients, they are especially vulnerable. Some hospitals offer group therapy and support sessions for anyone who has been involved with such challenging patients.

Authors of articles in the *Journal of Psychosocial Nursing and Mental Health Services* and *Critical Care Nurse* recognized the special role that nurses play and offered guidelines to help them manage factitious disorder patients. They advised avoiding any display of hostile or rejecting behavior; demonstrating that one can be aware of the deception without rejecting the patient; ensuring that expectations of the patient are realistic; providing an interdisciplinary approach to care; guarding against being overly fascinated by the patient or the syndrome; and being sure to support suspicions with facts. Nurses, like other health care providers, should be taught about factitious disorder from early on. This early education will not only help them when dealing with such patients, but may help them avoid becoming one of them, since nurses are at slightly increased risk. Nursing programs have come to realize these facts and to understand that nurses—like all professionals—need social support and programs that quietly fulfill their emotional needs.

Understanding Treatment: These are Patients AND Pretenders

Factitious disorder patients lose sight of what they are doing to their bodies and to those who care about them. They are fully aware of their actions, but they feel they must continue on this path. Their needs become the driving forces in their lives, overshadowing all they do. Everything and everyone else becomes secondary.

Friends, family members, and co-workers are suspended in a psychological twilight zone: unable to help the factitious disorder patient change his or her ways, and equally unable to reconcile their disenfranchised grief. As I have pointed out, families and friends pay an immense emotional toll when they find out that their personal sacrifice to help another person has been directed toward someone who has been feigning. How does a school superintendent explain to an assembly of students that a beloved teacher with cystic fibrosis was faking—a teacher to whom they had dedicated their basketball season and generously taken up donations. This very dilemma was posed to me at the beginning of my foray into the strange world of factitious disorder.

Factitious disorder becomes a lopsided game of chess in which the factitious disorder patient dictates the moves of the other players. Still, despite this illusion of mastery and control, there is no alternative but to view these great pretenders as real, not false, patients. Despite the cries of waste and repulsion by the medical community, humanity must prevail. As socially and medically unacceptable as their actions often are, factitious disorder patients deserve an opportunity to receive psychiatric treatment, even if it is ultimately rejected. I am aware of many spectacular success stories, even from individuals such as Roberta and Winona (below) whom most psychiatrists would undoubtedly have dismissed as untreatable.

Roberta's Advice

As a person who has essentially recovered from Munchausen syndrome, I feel a need to set out some guidelines and make some suggestions for those who are trying to help me and others recover. The availability of psychiatrists who will even attempt to treat me is severely lacking, mostly due to their belief that I am untreatable. I have made great strides towards complete recovery through a combination of my own self-help methods and limited psychiatric care.

First and foremost, I would like to emphasize that this illness is treatable. Patients need to try psychotherapy, approaching it with a positive attitude. Any therapy for factitious disorder that is determined at the outset to fail, will fail. The therapist must believe in the ability of the patient to recover. Too many times I have met with a psychiatrist who, from the beginning takes the attitude that treatment is doomed and recommends only maintenance support "therapy." Under the care of a psychiatrist who believes enthusiastically in a positive outcome, the patient can strive more easily towards that goal. I am living proof that chronic severe Munchausen syndrome can be treated and full recovery is not so unbelievable.

The factitious disorder patient has used these symptoms maladaptively to meet specific needs that are otherwise unmet in daily life. The focus for recovery, therefore, should be on developing ways for the patient to meet these needs in more appropriate ways. Because of the nature of the disorder, many of the needs initially will be met within the relationship with the therapist.

Hard-hearted (even hostile) confrontation has no place in this safe, somewhat nurturing therapy environment. Real and factitious symptoms should be acknowledged and treated. There should be a good working relationship with the patient's primary physician to enable physical complaints to be taken seriously there too, always under the understanding that they could be factitious so as to avoid harmful and unnecessary medical interventions. I highly recommend to patients that they have regular appointments with both the primary physician and the psychiatrist whether the patient has any medical complaints or not. This helps to alleviate feelings of abandonment and provides the contact with doctors that the patient craves without the need for a crisis to be created. This feeling of being safe and secure in a relationship with someone is the main key to success. That need being met regularly allows for the patient to focus on other aspects of their life that don't revolve around illness and the seeking out of nurturance.

It took me a long time in psychotherapy before I truly believed that I had a real illness and that I actually was a psychiatric patient, not just pretending. This behavior is like an addiction and the goals for behavior change should be small at first and perhaps one day at a time for the rest of the patient's life. Relapses should be expected. It is counterproductive to contract with the patient that, upon a relapse, therapy will be discontinued, and yet this happens all the time. The patient, still unable to completely control his behavior, is fearful that he will again fail and be abandoned. These are real crises, just disguised as something else. It is part of the therapist's job to see through the factitious behavior and try to understand the motivations for it. If the relationship is well-established, confrontation is very appropriate and useful. The relapse can be used effectively as a tool for further learning the motivations and needs met by the factitious behavior. If the patient feels he must hide his relapses from the therapist to protect himself from being rejected, then therapeutic benefit will halt.

Winona's Experience

I failed with numerous psychiatrists because they all forced contracts on me whereby any lapse back into factitious disorder led to their ending my treatment. These bad experiences left me deeply depressed, hopeless, and out of control. Every rejection by a health care professional led to a flurry of factitious activity. I would fake things intensely for about three weeks, going to as many as ten different hospitals and then do nothing but try to pick up the pieces of my normal life for the next three to four months. Often I got fired from my job even though when I worked I did excellently. However, I never lied to my family about anything and to this day they trust what I tell them as truth. Those relationships have always been sacred to me and have been a big part of my ability to come back to a healthier way of living.

My recovery was mostly through my own determination to find a better way to live, even though at the time I could not fathom what it would feel like or if it was worth it. Eventually, I found a psychiatrist who was willing to treat me without the use of contracts. He has been indispensable to my recovery. Although he did save my life many times when I was very suicidal, I feel his most important contribution was that he believed in me and accepted me unconditionally. He was always there when I needed him. Like a one-year-old child who needs to check that his parent is in the room to be able to take the risk and explore the other side of the room, I needed to feel that he was there so I could take the risk and adopt new healthy ways of coping. It's been the scariest adventure I've been on and I don't know how I would have done it without him. I feel the psychiatric community has to stop creating contracts for people like me ("Fake again and you're out!") and start creating safe environments as jumping-off points to taking healthy risks. Today, I am more aware of what triggers me and work hard to stay stable.

Roberta and Winona's first-person accounts, like all the others through this book, are vital. The main reason? Recommendations and opportunities for treatment within hospitals, clinics, and offices have been in short supply. However, this book has allowed professionals and the public to hear the intensely personal, quiet, but riveting voices of patients, family members, friends, and even casual acquaintances—all affected in their unique ways.

Change When You Least Expect It

Recovery, particularly in Munchausen cases, sometimes occurs as a result of a fortuitous life change (e.g., finding a caring life partner) rather than psychiatric treatment per se. One patient who had a history of self-induced sepsis, false blindness, and factitious fever of unknown origin had eagerly accepted a mistaken diagnosis of muscular dystrophy and became wheelchair-bound. She gradually abandoned the ruses as she started developing friendships through a church. These relationships, which existed only *outside* medical settings, provided the nurturance she had sought through factitious behavior.

As with other addictions, the impulse to continue the behaviors never goes away, even in successful cases. The temptation to misuse health care forever lingers. After all, it is part of the patient's history and thus relevant as they continue to live life. With time, many get to the point where they think only sporadically about factitious behavior.

Adelaine

I used to be a factitious disorder patient. This was a long time ago, or so it seems. I no longer "live" in the emergency room, and I don't thrive off of giving EMTs [emergency medical technicians] a chance to play the hero. Instead, I married a nurse. It may have been the best cure because he doesn't jump and overreact when I am in real pain. Besides that, though, I had to be in the waiting room once while he had a simple procedure done. It terrified me so much that he was under the knife that I don't see doctors anymore and have discussed a health care proxy with my husband to include practically no treatment for me. It is strange to think that I have pretty much flip-flopped in thought pattern.

Although I discussed my true diagnosis with my husband at one point in our lives, he's not a big fan of the psych field. His odd disbelief in the world of psychiatry and psychology may have proved to be part of my recovery. By constantly being told you're not a mental case, I began to believe it. His support was one of the key factors. Another was that of the children I had had before I met my husband. You can't have kids if you're hospitalized for weeks at a time, in the emergency room [ER] as often as twice a week, or "passing out" and "ceasing breathing." I actually lost custody of my daughter to my father and stepmother for nearly three years due to factitious disorder. Ironically, my factitious behavior then got worse for a while. All alone, I needed someone around me, someone who cared, someone to take care of me physically if not emotionally. My goal was to be in the ER, and after my psychiatric hospitalizations with manufactured illnesses, I felt trapped. I remember the staff's being torn between those who believed my symptoms were real and those who just knew me as a frequent flyer. At that same time, I was attempting to attend college as well as an EMT course. I was great at the course, too. When medical research has been your life (to make your feigning more realistic), that course seemed ridiculously easy to me.

But I'm sure you can see what happened. With all those "adrenaline junkies" in one room, it was too easy. A little epinephrine [injected adrenaline] can cause unusual tachycardia for such a seemingly healthy young lady. I even induced supraventricular tachycardia [potentially dangerous overactivity of the heart]. I took it far too many times and I was dismissed from working in the hospital—I was told my "health" could put other patients at risk. Understandable, but heartbreaking. It was only after I married my husband that I applied for a job at that very hospital, and they took me back. I had to prove myself to keep my job, and I did. I have stayed well. I know that working in the medical field for a factitious disorder patient can be a deterrent to recovery, but for me it wasn't. I gained the respect of most of the people who rolled their eyes at the sight of me. I found something that even my marriage didn't give me totally. I liked that feeling, and it's that that helps me from reverting back to those old behaviors.

Another powerful example of recovery comes from the case of Wendy Scott, which was previously described. After being admitted approximately 800 times to hundreds of different hospitals throughout Europe, she stopped the behavior only when she became responsible for the care of a pet cat in a hostel for the homeless. She knew that her readmission would lead to neglect of the animal by the other residents. Now viewing herself as a giver, not a recipient of care, she abruptly ended the deceptions.

A brush with death (as in the case of Nellie in the previous chapter) often helps patients realize–finally–the danger of their actions and the need for change. They learn that they are not so firmly in control of their medical signs and symptoms as they may have thought. These patients must then be ardently encouraged to reach out to others, using words rather than painful actions to get their needs met.

What are Acceptable Outcomes?

In general, the prognosis for factitious disorder patients, and especially for Munchausen patients, will remain guarded. Their inability to tolerate frustration and their tendency to lie contrasts sharply with individuals such as Colleen, who remained open to psychotherapeutic and behavioral treatments and was thus able to turn her life around. There are some reports that very lengthy psychotherapy makes a difference for certain patients, but the psychological underpinnings vary in each case and so the treatment must as well.

With many of these patients, I believe we must look at a holding action rather than a cure, meaning that the best we can hope for is a reduction in the number or the severity of their disease forgeries. At times, treatment means gratifying these patients' needs without ever permanently changing the underlying behavior. If a patient has a psychological disorder for which we have a specific treatment and the factitious disorder is only secondary, we can treat the primary disorder while simultaneously dealing with the issue of feigned illness. Patients whose factitious disorder stems from major depression have the best prognosis of all factitious disorder patients. Some of the milder cases or more situationally determined cases may respond to family therapy or some type of direct practical intervention, such as addressing the social milieu. Most Munchausen patients are very difficult to treat, so with them it's a matter of early recognition and damage control—trying to prevent the patient from bodily damage from repetitive operations and invasive diagnostic procedures.

Caregivers must tolerate lapses during which factitious disorder patients "fall off the wagon." These lapses don't mean that the doctor is a failure or that treatment should be abandoned. These disorders demand perseverance. Caregivers must also anticipate that when they prescribe medications for specific associated psychiatric diagnoses, the patient may not take the medication or may even end up misusing or abusing it. Physicians must continue to pursue whatever treatment appears to be effective and hope that the periods of health become longer and longer. If a physician can reduce hospitalizations in a single patient by 50 percent, treatment has been effective. It's enormously difficult to work with some of these patients because they may not have the motivation. To increase the chances of a positive outcome, physicians must also look at the potential for alternative social support for factitious disorder patients. Can they be hooked into a more nurturing social support system that will reduce the need for symptoms? A support network, even the small but powerful one that was waiting for Colleen, is crucial for a continued positive outcome.

Writing in the *American Journal of Psychotherapy*, Drs. James P. Mayo, Jr. and John J. Haggerty, Jr. noted that up to the time of their report, 37 factitious disorder patients were known to have agreed to extensive evaluation or treatment. Twenty-two of them received outpatient psychotherapy for months to a year or more and ten reportedly improved. Compared to the countless factitious disorder patients who enter hospitals every year, these are slim statistics, but they hold promise for other factitious disorder patients. And although some of these patients do not remain in therapy, they may benefit in limited ways. Drs. Mayo and Haggerty recount the story of one of these patients, a 22-year-old woman who called a hospital pretending to be a psychiatrist referring herself for inpatient treatment for "psychiatric Munchausen syndrome." While her admission was being arranged, she conned her way into the medical unit of the hospital by saying she had a peptic ulcer. She ultimately confessed to having Munchausen syndrome, but, when offered psychiatric hospitalization, she declined, accepting outpatient therapy instead. Surprisingly, this patient stayed in treatment for 70 sessions over 16 months. During that time, she had lapses during which she cancelled sessions and was also hospitalized several times for feigned illness. These hospitalizations neatly coincided with absences by her therapist, which she perceived as intolerable abandonment. Although she ultimately left treatment and moved on, she had shown definite signs of improvement in symptoms and behavior during the middle eight months of therapy. The candle glimmers, if only weakly, even in the most difficult of cases. The challenge for clinicians is to focus not on the darkness, but on the light.

The best form of treatment is prevention in all disorders. If we can find ways to reduce the neediness and desperation so many people feel, if their needs for attention and nurturance can be better met through social support and personal achievement, factitious disorder may become a disease of the past. And if it serves no other purpose, this book will counter the isolation of those who believe that they are the only ones who have been misled in this way.

How needy can these people be that they are willing to endure pain and shame to garner some moments of caring, concern, and control? This is the question that I, as a psychiatrist and researcher, explore and

that I, as an author, implore you to consider before judging the factitious disorder patient. As poet Elizabeth Barrett Browning wrote in
1857,

> I think it frets the saints in heaven to see
> How many desolate creatures on the earth
> Have learnt the simple dues of fellowship
> And social comfort, in a hospital.

Notes

Chapter 1

"Sandra's Tale" adapted with permission of the American Psychiatric Press. Feldman, M.D. (2001). Prophylactic bilateral radical mastectomy resulting from factitious disorder. *Psychosomatics 42*:519–521.

Chapter 10

The comments of Jolene are included with permission of Baywood Publishing. Rand D.C. and Feldman M.D. (2001). An explanatory model for Munchausen by proxy abuse. *International Journal of Psychiatry in Medicine 31*:113–126.

Chapter 12

"Barbara's Guise" and the other cases are adapted with permission of the *Southern Medical Journal* and the Southern Medical Association. Feldman, M.D. (2000). Munchausen by Internet: detecting factitious illness and crisis on the Internet. *Southern Medical Journal 93*: 669–672, and the *Western Journal of Medicine* and the British Medical Journal Publishing Group. Feldman, M.D., Bibby, M.A., Crites, S.D. (1998). 'Virtual' factitious disorders and Munchausen by proxy. *Western Journal of Medicine 168*:537–539.

Chapter 13

"The History of Paula and Derek" is adapted with permission of the American Psychiatric Press. Feldman, M.D. and Eisendrath, S.J. (Eds) (1996). *The Spectrum of Factitious Disorders*. Washington, DC, American Psychiatric Press.

Chapter 14

"The Case of Millie" is adapted with permission of Elsevier Science. Feldman, M.D. (1999). Factitious disease of periocular and facial skin. *American Journal of Ophthalmology* 128:392–393.

"Ashley's Hearing" is adapted with permission of the American Psychiatric Press. Feldman M.D. (1995). Factitious disorders and fraud. *Psychosomatics* 36:509–510.

Chapter 15

"Nellie's Words" is adapted with permission of the Southern Medical Journal and Southern Medical Association. Feldman, M.D. (1998). Breaking the silence of factitious disorder. *Southern Medical Journal* 91:41–42.

"The Red Flags" is adapted with permission of the American Psychiatric Press. Feldman, M.D. Eisendrath S.J. (Eds) (1996). *The Spectrum of Factitious Disorders*. Washington, DC, American Psychiatric Press.

Chapter 16

Some of the material in the section "Acceptance of Treatment" has been adapted with permission of American Psychiatric Publishing. Feldman, M.D., Hamilton, J.C., Deemer, H.N. (2001). Factitious disorder. In Phillips, K.A. (ed). *Somatoform and Factitious Disorders*. Washington, DC, American Psychiatric Press.

" Sarah's History" is adapted with permission of American Psychiatric Publishing. Feldman, M.D. & Duval, N.J. (1997). Factitious quadriplegia: A rare new case and literature review. *Psychosomatics* 38:76–80.

Selected Readings

This listing contains items from which some of the case material was drawn and adapted. In order to enhance readability, the text of the chapters does not include complete references. However, items of special interest can be located by scanning this section for identifying information given within the chapters. This information includes the first author's name; the particular topic under discussion; and/or the title of the article, journal, or book. For readers not familiar with the conventions of referencing, any librarian—particularly one within a hospital or university—should be able to help. Novels are indicated with brief annotations.

Ablow, K. *Compulsion*. (2003). New York: St. Martin's Press. Novel with coverage of factitious disorder.

Adshead, G., & Brooke, D., (Eds.) (2001). *Munchausen's Syndrome by Proxy: Current Issues in Assessment, Treatment and Research*. London: Imperial College Press.

Aduan, R. P., Fauci A. S., & Dale, D. D. (1979). Factitious fever and self induced infection. *Annals of Internal Medicine 90*:230–242.

American Psychiatric Association (2000). *Diagnostic and Statistical Manual of Mental Disorders, 4th Edition, Text Revision*. Washington, DC: American Psychiatric Association.

Artingstall, K. (1998). *Practical Aspects of Munchausen by Proxy and Munchausen Syndrome Investigation*. Boca Raton, Florida: CRC Press.

Asher, R. (1951). Munchausen's syndrome. *Lancet 1*:339–341.

Axen, D. M. (1986). Chronic factitious disorders. Helping those who hurt themselves. *Journal of Psychosocial Nursing and Mental Health Services* 24:19–20, 25–27.

Baile, W. F. Jr., Kuehn, C. V., & Straker, D. (1992). Factitious cancer. *Psychosomatics 33*:100–105.

Ballas, S. K. (1996). Factitious sickle cell acute painful episodes: a secondary type of Munchausen syndrome. *American Journal of Hematology 53*:254–258.

Barber, M. A. & Davis, P. M. (2002). Fits, faints, or fatal fantasy? Fabricated seizures and child abuse. *Archives of Disease in Childhood 86*:230–233.

Bauer, M. & Boegner F. (1996). Neurological syndromes in factitious disorder. *Journal of Nervous and Mental Disease 184*:281–288.

Bhugra, D. (1988). Psychiatric Munchausen's syndrome. Literature review with case reports. *Acta Psychiatrica Scandinavica 77*:497–503.

Bogazzi, F., Bartalena, L., & Scarcello, G. et al. (1999). The age of patients with thyrotoxicosis factitia in Italy from 1973 to 1996. *Journal of Endocrinological Investigation 22*:128–133.

Bools, C. N., Neale B. A, Meadow, S. R. (1993). Follow up of victims of fabricated illness (Munchausen syndrome by proxy). *Archives of Disease in Childhood 69*:625–630.

Bools, C., Neale B. & Meadow R. (1994). Munchausen syndrome by proxy: a study of psychopathology. *Child Abuse and Neglect 18*:773–788.

Bridges, K. W. & Goldberg, D. P. Somatic presentations of DSM-III psychiatric disorders in primary care. *Journal of Psychiatric Research 9*:583–586, 185.

Bryk, M. & Siegel P. T. (1997). My mother caused my illness: the story of a survivor of Munchausen by proxy syndrome. *Pediatrics 100*:1–7.

Bunim, J. J., Federman D. D., Black R. L. et al. (1958). Factitious diseases: clinical staff conference at the National Institutes of Health. *Annals of Internal Medicine 48*:1328–1341.

Byrne, B. (1997). *Foolish Notions*. Dublin, Ireland: Mather Publications. Novel about Munchausen syndrome.

Carswell, J. (1950). *The Romantic Rogue: Being the Singular Life and Adventures of Rudolph Eric Raspe, Creator of Baron Munchausen*. New York: Dutton.

Chew, B. H., Pace, K. T. & Honey, R. J (2002). Munchausen syndrome presenting as gross hematuria in two women. *Urology 59*:601.

Chua, J. D. & Friedenberg, W. R. (1998). Superwarfarin poisoning. *Archives of Internal Medicine 158*:1929–1932.

Churchill, D. R., De Cock, K. M. & Miller, R. F. (1994). Feigned HIV infection/AIDS: malingering and Munchausen's syndrome. *Genitourinary Medicine 70*:314–316.

Colie, J. (1913). *Malingering and Feigned Sickness*. London: Edward Arnold.

Cornwell, P. (1994). *The Body Farm*. New York: Charles Scribner's Sons. Novel with coverage of MBP.

Craven, D. E., Steger, K. A. & La Chapelle, R., et al. (1994). Factitious HIV infection: the importance of documenting infection. *Annals of Internal Medicine 121*:763–766.

Daily, W. J., Coles, J. M. & Creger, W. P. (1963). Factitious anemia. *Annals of Internal Medicine 58*:533–538.

D'Andrea, V. J. (1978). Cancer pathomimicry: a report of three cases. *Journal of Clinical Psychiatry 39*:233–240.

Davies, F. & Gupta, R. (2002). Apparent life threatening events in infants presenting to an emergency department. *Emergency Medical Journal 19*:11–16.

Davis, P., McClure, R. J., Rolfe, K. et al. (1998). Procedures, placement, and risk of further abuse after Munchausen syndrome by proxy, non-accidental poisoning, and non-accidental suffocation. *Archives of Disease in Childhood 78*:217–221.

Dickinson, E. J. & Evans, T. R. (1987). Cardiac Munchausen's syndrome. *Journal of the Royal Society of Medicine 80*:630–633.

Donovan, D. M. (1987). Costs of factitious illness. *Hospital and Community Psychiatry 38*:571–572.

Earle, J. R., Jr. & Folks, D. G. (1986). Factitious disorder and coexisting depression: a report of successful psychiatric consultation and case management. *General Hospital Psychiatry 8*:448–450.

Edwards, M. S. & Butler, K. M. (1987). "Hyperthermia of trickery" in an adolescent. *Pediatric Infectious Disease Journal 6*:411–414.

Eisendrath, S. J. (1994). Factitious physical disorders. *Western Journal of Medicine 160*:177–179.

Eisendrath, S. J. (1989). Factitious physical disorders: treatment without confrontation. *Psychosomatics 30*:383–387.

Eisendrath, S. J. (1996). When Munchausen becomes malingering: factitious disorders that penetrate the legal system. *Bulletin of the American Academy of Psychiatry and the Law 24*:471–481.

Faguet, R. A. (1980). Munchausen syndrome and necrophilia. *Suicide and Life Threatening Behavior 10*:214–218.

Fairbank, J. A., McCaffrey, R. J. & Keane, T. M. (1985). Psychometric detection of fabricated symptoms of posttraumatic stress disorder. *American Journal of Psychiatry 142*:501–503.

Feldman, M. D. (1994). The costs of factitious disorders. *Psychosomatics 35*:506–507.

Feldman, M. D. (1995). Factitious disorders and fraud. *Psychosomatics 36*:509–510.

Feldman, M. D. (1998). Breaking the silence of factitious disorder. *Southern Medical Journal 91*:41–42.

Feldman, M. D., Bibby, M. & Crites, S. D. (1998). 'Virtual' factitious disorders and Munchausen by proxy. *Western Journal of Medicine 168*:537–539.

Feldman, M. D. (1999). Factitious disease of periocular and facial skin. *American Journal of Ophthalmology 128*:392–393.

Feldman, M. D. (2000). Munchausen by Internet: detecting factitious illness and crisis on the Internet. *Southern Medical Journal 93*:669–672.

Feldman, M. D. (2001). Prophylactic bilateral radical mastectomy resulting from factitious disorder. *Psychosomatics 42*:519–521.

Feldman, M. D. & Brown, R. M. (2002). Munchausen by Proxy in an international context. *Child Abuse and Neglect 26*:509–524, 2002.

Feldman, M. D. & Duval, N. J. (1997). Factitious quadriplegia. A rare new case and literature review. *Psychosomatics 38*:76–80.

Feldman, M. D. & Eisendrath, S. J. (1996). *The Spectrum of Factitious Disorders*. Washington, DC: American Psychiatric Press.

Feldman, M. D. & Escalona, R. (1991). The longing for nurturance. A case of factitious cancer. *Psychosomatics 32*:226–228.

Feldman, M. D. & Feldman, J. M. (1995). Tangled in the web: countertransference in the therapy of factitious disorders. *International Journal of Psychiatry in Medicine 25*:389–399.

Feldman, M. D. & Ford, C. V. (1999). Factitious disorders. In Sadock, B. J. & Sadock, V. A. (Eds.), Kaplan and Sadock's *Comprehensive Textbook of Psychiatry, 7th Edition*, pp 1533–1543. Baltimore: Lippincott Williams & Wilkins.

Feldman, M. D. & Ford, C. V. (1994). *Patient or Pretender: Inside the Strange World of Factitious Disorders*. New York: John Wiley & Sons.

Feldman, M. D., Hamilton, J. C. & Deemer, H. N.: *Factitious disorder. In Somatoform and Factitious Disorders*. Phillips, K. A. (Ed.) (2001). Washington, DC: American Psychiatric Publishing, pp 129–166

Feldman M. D. & Sheridan, M. S. (in press). *In* Giardino, A. P. & Alexander, R. (Eds.), Munchausen syndrome by proxy. *In Child Maltreatment: A Clinical Guide, 3rd edition*. St. Louis: G.W. Medical Publishing, Inc.

Fink, P. (1992). Physical complaints and symptoms of somatizing patients. *Journal of Psychosomatic Research 36*:125–136.

Fink, P. (1992). The use of hospitalizations by persistent somatizing patients. *Psychological Medicine 22*:173–180.

Fink, P. & Jensen, J. (1989). Clinical characteristics of the Munchausen syndrome. A review and 3 new case histories. *Psychotherapy and Psychosomatics 52*:164–171.

Firstman, R. & Talan J. (1997). *The Death of Innocents: A True Story of Murder, Medicine, and High-Stakes Science*. New York: Bantam.

Fishbain, D. A., Goldberg, M., Rosomoff, R. S. et al. (1991). More Munchausen with chronic pain. *Clinical Journal of Pain 7*:237–244.

Fliege, H., Scholler, G., Rose, M., et al. (2002). Factitious disorders and pathological self-harm in a hospital population: an interdisciplinary challenge. *General Hospital Psychiatry 24*:164–171.

Folks, D. G. (1995). Munchausen's syndrome and other factitious disorders. *Neurologic Clinics 13*:267–281.

Folks, D. G., Feldman, M. D. & Ford, C. V. (2000). Somatoform disorders, factitious disorders, and malingering. In Stoudemire A., Fogel, B. S., & Greenberg, D. B. (Eds.), *Psychiatric Care of the Medical Patient, 2nd Edition*. New York: Oxford University Press.

Ford, C. V. (1983). *The Somatizing Disorders: Illness as a Way of Life*, pp 458–475. New York: Elsevier Biomedical.

Ford, C. V. (1992). Illness as a lifestyle. The role of somatization in medical practice. *Spine 17*:S338–343.

Ford, C. V. (1995). Dimensions of somatization and hypochondriasis. *Neurologic Clinics 13*:241–253.

Ford, C. V. (1996). *Lies! Lies!! Lies!!! The Psychology of Deceit*. Washington, DC: American Psychiatric Press.

Freyberger, H., Nordmeyer, J. P., Freyberger, H. J., et al. (1994). Patients suffering from factitious disorders in the clinico-psychosomatic consultation liaison service: psychodynamic processes, psychotherapeutic initial care and clinicointerdisciplinary cooperation. *Psychotherapy and Psychosomatics 62*:108-122.

Freyberger, H. J. & Schneider, W. (1994). Diagnosis and classification of factitious disorder with operational diagnostic systems. *Psychotherapy and Psychosomatics 62*:27-29.

Gault, M. H., Campbell, N. R. & Aksu, A. E. (1988). Spurious stones. *Nephron 48*:274-279.

Gavin, H. (1843). *On Feigned and Factitious Diseases, Chiefly of Soldiers and Seamen, On the Means Used to Simulate or Produce Them, and On the Best Mode of Discovering Imposters*. London: John Churchill.

Gill, G. V. (1992). The spectrum of brittle diabetes. *Journal of the Royal Society of Medicine 85*:259-261.

Gilliam, T. & McKeown, C. (1989). *The Adventures of Baron Munchausen*. New York: Applause Theatre Book Publishers. Novel based on the Munchausen tales.

Goodlin, R. C. (1985). Pregnant women with Munchausen syndrome. *American Journal of Obstetrics and Gynecology 153*:207-210.

Goodwin, J. (1988). Munchausen's syndrome as a dissociative disorder. *Dissociation 1*:54-60.

Gregory, J. (2003). *Sickened: The Memoir of a Munchausen by Proxy Childhood*. New York: Bantam.

Greenwood, T. (2001). *Nearer Than the Sky: A Novel*. New York: St. Martin's Press. Novel with coverage of MBP.

Gutheil, T. G. & Appelbaum, P. S. (2000). *Clinical Handbook of Psychiatry and the Law, 3rd Ed*. New York: Lippincott Williams & Wilkins.

Hall, D. E., Eubanks, L., Meyyazhagan, L. S., et al. (2000). Evaluation of covert video surveillance in the diagnosis of Munchausen syndrome by proxy: lessons from 41 cases. *Pediatrics 105*:1305-1312.

Halligan, P., Bass, C. & Oakley, D. (2003). *Malingering and Illness Deception*. New York: Oxford University Press.

Hamilton, J. C. & Janata, J. W. (1997). Dying to be ill: the role of self-enhancement motives in the spectrum of factitious disorders. *Journal of Social and Clinical Psychology 16*:178-199.

Hardie, T. J. & Reed, A. (1988). Pseudologia fantastica, factitious disorder and impostership: a deception syndrome. *Medicine, Science, and the Law 38*:198-201.

Harrington, T. M., Folks, D. G. & Ford, C. V. (1988). Holiday factitial disorder: management of factitious gastrointestinal bleeding. *Psychosomatics 29*:438-442.

Highland, B. K. & Flume, P. A. (2002). A "story" of a woman with cystic fibrosis. *Chest 121*:1704-1707.

Hirayama, Y., Sakamaki, S., Tsuji, Y., et al. (2003). Fatality caused by self-bloodletting in a patient with factitious anemia. *International Journal of Hematology 78*:146-148.

Jonas, J. M. & Pope, H. G., Jr. (1985). The dissimulating disorders: a single diagnostic entity? *Comprehensive Psychiatry 26*:58–62.

Jones, A. B. & Llewellyn, J. (1917). *Malingering or the Simulation of Disease*. London: William Heinemann.

Joseph-Di Caprio, J. & Remafedi, G. J. (1997). Adolescents with factitious HIV disease. *Journal of Adolescent Health 21*:102–106.

Kahan, B. & Yorker, B. C. (1991). Munchausen syndrome by proxy: clinical review and legal issues. *Behavioral Sciences & the Law 9*:73–83.

Kass, F. C. (1985). Identification of persons with Munchausen's syndrome: ethical problems. *General Hospital Psychiatry 7*:195–200.

Kellerman, J. (1993). *Devil's Waltz*. New York: Bantam Books. Novel with coverage of MBP

Kellner, C. H. & Eth, S. (1982). Code blue—factitious cyanosis. *Journal of Nervous and Mental Disease 170*:371–372.

King, B. H. & Ford, C. V. (1990). Pseudologia fantastica. *Acta Psychiatrica Scandinavica 77*:1–6, 1988

Kinsella, P. Staged fright. *Nursing Times 86*:26–29.

Kirkmayer, L. J. & Robbins, J. M. (1991). *Current Concepts of Somatization: Research and Clinical Perspectives*. Washington, DC: American Psychiatric Press.

Klonoff, E. A., Youngner, S. J., Moore, D. J., et al. (1983). Chronic factitious illness: a behavioral approach. *International Journal of Psychiatry in Medicine 13*:173–183.

Knockaert, D. C., Vanneste, L. J., Vanneste, S. B., et al. (1992). Fever of unknown origin in the 1980s. An update of the diagnostic spectrum. *Archives of Internal Medicine 152*:51–55.

Krahn, L. E., Li, H. & O'Connor, M. K. (2003). Patients who strive to be ill: factitious disorder with physical symptoms. *American Journal of Psychiatry 160*:1163–1168.

Kroenke, K. & Mangelsdorff, A. D. (1989). Common symptoms in ambulatory care: incidence, evaluation, therapy, and outcome. *American Journal of Medicine 86*:262–266.

Lasher, L. J. (2003). Munchausen by proxy (MBP) maltreatment: an international educational challenge. *Child Abuse and Neglect 27*:409–411.

Lasher, L. J. & Sheridan, M. S. (2004). *Munchausen by Proxy Maltreatment: Identification, Intervention, and Case Management*. Binghampton, NY: Haworth Press.

Levin, A. V. & Sheridan, M. S., (Eds.). (1995). *Munchausen Syndrome by Proxy: Issues in Diagnosis and Treatment*. New York: Lexington.

Libow, J. A. (1995). Munchausen by proxy victims in adulthood: a first look. *Child Abuse and Neglect 18*:1131–1142, 1995

Libow, J. A. (2000). Child and adolescent illness falsification. *Pediatrics 105*:336–342.

Light, M. J. & Sheridan, M. S. (1990). Munchausen syndrome by proxy and apnea (MBPA). A survey of apnea programs. *Clinical Pediatrics 29*:162–168.

Locke, S. E. (1997). Treating somatization: an update. *Behavioral Health Management* 17:22–24.

Louis, D. S., Lamp, M. K. & Greene, T. L. (1985). The upper extremity and psychiatric illness. *Journal of Hand Surgery* 10:687–693.

Lowenstein, L. F. (2002). Recent research into dealing with the problem of malingering. *Medico-Legal Journal* 70:38–49.

Ludwigs, U., Ruiz, H., Isaksson, H., et al. (1994). Factitious disorder presenting with acute cardiovascular symptoms. *Journal of Internal Medicine* 236:685–690.

Marriage, K., Govorchin, M., George, P., et al. (1988). Use of an amytal interview in the management of factitious deaf mutism. *Australian and New Zealand Journal of Psychiatry* 22:454–456.

Mayo, J. P., Jr. & Haggerty, J. J., Jr. (1984). Long-term psychotherapy of Munchausen syndrome. *American Journal of Psychotherapy* 38:571–578.

Mayou, R., Bass, C. M. & Sharpe, M. (1995). *Treatment of Functional Somatic Symptoms*. New York: Oxford University Press.

McCahill, M. E. (1997). Somatoform and related disorders: delivery of diagnosis as first step. *American Family Physician* 52:193–204.

McCann, J. T. (1998). *Malingering and Deception in Adolescents: Assessing Credibility in Clinical and Forensic Settings*. Washington, DC: American Psychological Association.

McClure, R. J., Davis, P. M., Meadow, S. R., et al. (1996). Epidemiology of Munchausen syndrome by proxy, non-accidental poisoning, and non-accidental suffocation. *Archives of Disease in Childhood* 75:57–61.

Meadow, R. (2002). Different interpretations of Munchausen Syndrome by Proxy. *Child Abuse and Neglect* 26:501–508.

Meadow, R. (1977). Munchausen syndrome by proxy: the hinterland of child abuse. *Lancet* 2:343–345.

Meadow, R. (1984). Fictitious epilepsy. *Lancet* 2:25–28.

Meadow, R. (1999). Unnatural sudden infant death. *Archives of Disease in Childhood* 80:7–14.

Meagher, D. J. & Collins, A. G. (1997). The use of aliases by psychiatric patients. *Psychopathology* 30:324–327.

Mechanic, D. & Angel, R. J. (1987). Some factors associated with the report and evaluation of back pain. *Journal of Health and Social Behavior* 28:131–139.

Meessen, N. E. L., Walenkamp, G. H. I. M. & Jacobs, J. A. (1998). Munchausen's Microbes? *New England Journal of Medicine* 339:1717–1718.

Menninger, K. (1934). Polysurgery and polysurgical addiction. *Psychoanalytic Quarterly* 4:173–199.

Meropol, N. J., Ford, C. V. & Zaner, R. M. (1985). Factitious illness: an exploration in ethics. *Perspectives in Biology and Medicine* 28:269–281.

Miller, M. & Cabeza-Stradi, S. (1994). Addiction to surgery: a nursing dilemma. *Critical Care Nurse* 14:44–47.

Mohammed, R., Goy, J. A., Walpole, B. G., et al. (1985). Munchausen's syndrome. A study of the casualty "Black books" of Melbourne. *Medical Journal of Australia* 143:561–563.

Nadelson, T. (1979). The Munchausen spectrum: borderline character features. *General Hospital Psychiatry 1*:11–17.

Nadelson, T. (1985). False patients/real patients: a spectrum of disease presentation. *Psychotherapy and Psychosomatics 44*:175–184.

Newmark, N., Adityanjee, & Kay, J. (1999). Pseudologia fantastica and factitious disorder: review of the literature and a case report. *Comprehensive Psychiatry 40*:89-9.

Nichols, G. R. II, Davis, G. J. & Corey, T. S. (1990). In the shadow of the Baron: sudden death due to Munchausen syndrome. *American Journal of Emergency Medicine 8*:216–219.

Nickoloff, S. E., Neppe, V. M. & Ries, R. K. (1989). Factitious AIDS. *Psychosomatics 30*:342–345.

O'Dowd, M. (2001). Editorial comment: factitious HIV syndrome—back to basis in diagnosis. *AIDS Reader 11*:280.

Pankratz, L. (1998). *Patients Who Deceive: Assessment and Management of Risk in Providing Health Care and Financial Benefits*. Springfield, Illinois: Charles C. Thomas.

Papadopoulos, M. C. & Bell, B. A. (1999). Factitious neurosurgical emergencies: report of five cases. *British Journal of Neurosurgery 13*:591–593.

Parnell, T. F. & Day, D. O., (Eds.) (1998). *Munchausen Syndrome by Proxy: Misunderstood Child Abuse*. Thousand Oaks, California: Sage.

Phillips, M. R., Ward, N. G. & Ries, R. K. (1983). Factitious mourning: painless patienthood. *American Journal of Psychiatry 140*:420–425.

Plewes, J. M. & Fagan, J. G. (1994). Factitious disorders and malingering. In Hales, R., Talbott, J. A. &, Yudofsky, S. C. (Eds.), *The American Psychiatric Press Textbook of Psychiatry,* pp 623–632. Washington, DC: American Psychiatric Press.

Pope, H. G., Jr., Jonas, J. M. & Jones, B. (1982). Factitious psychosis: phenomenology, family history, and long-term outcome of nine patients. *American Journal of Psychiatry 139*:1480–1483.

Powell, R., & Boast, N. (1993). The million dollar man. Resource implications for chronic Munchausen's syndrome. *British Journal of Psychiatry 162*:253–256.

Rabins, P. V. (1983). Reversible dementia and the misdiagnosis of dementia: a review. *Hospital and Community Psychiatry 34*:830–835.

Rand, D. C. & Feldman, M. D. (1999). Misdiagnosis of Munchausen syndrome by proxy: a literature review and four new cases. *Harvard Review of Psychiatry 7*:94–101.

Raspe, R. E. & Cruikshank, G. (1989). *The Travels and Surprising Adventures of Baron Munchausen*. New York: Dedalus/Hippocrene.

Reich, J. D. & Hanno, P. M. (1997). Factitious renal colic. *Urology 50*:858–862.

Reich, P. & Gottfried, L. A. (1983). Factitious disorders in a teaching hospital. *Annals of Internal Medicine 99*:240–247.

Rogers, R. (Ed.) (1997). *Clinical Assessment of Malingering and Deception, Second Edition*. New York: Guilford Press.

Rosenberg, D. A. (2003). Munchausen syndrome by proxy: medical diagnostic criteria. *Child Abuse and Neglect 27*:421–430.

Rosenberg, D. A. (1987). Web of deceit: a literature review of Munchausen syndrome by proxy. *Child Abuse and Neglect 11*:547–563.

Rumans, L. W. & Vosti, K. L. (1978). Factitious and fraudulent fever. *American Journal of Medicine 65*:745–755.

Sabot, J. F., Bornet, C. E., Favre, S., et al. (1999). The analysis of peculiar urinary (and other) calculi: an endless source of challenge. *Clinica Chimica Acta 283*:151–158.

Samuels, M. P., Poets C. F., Noyes, J. P., et al. (1993). Diagnosis and management after life threatening events in infants and young child who received cardiopulmonary resuscitation. *British Medical Journal 306*:489–492.

Sansone, R. A., Weiderman, M. W., Sansone, L. A., et al. (1997). Sabotaging one's own medical care. *Archives of Family Medicine 6*:583–586.

Sarwari, A. R. & Mackowiak, P. A. (1997). Factitious fever: a modern update. *Current Clinical Topics in Infectious Diseases 17*:88–94.

Savvidou, I., Bozikas, V. P. & Karavatos, A. (2002). False allegations of child physical abuse: a case of Münchausen by proxy-like syndrome? *International Journal of Psychiatry in Medicine 32*:201–208.

Schreier, H. (2002). On the importance of motivation in Munchausen by Proxy: the case of Kathy Bush. *Child Abuse and Neglect 26*:537–549.

Schwartz, S. M., Gramling, S. E. & Mancini, T. (1994). The influence of life stress, personality, and learning history on illness behavior. *Journal of Behavior Therapy and Experimental Psychiatry 25*:135–142.

Schwarz, K., Harding, R., Harrington, D., et al. (1993). Hospital management of a patient with intractable factitious disorder. *Psychosomatics 34*:265–267.

Sheridan, M. S. (2003). The deceit continues: an updated literature review of Munchausen syndrome by proxy. *Child Abuse and Neglect 27*:431–451.

Silver, F. (1996). Management of conversion disorder. *American Journal of Physical Medicine and Rehabilitation 75*:134–140.

Snowdon, J., Solomons, R., Druce, H. (1978). Feigned bereavement: twelve cases. *British Journal of Psychiatry 133*:15–19.

Snyder, S. (1986). Fabricated 'eating disorder.' *Psychosomatics 27*:662.

Solyom, C. & Solyom, L. (1990). A treatment program for functional paraplegia/Munchausen syndrome. *Journal of Behavior Therapy and Experimental Psychiatry 21*:225–230.

Southall, D. P., Plunkett, M. C., Banks, M. W., et al. (1997). Covert video recordings of life-threatening child abuse: lessons for child protection. *Pediatrics 100*:735–760.

Spiro, H. R. (1968). Chronic factitious illness. Munchausen's syndrome. *Archives of General Psychiatry 18*:569–579, 1968

Spivak, H., Rodin, G. & Sutherland, A. (1994). The psychology of factitious disorders. A reconsideration. *Psychosomatics 35*:25–34.

Stanziale, S. F., Christopher, J. C. & Fisher, R. B. (1997). Brodifacoum rodenticide ingestion in a patient with shigellosis. *Southern Medical Journal 90*:833–835.

Stone, M. H. (1977). Factitious illness. Psychological findings and treatment recommendations. *Bulletin of the Menninger Clinic 41*:239–254.

Suresh, T. R. & Srinivasan, T. N. (1990). Claimed simulation of insanity. A coping strategy in mania. *British Journal of Psychiatry 157*:603–605.

Sutherland, A. J. & Rodin, G. M. (1990). Factitious disorders in a general hospital setting: clinical features and a review of the literature. *Psychosomatics 31*:392–399.

Toth, E. L. & Baggaley, A. (1991). Coexistence of Munchausen's syndrome and multiple personality disorder: detailed report of a case and theoretical discussion. *Psychiatry 54*:176–183, 1991

Truman, T. L., Ayoub, C. C. (2002). Considering suffocatory abuse and Munchausen by Proxy in the evaluation of children experiencing apparent life-threatening events and Sudden Infant Death Syndrome. *Child Maltreatment 7*:138–148.

van Moffaert, M. M. (1991). Integration of medical and psychiatric management in self-mutilation. *General Hospital Psychiatry 13*:59–67.

Warner, J. O., Hathaway, M. J. (1984). Allergic form of Meadow's syndrome (Munchausen by proxy). *Archives of Disease in Childhood 59*:151–156.

Westfall, V. V. (2001). *Almost Love, Almost Death*. 1stBooks.com (online). Novel with coverage of MBP.

Zitelli, B. J., Seltman, M. F. & Shannon, R. M. (1987). Munchausen's syndrome by proxy and its professional participants. *American Journal of Diseases of Children 141*:1099–1102.

Zuger, A & O'Dowd, M. A. (1992). The baron has AIDS: a case of factitious human immunodeficiency virus infection and review. *Clinical Infectious Diseases 14*:211–216.

Selected Websites

Dr. Feldman cannot vouch for website content that he has not personally written. However, the websites that follow appear credible and should be of interest to readers. Unfortunately, website addresses do change regularly and without notice, so resources listed here may no longer be found online at the time of publication.

Factitious Disorder, Munchausen Syndrome, and Malingering

- http://www.munchausen.com
  Dr. Feldman's website for the public on all the phenomena discussed in this book
- http://www.drmarcfeldman.com/
  Dr. Feldman's website for attorneys interested in the legal aspects of the phenomena
- http://www.shpm.com/articles/chronic/factit.html
  A brief overview article about factitious disorder, including a case of factitious cancer
- http://healthinmind.com/english/factittxt.htm
  A one-page article about factitious disorder (Note that treatment with long-term hospitalization is very controversial.)
- http://my.webmd.com/content/c4_asset/merriam-webster_medical_dictionary_165330
  A medical dictionary entry on Munchausen syndrome
- http://www.merck.com/pubs/mmanual/section15/chapter185/185d.htm
  The Merck Manual entry on Munchausen syndrome

- http://www.allsands.com/Health/Diseases/
    munchausensyndr_xda_gn.htm
    A fine overview article about Munchausen syndrome
- http://www.behavenet.com/capsules/disorders/factitiousdis.htm
    A site with the Diagnostic and Statistical Manual of Mental Disorders
    criteria for factitious disorder, as well as a collection of the pejorative
    terms sometimes used in the literature to refer to these disquieting
    patients
- http://www.sma.org/smj1998/jansmj98/9text.htm
    A woman's first-hand account of severe factitious disorder
- http://www.priory.com/psych/fact.htm
    A case of factitious bereavement
- http://www.selfhelpmagazine.com/articles/chronic/faking.html
    A brief article about Munchausen by Internet
- http://groups.yahoo.com
    Type "Munchausen" into the Search box and find numerous discussion
    groups dedicated to all things Munchausen (including Munchausen by
    proxy and the Munchausen tales)
- http://www.villagevoice.com/issues/0126/russo.shtml
    A longer article from a major newspaper about Munchausen by Internet
- http://my.webmd.com/printing/article/1728.55062
    A report about children and adolescents with factitious disorder
- http://www.kfshrc.edu.sa/annals/154/94280/94280.html
    An article illustrating the international dimensions of factitious disorder
- http://www.forensic-psych.com/articles/artPretender.html
    An article about a famous recovered Munchausen patient, Wendy Scott
- http://www.mtsinai.org/pulmonary/books/house/history-m.html
    A doctor's account of a Munchausen patient (skip to "A Case of
    'Munchausen'")
- http://www.physweekly.com/archive/96/07_22_96/cu4.html
    A brief article about factitious Cushing's syndrome
- http://www.sma.org/smj/97aug13.htm
    A case report of a factitious blood-clotting disorder
- http://www.electronicipc.com/JournalEZ/
    detail.cfm?code=02250010681115&cfid=&cftoken
    An abstract about factitious dental problems
- http://www.healthatoz.com/healthatoz/Atoz/ency/malingering.html
    A quick description of malingering and its diagnosis
- http://www.reidpsychiatry.com/columns/Reid07-00.pdf
    A sometimes irreverent look at malingered psychiatric symptoms
- http://www.karger.ch/journals/PSP/PSP306/PSP0324.htm
    An abstract about the use of aliases in medical deception
- http://www.pownetwork.org/phonies/phonies.htm
    A site from the P.O.W. Network that exposes false prisoners of war, Medal
    of Honor winners, and other "fake warriors"

Munchausen by Proxy (MBP)

- http://www.mbpexpert.com
  MBP consultant Louisa Lasher's website
- http://www.mbpsnetwork.com
  A website founded by an adult survivor of MBP maltreatment
- http://www.juliegregory.com
  A website established by the celebrated author of Sickened: The Memoir of
  a Munchausen by Proxy Childhood
- http://www.ashermeadow.com
  A large site including news, books, and other information and resources
  related to MBP
- http://www.smith-lawfirm.com/mandatory_reporting.htm
  A detailed examination of state laws governing abuse reports, with
  information on whom to contact
- http://www.childhelpusa.org
  A site listing contacts to child protective agencies throughout the United
  States
- http://www.medicine.uiowa.edu/pa/sresrch/Huynh/Huynh/sld001.htm
  A fine, comprehensive slideshow on MBP
- http://www.cnn.com/US/9907/20/florida.operation.01/
  Information about the celebrated case of Kathy and Jennifer Bush
- http://www.vachss.com/help_text/archive/kathy_bush.html
  A short article about the failed appeal in the Bush case
- http://nsweb.nursingspectrum.com/ce/ce209.htm
  An excellent self-study module intended primarily for nurses
- http://home.coqui.net/myrna/munch.htm
  A pediatrician's brief review article about MBP
- http://webserver.pulsus.com/clin-pha/03_01/khat_ed.htm
  An abstract demonstrating how drug monitoring can help in MBP
  detection
- http://www.bullyonline.org/workbully/munchaus.htm
  An article that points out some of the factors underlying MBP and the
  barriers to its being reported
- http://www.syracuse.com/features/apnea
  An investigative series about apparent Sudden Infant Death Syndrome
  (SIDS), apnea, and suffocation
- http://www.aap.org/policy/re0036.html
  An American Academy of Pediatrics policy on the risks of misdiagnosing
  fatal child abuse as SIDS
- http://www.vachss.com/help_text/archive/sanjose_mom.html
  An article about a California mother who used MBP as a defense in her
  child abuse trial
- http://strangerbox.topcities.com/disorders.html
  Information on why some victims seem to collude in their MBP abuse (skip
  to "Stockholm syndrome")

- http://www.chron.com/content/chronicle/metropolitan/96/01/05/
  padron.html
  A legal case in which the mother admitted to the MBP maltreatment
- http://www.kfshrc.edu.sa/annals/182/97-327.html
  An article that notes that MBP has been found internationally
- http://www.ipt-forensics.com/journal/volume2/j2_2_4.htm
  An article that argues that false allegations of victimization of a child can
  be a variant of MBP
- http://childabuse.gactr.uga.edu/both/lasherfeldman/
  lasherfeldman1.phtml
  An article on MBP presenting as child sexual abuse, it also discusses general
  MBP intervention
- http://www.texnews.com/1998/texas/visit0515.html
  A Texas case in which custody and visitation were contested
- http://www.texnews.com/1998/texas/mun0601.html
  More information about the Texas case, in which the mother eventually
  pled guilty.
- http://www.phillymag.com/Archives/1998April/noes.html
  An article about a Philadelphia case in which the mother killed 8 of her
  own children in a MBP pattern
- http://specialchildren.about.com/library/
  blchatMF.htm?terms=Munchausen
  The transcript of an on-line chat with Dr. Feldman about MBP.
- http://lectlaw.com/files/cri15.htm
  An overview of investigative issues for law enforcement in MBP
- http://www3.oup.co.uk/harrev/hdb/Volume_07/Issue_02/
  070094.sgm.abs.html
  An abstract about misdiagnoses of MBP

The Munchausen Tales

- http://www.rickwalton.com/authtale/munch01.htm
  A thorough discussion of the origin of the stories attributed to Baron
  Münchhausen
- http://www.munchausen.org
  A site prepared by German devotees of the Baron, his hometown, and his
  legacy
- http://us.imdb.com/M/title-
  exact?±Adventures±of±Baron±Munchausen,±The
  The tales of the Baron as adapted as a 1989 film by director Terry
  Gilliam.
- http://us.imdb.com/Title?0080037
  The tales as presented in a 1979 Russian film version
- http://us.imdb.com/Title?0036191
  The tales as presented in a 1943 German (Nazi) film version
- http://us.imdb.com/Title?0001488
  The tales as presented in a 1911 French film version

- http://us.imdb.com/Title?0054665
  The tales as presented in a 1961 Czech film version
- http://us.imdb.com/Title?0024320
  The tales as presented in a 1933 American film version
- http://www.gamecabinet.com/rulesText/Munchhausen.txt
  A card game named for Baron Münchhausen
- http://www.tradecards.com/articles/munchausen/index.html
  Colorful trading cards associated with the Baron's adventures have become
  collectibles.

Index

A

Abuse
    diagnosis of, 200
    documentation of, 194
    main types of, 122
    and MBP, 128–129
    MBP as, 122
    videotaped documentation of, 194 (*see also* Video camera
        surveillance)
Addiction, factitious disorder as, 218, 232, 238, 240
Addison's disease, 96
Adolescents
    anorexia nervosa in, 66
    with factitious disorder, 61
    false sexual abuse claimed by, 118–120
    as MBP victims, 151
    pseudologia fantastica in, 40–41
"Adrenaline junkies," 241
Adults, MBP victims as, 151
Aggravations
    in disease forgery, 21
    in MBP, 129
AIDS, factitious, 114, 115
Ailments, induced in MBP, 129
Alcohol abuse, and factitious disorder patients, 108

D